Cottons and Casuals

The gendered organisation of labour in time and space

Miriam Glucksmann

sociologypress

Published by:
sociologypress
British Sociological Association,
Units 3F/G, Mountjoy Research Centre, Stockton Road, Durham, DH1 3UR
http://www.britsoc.org.uk/sociologypress

sociologypress is supported by the British Sociological Association. It furthers
the Association's aim of promoting the discipline of sociology and disseminating
sociological knowledge.

British Library Cataloguing in Publication Data
A catalogue record for this book is available from the British Library
Library of Congress Cataloging-in-Publication Data applied for

ISBN 1 903457 00 9

Printed and bound in the United Kingdom by York Publishing Services Ltd, 64 Hallfield
Road, Layerthorpe, York YO31 7ZQ, UK

Contents

List of tables

Acknowledgements

The original research for this book was undertaken while I held a Hallsworth Research Fellowship in the Sociology Department of the University of Manchester. I remain deeply grateful for the opportunity of that period of uninterrupted research, especially to Huw Beynon, the then Head of Department, for his continuing support.

I relied on many people and organisations in Bolton and Manchester to put me in contact with potential interviewees: Age Concern; Citizens' Advice Bureaux; Manchester Employment Research Group; General, Municipal and Boilermakers' Trades Union branches; the Workers' Education Association. Other helpful leads and information were provided by Salford and Ordsall local history libraries and groups; 'Bridging the Years' oral history project in Ordsall docks; Manchester Women's History Group; Manchester Studies project on Trafford Park; Documentary Photography Archive; Salford Working Class Movement Library; The Manchester Jewish Museum. Bolton Libraries Archives and Local Studies Services gave access to transcriptions of the 'Growing up in Bolton 1900–1940' oral history project. Thanks also to Andrew Davies and Ian McIntosh for helping to track down sources and people, and for allowing me to refer to their unpublished work.

My main debt, however, is to all the people I interviewed, without whose testimony there would be no book. They welcomed me into their homes and gave generously of their time and memories, answering questions, telling their life stories and work histories, showing family photographs and lending all sorts of documents. I am only sorry that I cannot thank them by name: they have been given pseudonyms in the text so as to ensure confidentiality.

The final writing up was immensely facilitated by two Fellowships held in 1998: in the Sociology Program of the Research School of Social Sciences at the Australian National University and at the Swedish Collegium for Advanced Study in the Social Sciences in Uppsala. Special thanks are due to my 'hosts' Judy Wajcman and Göran Therborn respectively, not least for creating the perfect balance of stimulating seminars, lively mealtimes and peaceful isolation. Without the generosity of Joan Busfield, who took on my administrative duties, I would not have been able to go to SCASSS, and for this and for numerous discussions over the years I am grateful to her and to all my colleagues in the Sociology Department at Essex. Many of the ideas in the book took shape in discussion with graduate students: the intellectual input and empathy of my PhD students with agonisings over details of interpretation are much appreciated. Walks and talks along the Colne estuary with Catherine Hall helped dissolve those headaches that inevitably afflict the writing process and revived the spirit for further work.

John Holmwood has been the best editor an author could wish for. His encouragement, minimally interventionist but always constructive suggestions, calm efficiency and eye for detail made for an unexpectedly smooth transition from draft to final publication. sociologypress is an exciting and forward looking venture enabling the publication of research-based analyses which do not conform to the undergraduate textbook format currently constraining so many commercial publishers. I am honoured that *Cottons and Casuals* is the first in what I trust will be a stimulating and successful series of publications.

My final thanks are to Mark Harvey who has lived (too often at long distance) with this project throughout all the stages of its life. He has read and reread and commented on so many occasions that he must be almost as familiar with every person, word and argument as I am. The book would not have been completed without his intellectual contribution and unswerving support.

All Humphrey Spender photographs are reproduced with kind permission of Bolton Museum and Art Gallery.

Chapter 1
On working on 'work'

This book can be read in a number of ways which relate to its various aims. At the most straightforward level, of content and narrative, it is 'about' women, gender and work, and the connections, for different groupings of women, between the gendered divisions of different spheres of their lives. Its central subject matter and its central questions, and answers, therefore, are substantive ones, and historically specific. It develops an analysis on the basis of oral history research conducted in the 1990s with retired women who began work in Lancashire during the inter-war years and whose experience broadly laps over the second third of the twentieth century.

But their testimonies, and my analysis, are also deployed as a means by which to engage with a contemporary range of intellectual issues and debates in the social and human sciences, especially those of particular concern to sociology and feminist theory. Stated broadly, one key issue at stake is how, in practice, to move beyond dualistic modes of theoretical analysis that rely on either/or binary concepts. Another concerns diversity, and the positive challenge this poses for explanatory modes of analysis when the relatively easy explanations of modernist 'grand narratives' have been abandoned. Then there is the problem of how to conceptualise the linkages and intersection between, and relative significance of, different forms of social division and inequality. A further series of questions relates to time and temporality and to space, place and locality and to the interconnection of these with cultural forms and social relations. Also at issue is multi- or inter-disciplinarity and the challenge of doing justice to the social, cultural, historical, economic and spatial character of the subject matter without compromising analytical coherence. The central research questions for this research about the past arise from present-day theoretical and political concerns, and so, as well as being analysed in its own terms and own right, the historical material is used additionally to explore issues such as gender identity, and the meaning of work, which exercise thinkers today. In this way the text aims to contribute to contemporary intellectual debate.

The book is written with a further, and equally important, aim of 'opening up' the research process and reflecting on the 'production' of knowledge. Rather than simply presenting conclusions about the research in the form of final product, or neatly worked out analysis, which has the appearance of being 'fully constituted knowledge', I attempt to give a picture of 'interpretation in the making', commenting on the research process and its sources, and focusing especially on the 'in between' stages of processing and interpreting material. This is done not only out of concern for reflexivity. Rather, the hope is to bring into the open some of the fundamental problems which inevitably tax anyone doing empirical research but which do not feature nearly so prominently in methodology handbooks as does the earlier stage of material collection, and which are usually all but buried without trace, and forgotten, by the time the final write-up (on which their resolution rests) sees the light of day. Whatever her or his level of experience, problems of data processing and interpretation are bound to confront every researcher in every research project. Yet this is probably the most difficult phase for research methods experts to offer advice about since each researcher's problems necessarily refer to particular sources and specific contents for which general guidelines may be just too general.

Pointing to the existence of such questions is intended as just that: opening up the issue through discussion of the specific problems of interpretation and matching of source materials that arose in the course of this research project. No 'solutions' are suggested, but then that would be impossible. However, maintaining silence about this raft of problems and presenting research results as if they did not exist only pushes them further under the carpet, and reinforces the fiction of a 'virgin birth' analysis. A mode of writing up is attempted, therefore, with such issues in mind, in order both to demystify 'social analysis in the making' and reflect on the process of production of knowledge, and also to render the book of methodological relevance and interest. Premises and conceptual underpinnings of arguments are made explicit so as to avoid presenting them only in their fully finished end-state. Epistemological issues arising from the use of different types of source material (including official statistics, archive data, and qualitative interviews) are addressed, with comment on their respective inadequacies or advantages, as well as on the often vexed problem of synthesising an analysis from such materials of disparate style and content.

Tracing a trajectory

The research itself explores the connection between paid employment of different kinds and domestic labour, focusing on women's work in Britain in the 1930s. This was a time before married women were employed as wage workers on a mass scale and also before the widespread availability of the consumer commodities and domestic appliances that are often understood to be associated with women's mass entry to the labour market, as both condition and consequence. The anomalous situation of married women in Lancashire who were employed full-time in a period before this was general represents the starting point for analysis. What made their situation viable and how did they cope?

At a more general level the project is concerned with the relation between the household and market economies, and historical transformations of that relationship, a topic of key concern across the social sciences, to economists, anthropologists and historians, as to sociologists and gender theorists. As two of the most important sites for labour activity and for the production of goods and services in any socio-economic system (though not the only ones), particularly in industrial society, the nature of their structural connection tells much about other aspects of the society. The boundaries between these two sectors are not pre-given or fixed. What sort of labour and how much is expended in each is not predetermined. What is produced in each varies over time and between places, as does the labour socially allocated to each, which may or may not have a gendered character. Thus, anthropologists document the many complex and varied ways in which different kinds of activities involving labour connect to each other in pre-industrial or non-literate societies. Development economists chart the increasing definition of and differentiation between the two sectors that tends to accompany the emergence and expansion of a wage economy, industrialisation, integration with the world market and economic development, and the often far-reaching impact of such differentiation for households, people, genders, and well-being. Historians have done the same for the now long-industrialised world, drawing attention to the construction of new kinds of divisions between home and work, public and private, production and reproduction, and women and men that accompanied the development of the market, commodity, wage economy, and its separation off from the household, which in turn gradually ceased to constitute a central locus for production and consumption. For sociologists the more likely starting point is the already existing differentiation of a socio-economic system where priority has been accorded to work in the market economy, and to the economic significance of commodities produced and exchanged in this sector, rather than to labour expended, and goods and services produced, primarily by women, in the household which even now sometimes has difficulty in being recognised as a form of 'economy'.

But no two countries studied by social scientists are identical in this respect and within any one the pattern of connections is not static. In previous research (Glucksmann, 1990) I explored the structural transformation of the relationship between household and formal economies which occurred with the introduction of mass production and consumption in inter-war Britain, discerning two schematic patterns of relationship, characteristic of the periods before and after mass production respectively. In the later pattern, consolidated after the Second World War in the 1950s and 1960s, women assumed a heightened significance to new growth areas of industry both as consumers and producers. Moreover, one of the main findings in *Women Assemble* was that women assemblers working in the new mechanised industries of the inter-war period prefigured patterns of domestic and wage labour that were to become much more generalised after the war. They worked in factories producing new products such as domestic appliances, ready-made clothing and factory-prepared food that were specifically destined for use in the household and for whom women were the targeted market. This was how women became linked to the new products both as producer and consumer. These developments also implied an extensive alteration of the relationship between the household economy and the world of commodity production, the web of circuits connecting them gradually becoming more intertwined and denser as domestic labour came to be effected more on the basis of purchased commodities, as more women earned money wages, and as a higher proportion of household income was recirculated back to industries producing goods used to aid or replace the labour previously undertaken by women on a more labour-intensive basis.

But the 'new industries' were primarily located in the South East and in Greater London, areas where economic recovery from recession and the restructuring of industry were concentrated. The North West stood in sharp contrast, its old established staple industries in decline, unable to survive the slump, and with far fewer new industries being set up to replace them. An aim of the present research, then, was to continue exploration of long-term developments in the relationship between the household and the market economies occurring between the 1920s and 1960s by looking at another part of the country where a different set of circumstances obtained. If the economy of the South East was expanding while that of the North West was in decline, should we expect transformation of the relation between household and market economies to occur later in the latter than the former, perhaps only after the war? High levels of unemployment in the 1930s might militate against the changes for women working in the new industries in the South East (especially their increased domestic consumption) being possible in the North West, and suggest that changes might have begun to occur in the 1950s rather than in the 1930s. On the other hand, however, there was also a countervailing factor in the North West, which could complicate the picture, namely, the long tradition of women remaining in employment after they married and after they had children, particularly in the textile industry. Indeed, contemporary commentators like Joan Beauchamp (1937) had already drawn attention to the propensity of women workers in Lancashire to purchase laundry services and cooked dinners. So, who took responsibility for domestic labour when married women were in full-time employment and how was it effected in the absence of post-war 'labour-saving' devices? The present work, therefore, aims to advance and refine earlier analysis on the basis of new material, adding more of a spatial slant, introducing greater complexity into the relationship between household and wage economies, and linking this more structural dimension of analysis with that of different occupational groups of women worker. At the level of individuals, interest centres not on details of their jobs or the labour process but rather on interconnections between their paid work and their domestic labour and household economy, the links between gender divisions and inequalities at work and at home, with the aim of elucidating the configurations of home, family, community and work for different groups of women.

Inter-war Britain has often been characterised as a country of 'two nations' (e.g. Priestley 1934), the economic devastation, unemployment and poverty of Scotland, Wales and large parts of northern England contrasting with renewal and modernisation in the South and Midlands. In the latter, standards of living were improving for those sections of the population linked to the rapidly developing sectors of finance and commerce, retail, the professions and public administration, or to the new motor and consumer goods industries. New trading and housing estates were built, a renewal of infrastructure was undertaken, including the installation of electricity for both commercial and domestic use, and the occupational structure was transformed with the emergence of new kinds of jobs in offices, banks, shops and factories, many of which were filled by women. An emphasis on domesticity and the 'ideal home' with its 'non-working' wife accompanied the shift to consumer goods production and rising levels of disposal income. A new relation was in the process of being formed between woman and home, in practice and in ideology, and particularly for middle class women in a decade which witnessed the demise of the residential domestic servants which many of their mothers would have employed. The importance of scientific household management and the social value of housewives in caring for home, husband and children were resoundingly acknowledged in public discourse. All this was a far cry from the social conditions in the regions of economic decline where worsening levels of housing, nutrition, health and mortality rates accompanied mass unemployment and led to increasing divergence between the two parts of the nation.

But there were also sharp variations within regions, not just between them, so that areas characteristic of each of the 'two nations' could exist almost adjacent to each other. The thumbnail sketch is, thus, a gross oversimplification, parts of the South East also being poverty stricken, particularly older inner city areas, while sections of the North were flourishing, social conditions mirroring uneven decline and development wherever it occurred.[1] Certainly, the new industries were concentrated in the southern part of the country and those in decline were concentrated in the north. Coal mining, textiles, shipbuilding, and mechanical engineering had been the backbone of 'the first industrial nation' and the pre-eminent industries until the First World War, oriented to the manufacture and export of capital goods, and it was the closure of coal pits, shipyards, and heavy engineering factories that threw millions of men out of work, and of mills and weaving sheds that had a similar effect for women (and men). But at the same time as the unemployed organised hunger marches in many parts of Lancashire during the 1930s, parts of central Manchester prospered with a veritable boom in retail sales and employment and Trafford Park, the largest industrial estate in the world, continued to attract foreign investment, and in its wake, new factories, and a corresponding expansion of employment.

Any brief overview of women's employment during the inter-war years is similarly bound to gloss over important variations between places, making it difficult to distinguish between contradictory trends, especially between long established patterns which were diminishing in strength and newly emerging ones that were gaining prevalence. In general most women who engaged in waged work were young and single.[2] Most married women did not work in paid formal employment. This was partly a result of the marriage bars operated by civil service, local government and many factories, shops and offices. But looking after household and family was extremely demanding of both time and labour. And the normal working week expected of employees was 48 hours. Part-time work did not exist. So, it is not surprising that official statistics show as gross national figures for 1931, that only 10 per cent of married women were in paid employment, compared with 70 per cent of single women. Put the other way, 16 per cent of working women were married, while 77 per cent were single (Gales and Marks, 1974: 63; Hakim, 1979: 11–12).

But the situation was not static. In the 20 years to 1951 the number of occupied women officially enumerated rose from 5.6 to 6.3 million (*Census of Population*, 1931, Occupation Tables: 673; *Census of Population*, 1951, General Report: 130).[3] Married women represented a slowly growing proportion of the total labour force between 1918 and 1939, as did the proportion of married women who engaged in waged work. This trend, which preceded the Second World War (Glucksmann, 1990: 10, 37–8), was particularly marked in the new industries and for younger married women who tended to remain at work until the birth of their first child (Glucksmann, 1990: 57–65).

Marked regional differences further complicate the variations in women's participation by age and marital status. In the two regions which have been a particular focus for my research, the South East and North West, the employment of women, including married women, was higher than the national average as a proportion both of the female population and of the total labour force. But the underlying reasons were different in the two cases and the trends were, to some extent, moving in opposite directions. Taken together these two regions accounted for 56 per cent of all women occupied in 1931 (2.1 million, or nearly 37 per cent in the South East of the total of 5.6 million, and 1.1 million or 19 per cent of the total in the North West). Both regions had the highest levels of female participation at 36.1 and 41.9 per cent respectively of the total number of women aged 14 and over, against a national average for England and Wales of 34.2 per cent. But while the out of work amounted to 15.4 per cent of all occupied women in the North West, the proportion in the South East was much lower at 5.7 per cent (*Census of Population*, 1931, Occupation Tables: 154–5, General Report: 119). Older and married women were concentrated in the now declining industries of the North West such as textiles, which had a long tradition of employing them, but in the South East it was precisely the newly emerging areas of employment that retained or recruited married women, in a clear break with established practice in that part of the country. Any convergence in the pattern of participation for older or married women across the two regions was thus due to the intersecting of two contradictory trends. Taken to their logical conclusion these would result in the dominance of the married woman wage worker in the South East and her disappearance in the North West. (But in reality, of course, this did not happen.)

Although the numbers of women employed in textiles and textile goods increased slightly between 1921 and 1931 by 4.2 per cent from 662,384 to 690,395 (*Census of Population*, 1931, Industry Tables B: 714–19), the following 20 years saw a very steep decline, of 12.6 per cent in the number of women employed in textiles from 543,257 to 474,657, a loss of 68,600 (*Census of Population*, 1951, Industry Tables C: 644–8). And, while new employment opportunities for women continued to grow in the South East throughout the period, such that the number of people in insured occupations grew by almost 60 per cent between 1923 and 1938 (*Ministry of Labour Gazette*, December 1938: 469), the jobs lost in textiles and manufacture in the North West were far from compensated for by the creation of new employment opportunities.

Switching tracks

Having already researched women workers in the expanding industries of the South East my original plan for the new project was to do a comparative study in the North West of a similar occupational group, attempting a more generational contrast between those who had commenced employment in the 1930s and in the 1950s respectively. Holding the type of employment fairly constant, I would focus less on the content of paid work but more on the connection between their employment circumstances and their household economy, that is, their nexus of relations as 'producer and consumer' and changes in that nexus of relations. The award of a research fellowship at Manchester University[4] for a year provided a perfect opportunity for pursuing lines of inquiry arising from *Women Assemble* and for doing empirical work about the place where I would be based. The ideal research scenario envisaged was pairs of mothers and daughters, born around the 1910s and 1930s respectively, who would have begun work in the 1930s or 1950s. This way I could test out the pre-war/post-war question about married women, employment and consumer goods for the North West, as well as doing regional comparison. I would be able to pinpoint changes between the generations by interviewing mother and daughter together, and also have a longer-term perspective towards both the past and the future through the mothers' recollections of their own mothers, and the daughters' familiarity with the situation of their own daughters.

Trafford Park seemed like one of the best places to start looking for women to interview: lots of factories, many of them newly established in the inter-war years, and bound to employ women in similar semi-skilled operative positions to the ones I was familiar with from the South East in electrical engineering and food processing. It would be far easier to trace retired workers here than in the London area, I thought, because people had probably lived in closer proximity to their work place and there may well have been less geographical mobility in the intervening years. All I needed was to do some preliminary background reading on women's work in the area and then I'd be ready to get going.

Wonderful plans if they had worked! With hindsight they were naïve and unrealistic, hatched in ignorance, utopian and impossible. For a start, much less relevant information was available than I had imagined on the history of women's employment in the area, despite the abundance of formal labour and labour movement histories and the existence of a number of trade union archives. No background source existed as such so it proved necessary to track down the preliminary information too. Eventually I gave up the search for 'the' definitive labour history of women's work in Manchester and just had to accept that it did not exist.

Then it emerged that the factories in Trafford Park had not been large employers of women after all and/or that documentary and archive material was not available. In the 1930s there had been some mills, food manufacturers (e.g. Kellogg), soap, rubber goods and electrical engineering factories. Most, however, were heavy engineering firms that employed men. Although large numbers of women were drafted in during the Second World War, especially to Ford which set up a plant for the duration, it appeared that very few women had worked on assembly type work in Trafford Park before the war (McIntosh, 1991). Those I did manage to contact who had worked on the estate throughout their lives (Mary Gouden, Amy Fowler) were single, thus suggesting a marriage bar too. In any case, the consensus amongst local women was that Trafford Park was primarily a place for men, and not for married women to work. So, although I collected much documentary material about the history of the industrial estate, the firms operating there, Ford during the war, the housing estate and reminiscences of its residents (including my own interview with Connie Mitchell) this was to be of limited use.

Detailing further 'the research project that never happened' would be extremely tedious.[5] I did interview one mother and daughter pair (Clarice Holmes and Doreen Baker) and I retained the original themes for analysis, the generational perspective and regional comparison, but the eventual research 'subjects' were not those I originally had in mind. It was not feasible to concentrate the study on women assemblers in Manchester. The city had experienced early industrial diversification and prospered (whilst cotton and its associated problems moved northwards). Young people moved in and out of jobs fairly easily during the inter-war period with relatively low levels of unemployment, and although employment in the cotton industry still accounted for a fair proportion of jobs, expansion was concentrated in office work and the distributive trades, rather than in other factory work (*Census of Population*, 1931; Harley, 1937; Fowler, 1988). Labour markets were geographically circumscribed and discrete, Salford, Eccles and Stretford being distinct from Manchester. It had been unrealistic, therefore, to conceive of 'a' single labour market comprising Manchester and surrounding area. Certainly, local people spoke in terms of geographically bounded and small labour markets, having looked for work virtually only within walking distance (or a short bus ride) from home.

For these reasons most of the eventual interviewees had engaged in occupations other than assembly. Nor were they confined to central Manchester. Practical problems had forced greater flexibility onto the research, experience of industrial employment in the inter-war years becoming the bottom line criterion for selecting suitable respondents. But, interestingly, the sample turned out to comprise, and not by any prior design, two broad occupational groups, the 'cottons and casuals' of the title. Why this should have been so is discussed later on. Most of the cotton workers came from Bolton and surrounds and had engaged in full-time paid employment throughout their working lives. The other grouping, more diverse in terms of occupation and pattern of employment, included women, several of whom lived in Salford, who had engaged in formal waged work before marriage but in casual work afterwards. In addition a third, smaller, grouping of single women was distinguished who differed from both cottons and casuals. Once all the testimony was subjected to detailed scrutiny, and the same transcript revisited through several different sets of lenses, other differences also appeared, in addition to their work histories which varied systematically between the groupings. It was these patterns of systematic similarity and difference that led to the research focus on comparison of the connection between employment, domestic arrangements and identity.

Since the Lancashire textile industry has been well documented (e.g. Jewkes and Grey, 1935; Saul, 1960; Chandler, 1980; Pollard, 1983; Pagnamenta and Overy, 1984) there was no problem in contextualising the experience of the weavers I met against the history of the industry. We know now that this kind of work was decreasing in dominance as a female occupation (for every 1,000 occupied women 110 were textile workers in 1921, 104 in 1931 but only 57 in 1951 (*Census of Population*, 1931, Occupational Tables G: 673–80; *Census of Population*, 1951, General Report, Table 62: 134–5), and that the industry exemplified many of the problems[6] implicated in the demise of the traditional staples during the inter-war years. But it still provided a livelihood for many hundreds of thousands of women and to them at the time it did not necessarily appear to be entering terminal decline.

Placing the more casually employed workers in their context, however, is virtually impossible, since no reliable statistics were collected about them and no histories written. Only regular forms of full-time employment counted for Census purposes and although oral evidence (e.g. Roberts, 1984, 1995b: 40–2) suggests that it was common for working-class women to earn money on a part-time basis at some point in their married life, they were not included amongst the 'economically active' in Census employment figures. The history of casual workers is virtually unknown and represents a gaping hole in knowledge about women's work and women's history that it would now be extremely difficult to reconstruct. In the absence of such essential background information comparable to that existing for the cotton workers, it will be important to avoid writing about casual workers as 'a discovery', and in so doing reinforce the received impression that in some sense theirs was not 'proper' work, of secondary status, or that they were marginal people.

The sample was small and not intended to be representative of either the occupational groups or the towns. Although the following chapters include many partial histories, and fragments of histories, the study is not intended as 'a social history', and it is not comprehensive. Many issues that would be essential to a self-respecting social history of Salford or Bolton or textile workers or young workers are barely touched on, for example religion. The division between Catholics and Protestants is mentioned but no detailed appraisal is undertaken. Similarly, no extensive civic history of Manchester or Bolton is provided, nor an account of the demise of textiles. No systematic decade by decade 'historical time' analysis is offered, although information about interviewees does span their entire life history. These omissions would matter to some kinds of study but they are not critical here. They are not essential to the chief purpose of this project, which is to elucidate the pattern of connections between different parts of people's lives, exploring the manner of intersection of the various forms of difference and inequality, explaining their conditions of existence, comparing them and how they were subjectively lived, felt and understood by particular individuals. Such an analysis will provide the material by which to attempt an answer to the bigger questions outlined above as well as to refine the conceptual framework, outlined below, for analysing all forms of labour.

Since the people interviewed are the main characters in the cast, most are introduced here in the main text as a central reference point for the reader, rather than being relegated to a methodological appendix. Hopefully, the Interview grid (Tables 1–3) supplys sufficient detail to give a picture of each player as a real person as well as to suggest some of the similarities and differences between and across groups that form the basis for in-depth examination. As the various categories may suggest, the interpretation relied on going over and over the testimonies with different sets of questions in mind, some questions giving rise to others. To a large extent the grid is a product of the analysis, rather than its starting point, the categories indicating features that came to be recognised as significant only through the lengthy process of qualitative analysis.

Explanatory notes on the Interview Grid, Tables 1–3

- The tables include the twenty interviewees mentioned most frequently in the text and whose testimony was the fullest. See Appendix for details of the interviews.

- People have been grouped as textile workers, single women, and other occupations (than textiles) which includes casual work. There would, of course, be other ways of sub-dividing (for instance by where they came from) or leaving them ungrouped.

- Amy Fowler is placed with the single women. Even though she did eventually marry, aged 57, her circumstances closely resemble those of the other unmarried women. Her husband Harry Fowler is the only man included in the tables or interviewed at length. He sat in on her session and was keen to tell his life story too.

- Name: all are pseudonyms in order to respect the confidentiality of testimony. Within the groupings people are listed in order of date of birth, rather than alphabetically, this seeming excessively artificial given that these are not their real names.

- Siblings: the number excludes the interviewee, so add one for the total number of children in the family of origin.

- Husband housework: refers to whether, and how much, husbands shared domestic labour and child care.

- Work after marriage: indicates whether or not she engaged in waged work.

- Childcare: who looked after the children and whether they were remunerated.

- A Tip-up/B Housekeeping: relates to financial arrangements. In system A the man hands over his entire pay packet to his wife, while in B he gives her housekeeping money, retaining an often unknown amount for personal use. See Pahl (1989) for modes of intra-familial money management.

- Washing machine: date they acquired a washing machine in their own home, or what other method was used.

- Vacuum cleaner: attempts to get at when electricity was installed, or when they first had electric domestic appliances, refrigerator or vacuum cleaner.

- Bath: date and stage in life at which they first had indoor facilities of toilet and bath.

- Special: highlights something particular about each person which will feature later on, though this is not necessarily their most noteworthy aspect.

Interview Grid: Table 1 Textile workers

	Clarice Holmes	Edith Ashworth	Lily Hunt	Marjorie Fisher	Alice Foster	Nellie Lynch	Doreen Baker
Date of birth	1895	1907	1911	1914	1917	1918	1919
Siblings	6	4 surviving + 2 died	2	7 surviving + 4 died	1	13: a 'mixed family'	None
Father's job	Engineer	Building labourer	Road paver	Iron moulder in foundry	On the railway	Foundry	Spinner Quarry
Mother's work	Card room in mill	Weaver	Card room in mill Took in washing	Ring spinner Took in washing	Mother deserted when AF was 11 Father remarried	Died in childbirth when NL was 10	Weaver (Clarice Holmes)
Date of marriage	1916	1932	1939	1936	1940	1945	1939
Home	Bolton	Little Hulton	Oldham	Rochdale Timperley	Bolton	Bolton	Bolton
Own job	Weaver	Weaver	Weaver Pub work Weaver	Spinner Engineering after children	Spinner Weaver	Doffer Weaver	Winding
Husband's job	Spinner Quarry, often unemployed d.1937	Miner: coal cutter	Pub Mill warehouse	Fitter, Metrovicks	Foundry	Little piecer Army Pit	Painter/decorator
Husband housework	'A bit' dismissive about husband	Washing up only. EA had 'strict routine'	Washing up	DIY only	Yes	No	Impl es not: in the army
Work after marriage	Continuous	Continuous	Continuous	Part-time 1943–59 Then full-time	Continuous	'No, he wouldn't allow it' Part-time cleaning	Part-time Resistance of husband
Children	1: 1919	2: 1933, 1937	None	2: 1937, 1939	1: 1945	4: 1946–59	1: 1943
Childcare	Paid mother	Paid mother, boarded during week	N/A	Mother	Board with sister, cost half AF's wages	Self	Neighbour, cost 5 shillings a week Nursery school
A. Tip-up B. Housekeeping	Father A Husband A	Father B Husband A	Father A Husband A	Father B Husband A 'no quarrels'	Husband A	Husband B	Husband probably A, DB knew his earnings
Washing machine		1936 [!!]	Laundrette only	Before 1960	1950	1954	1960s
Vacuum cleaner		Late 1930s	Fridge 1950	Fridge 1960	1979	1954	Soon after war
Bath	1960s	1933 in rented house	Post-war	1936, in new house with WC	Bored at home after birth of child	Child labourer	1960s
Special	Political activist in 1930s. Mother of Doreen Baker	Felt exploited when young	Left Oldham in search for work in 1930s	Sole support of parental family in 1930s			Stresses conflict with husband over her working

Interview Grid: Table 2 Casual and other occupations

	Connie Mitchell	Flo Nuttall	Hilda Walker	Annie Preston	Kath Hinton	Winnie Smith	Agnes Brown	Mabel Paget	Vera Rogers
Date of birth	1911	1916	1916	1917	1918	1918	1920	1923	1924
Sibs	4	4	1	2	2	?	5 surviving + 6 died: 'eldest of 12'	Only child	1
Father's job	Navy, deserted mother and 5 children	Cruel stepfather, mostly out of work	Dock labourer	Timber yard, invalided by injury	'Work-shy'	? (Died young)	Docker	Draughtsman	Engine driver in docks
Mother's work	Took in washing	Office cleaning	Worral's Dyeworks	Died when AP was 11	Hairdresser	? (Died young)	Cotton mill worker until birth of AB; 'of course she couldn't go after'	Dress fitter	Rope works before marriage Office cleaning
Date of marriage	1936	1933	1941	1939	1950	1944	1946	1948	1947
Home	Trafford Park, Salford	Salford	Salford	Salford	Ancoats 1954 Middleton 1965 Oldham	Oldham	Salford	Salford Timperley	Salford
Own job	Brooke Bond tea blending Ford during war	Woolworth Factory canteens, 1949 onwards	Bonus clerk at Metrovicks	Mill, weaver, 14 to 21 years Night-cleaning and 'all sorts'	Electrical factories, Ferranti from 1957	Sewing machinist on piecework, same mill from 1944–69	Spinner, Metrovicks, cable factory, mill, then buses 1950–78	'Draughtsman' at Metrovicks during war	Clerical Sales (part-time after children)
Husband's job	Welder at Trafford Park	Lorry driver	Lathe turner, skilled engineer at Metrovicks	Army Building Crane-driver at Metrovicks	Labourer, night work	Engineer at Ferranti	Bricklayer, seasonal	Engineer	Maintenance stores manager
Husband housework	No	No	Yes	No	Only later	No	No, 'old brigade'	Little	No
Work after marriage	Continuous	Stopped work after children, went full-time when grew up	Left 1941, at childbirth, returned 1950, part-time	Yes, continuously	Yes, 'necessity'	Continuous	Continuous	Occasional contracts for drawing offices	Part-time
Children	None	6, from 1935	2: 1941, 1943	4, plus one died: 1942–59	3: 1946 unmarried, 1956, 1959	None	1: 1947	1: 1956	Five: 1948–64

Interview Grid: Table 2 Casual and other occupations continued

	Connie Mitchell	Flo Nuttall	Hilda Walker	Annie Preston	Kath Hinton	Winnie Smith	Agnes Brown	Mabel Paget	Vera Rogers
Childcare	N/A	Looked after by self	Mother, lived opposite, did not pay	Sister, paid £2 per week for 3 children	Paid neighbours	N/A	Mother next door, paid firth of wages, + electricity bil + rent	Self	Paid mother
A. Tip-up B. Housekeeping	Husband B	Stepfather B Husband B	Husband B 'No complaints'	Husband B	Husband A		Husband B Says this is local custom	Father A Husband B	Father B Husband B
Washing machine	Used wash-house	1958	Wash-house, until 1970s	Wash-house until 1971	Gas boiler at home		1974. Eulogy of wash-house	1956	Before 1950
Vacuum cleaner				1960s, fridge 1970s	Late 1950s	Fridge, late 1950s	Electricity, c 1948	Fridge 1953	
Bath	1936, in own rented house on TP estate	1956	New house 1970	1971, when rehoused		1950, bought house with bath		Early 1930s, after move to Timperley	Bath 1960
Special	Emphasised no work for married women in Salford	'Thrilled to bits with outside loo' 1956	Still lives near birthplace Opposed to mothers working	Eulogy of wash-house Cousin of Ivy Turner	'Wore out shoes' looking for work Vague memory re child minders except for pay	'Walked our feet off looking for work' Too young to qualify for dole	On paying mother for child care: 'helped her, helped me'	Husband's presence inhibited interview	Post-war work pattern

Interview Grid: Table 3 Single women and husband

	Ivy Turner	Amy Fowler	Mary Gouden	Harry Fowler
Date of birth	1914	1919	1920	1923
Sibs	7: the youngest of 8	4 surviving + 1 died	1	6: the youngest of 7
Father's job	Lorry driver Docks	Cranedriver in docks	Trams	Labourer at Worrals
Mother's work	Cook before marriage	Printing before marriage	Maid before marriage	Took in washing 'Unofficial midwife'
Date of marriage	Single	1976*	Single	1976*
Home	Salford	Salford	Salford	Salford
Own job	Co-op tea factory for 48 years, 1928–76	Box works Cable factory for 35 years Various	Sewing Metrovicks, 1940–80: manual then clerical	Apprentice, then engineer Retired 1980
Husband's job	N/A	Engineer	N/A	
Husband housework	N/A	N/A	N/A	
Work after marriage	Continuous	Continuous	Continuous	None
Children	None	None	None	None
Childcare	N/A	N/A	N/A	
A. Tip-up B. Housekeeping	Father 1934 IT supported mother	Father B	Father A	Father A
Washing machine	Bag wash at laundry	Copper Launderette	Mother washed by hand at home Launderette	At home until 1968; then launderette
Vacuum cleaner				1968, only when re-housed
Bath	1960s, after mother died	1966	1980, also inside WC	
Special	Marriage bar at Co-op 'Mother tied me to her apron strings'	*She (and husband) cared for elderly mothers, married very late	Rehoused only in 1980 when 61 and retired	*Cared for mother. Single till late when married Amy. Kept interrupting her interview, so did him too!

Questioning theory

Reforming the relation between concepts, theory and empirical analysis is perhaps one of the most urgent tasks facing sociology today, a virtual necessity if the discipline is to survive yet still take to heart the end of century's thorough-going challenges to post-Enlightenment modernist European thought. Modes of thinking which deploy 'grand narratives', imply determinism, universalism or essentialism, rely on binaries as a basic analytical procedure have characterised sociology as much as any other discipline. For example, dualisms (of individual versus society, action versus structure, or structure versus culture, meaning versus materiality, or idealism versus materialism, subject versus object, and so on) have furnished some of the central frames for sociological analysis for well over a century. They will have been familiar to generations of students who confront them at a particular stage in their seemingly endlessly repeated life-cycle in which one side of the dualism represents the dominant way of thinking, superseded after some years by the other, followed by the attempt to combine the two together in an effort to overcome the dualism, before starting on the round all over again, with each new cycle having slightly altered emphases and terminology.

Perhaps one reason why these dualisms and the debates deriving from them have remained so intractable, replaying themselves with such regularity but without appearing (to me) to move forward is to do with their positioning within one side of an even deeper and more fundamental dichotomy between 'theory' and empirical material. Probably causing more intellectual paralysis than all the other debates over the 'sub-binaries', this dichotomy clearly connotes abstract versus concrete, and also has associations, in academic circles, of superior versus inferior, complex versus simpler, and, more arguably, of male versus female. The more abstract, the less touched by substantive considerations, the better, it seems to be suggested, and the more likely that its practitioners (until recently) would be male. Rather than rising to the challenge of empirical data, an effect of this division, which elevates and isolates theory as something to be perfected in and for itself, is to reduce substantive material to being little more than an instance or demonstration of a theoretical position, lacking in significance itself. This criticism, I hope it is clear, is not addressed towards theory itself but rather towards theoreticism.[7] It is ironic that the critiques of dualistic thinking should have made so little inroad into this most basic of dualisms: by conducting their attacks within one side of the opposition, largely within theory, they effectively reinforce the one dichotomy underlying all the others they aim to undermine, and in so doing reproduce the exclusive status accorded to pure 'theory'.

A number of feminists (including Collins, 1990; Bradley, 1996) have suggested the adoption of a 'both–and' approach in preference to the more conventional dualistic 'either–or' perspective, and in the chapters that follow I pursue a broadly similar path. In place of the theory versus empirical data couple, with the latter as illustration or proof of the former, I prefer to think of knowledge as being generated through interplay between the concepts of a broad conceptual framework and analysis of the substantive subject matter that they were designed to conceptualise, using theoretical constructs to make sense of the data and in turn developing theoretical analysis on the basis of substantive material. Instead of formulating general theoretical propositions, whose validity is assessed by reference to empirical instances, this approach attempts to refine and develop the concepts through analysis of empirical material, connecting abstract and concrete, and concept and data, rather than opposing them. I have found it more intellectually demanding, personally, to enter the uncharted waters of producing and making sense of empirical data, in order to theorise it, than to critique or extrapolate theoretical positions, manipulating one in terms of another.

But if the primary concern of a project is to analyse and explain the social processes and dynamics that confront us, rather than to develop a timeless theory, a particular way of slicing up and relating together data, theory and concepts would be called for, one where the main route of traffic is between concepts and conceptual framework on the one hand, and, on the other, analysis of particular historical circumstances and empirical data. The process of theorising these not only contributes to the accumulation of new knowledge, but also assists in refining and improving concepts and frameworks. This does not mean ruling out consideration of the dilemmas for social analysis traditionally expressed by the various dualisms and binaries. What they are about, their content, is bound to remain a continuing parameter for social analysis, but perhaps they are to be viewed most fruitfully as world outlooks, philosophies or ontologies, frames for thinking about social life but which are not capable of resolution either theoretically or at any empirical level. The 'total social organisation of labour', outlined in the next section, and deployed throughout the book, represents the attempt at such a broad conceptual/ empirical schema along the lines suggested, which permits an inclusive way of thinking about 'work' and provides a set of conceptual tools formulated to assist the analysis of labour activity, whatever form this takes. Actual instances of work could never be 'case studies' or 'proofs' of the conceptual framework anymore than the framework could have been formulated purely in the abstract.

In terms of their content, several of the binaries or 'sub-dualisms' are indeed directly relevant to the subject matter of this research. The 'individual versus society' and 'agency versus structure' dichotomies could certainly figure, with attention focused, on one side, towards meaning, subjectivity or identity, and on the other, towards materiality or objective conditions. But in looking at individual people and their life histories the approach I intend to adopt will be to view particular persons neither as 'reflecting' external forces and social conditions nor as capable of (re)inventing themselves, but rather as formed by, responding to, and living the conditions in which they find themselves. While being a unique person with her own specific history and identity, the individual can also reveal much about the social structure of which she is and constitutes a part, and about the constraints imposed on her and opportunities available to her that extend far beyond her particular circumstances. Similarly, in approaching another key distinction, between public and private, the aim will be to focus on their inter-relation, on the premiss that the workings of one could not be understood in isolation from the other. If 'public' is constructed in contrast, and has meaning only in opposition, to 'private', and vice versa, then they must be approached not singly and separately but together in combination.

'Difference' became one of the most commonly used terms of 1990s social and cultural analysis, and it is also central to this study. The meaning of the concept varies in different discourses and disciplines, and it has been deployed at varying levels of analysis and generality. Within feminist theory it has been widely used to refer to experience, social relations, subjectivity, and identity, indicating to the various ways in which specific discourses (in particular) of difference are constituted, contested, reproduced, or resignified (Barrett, 1987; Brah, 1997: 125). Acknowledgement of difference, especially when combined with a theoretical outlook which emphasises fragmentation (of identities and social relations), and the transient, fleeting, ever-changing and hence unstable nature of meaning, has frequently been associated with a rejection of the attempt to explain phenomena, and of the quest for causal analysis, this being viewed as an inadmissable or impossible project. The 'differences' that I shall be exploring are not just ones of discourse (though they may be that too) but of lived experience, social relations, and subjective understanding of those experiences and social relations. Things and words (Barrett, 1992), or materiality and meaning, are different but can hardly be separated (Bradley, 1996: 10).

Diversity of experience, even amongst women who might appear to be very similar when viewed from the outside, is one of the main arguments of the book. A focus on the multiplicity of femininities and feminine identities will be to the fore, open to the possibility that in the working class areas of Salford or Bolton in the 1930s there were many different ways of being a woman, and many different ways of understanding that being. Such a focus, however, need not entail the abandonment of explanatory analysis. Nor does acknowledgement of difference, in itself, undermine concepts relating to structure. The choice (a new binary?) is not between, on the one hand, a flawed modernist meta-narrative which offers a deterministic, unitary, universalising account and, on the other, exclusive concentration on discourse and re-description, refusing all categories, systematicities, and causes. These opposing and mutually exclusive alternatives are not the only ones open to social theory in an era of 'post-post-modernism' (Walby, 1992). A different response would be to construct better theories than the discredited modernist versions (Holmwood, 1994; Marshall, 1994), to see internal differentiation within a category not as reason for abandoning the category, but as a stimulus to conceptual refinement (Maynard, 1994: 22), which works on the notion of causality, rather than dropping it, in the face of the complexity of the social world (Walby, 1992: 48), and that sees the multiplicity of inequalities, fragmentation and polarisation, as explicable tendencies (Bradley, 1996: 204). This is broadly the approach taken here, diversity, multiplicity, difference and complexity being welcomed as positive challenges to analysis, including explanation.

In concrete terms, this means thinking about the ways in which different forms of social division intersect with each other, for different people, and how widely, and by whom, particular configurations of intersection are shared. Occupation, gender, economic standing, class, marital status, age, and locality are the main social relations at issue. 'Race' and ethnicity play relatively less part in the story, though in Chapter 6 I shall suggest the quasi-ethnic undertones of discourses of local difference.[8] All the women interviewed were white 'native' Lancastrians. Some of their parents or grandparents had migrated to the area from other parts of Great Britain and Ireland but these migrant origins seemed of less significance to their present selves than their own current local residence.

However, issues of 'race'/ethnicity and their linkage with other forms of social division do enter the analysis in another way. Many of the frameworks on which I draw for thinking about the overlap and criss-crossing of different forms of inequality were developed in the highly productive aftermath of 'the black critique of white feminism' when concerted attempts were made to reconceptualise the intersection of 'race'/ethnicity with other social markers of difference and forms of social division. Anthias and Yuval-Davis (1983, 1992) stressed the importance of divisions of class and ethnicity that might cut across gender, or of gender within ethnicity or class, arguing for a framework that treats class, gender, ethnicity, racism as 'contexts' for each other. Gender, they insist, should always be contextualised in terms of class and ethnicity, and vice versa, permitting a conception of overlapping divisions, capable of coping with unequal power relations within the same ethnic or gender or class grouping. A similar framework was suggested by Collins's (1990) notion of a 'matrix of domination', which, like Anthias and Yuval-Davis, rejects additive models of oppression based on a unitary scale in favour of an inclusive 'both–and' approach towards interlocking features and divisions. From this conceptual stance, and depending on the context 'an individual may be an oppressor, a member of an oppressed group, or simultaneously oppressor and oppressed' (Collins, 1990: 225). The emerging concept of 'intersectionality', elaborated most fully (Brah, 1996: chapter 5; Lewis, 1996; Phoenix, 1998) in order to grasp complex intersections of gender and ethnicity, or gender and nationality, is of direct relevance to this study and one that I shall be working with and hoping to develop. An intersectional approach (if not always the term itself) is central to the attempt at highlighting the multi-faceted character of connections and divisions.

Thinking beyond dualisms; developing concepts on the basis of substantive material; a focus on difference and diversity and how to explain them; the variety of possible connections between forms of social division and inequality. These, in summary, are amongst the most pressing questions confronting social theory 'in general'. Whether or not they could ever be solved or answered in general is another matter. An implication of the foregoing discussion is that they could not, and that the attempt to do so would be based on a misunderstanding of the critiques from which they arise. Rather than seeking single, general, or definitive answers these are questions that can be answered only specifically, in practice, in relation to substantive analysis.

'Total social organisation of labour'

Since it represents a practical demonstration of many of these questions for theory, and is also a basic framework of analysis for the chapters that follow, this is an appropriate juncture to elaborate further the 'total social organisation of labour'. Recognition that 'work' is not simply synonymous with paid employment, and does not take place only in a structurally distinct 'economy' in industrial societies, but may be undertaken within a variety of socio-economic relations and take a variety of forms, raises questions that go to the very heart of the concept of 'work'. Work may be embedded in non-work activities, and the identical activity may constitute 'work' in some situations but not others. How is it now to be approached and defined in a manner which can take into account its fuzzy edges, its lack of differentiation from other activities and its location within and across the different sectors and institutions in complex societies. The 'total social organisation of labour' (an unfortunately cumbersome mouthful[9]) is a conceptual framework intended to solve some of these problems by a reorientation of perspective. Total social organisation of labour (TSOL) refers to the manner by which all the labour in a particular society is divided up between and allocated to different structures, institutions, activities and people. The TSOL is a kind of higher level division of labour, referring not to the technical division of tasks within one institution or work process, but rather to the social division of all of the labour in a given society of whatever kind between institutional spheres. It is the organisation of activities from the standpoint of their economic constraints and relations.

This idea was originally formulated in *Women Assemble* as a means of conceptualising the transformation of the relationship between the domestic and market economies during the inter-war years, and the associated large-scale changes in the gender allocation of labour between sectors. Since the various activities undertaken in domestic and more formal economic institutions were bound together, but in a changing nexus of relations, I considered that they were best understood as belonging to a wider system of 'labour' or work carried out under conditions that bound the two areas together.

Despite this substantive grounding, the 'total social organisation of labour' could be of more general applicability (as argued in Glucksmann 1995, 1998). The configuration by which labour is organised on a societal scale could be analysed either synchronically, as the pattern of differentiation existing at a particular historical conjuncture in a particular country, or diachronically, as the transformation between one form of the total social organisation of labour and another, or comparatively, as the different configurations of structures that characterise different social formations. A concrete analysis of the TSOL at any particular historical conjuncture would be concerned with the distribution of labour between different kinds of function: production, services, welfare, education and so on, and with the institutions and forms of labour in which such functions are carried out. Historical developments such as the emergence of specific sectors like healthcare and education could be accommodated within this framework. It would study the separating out and differentiation of sectors, the circuits connecting them, and the relations of determinacy operating between different sectors, as well as the internal divisions of labour and hierarchies of inequality within each. To pursue the earlier example, the market and household economies could be conceptualised as two sectors, but not the only two, of a larger structure of production and reproduction in industrial societies. At any given time a particular form of structural division and connection exists between them such that they are articulated in a particular manner. In addition to the internal organisation of each, then, there is also a structure to the relation between them. What occurred in one would be affected by and in turn affect the other so that they are interdependent. By focusing on the articulation of sectors that are distinct but not autonomous, it becomes possible to conceptualise links between hierarchies of inequalities in each.

At a theoretical level, an inclusive approach towards labour helps to overcome the divisions, both actual and conceptual, between public/private, work/home and commodity/non-commodity and so on, thus challenging analysis in terms of binaries or dualisms. As a relational concept, designating the interrelatedness of sectors and of the labour undertaken within them, the view of the TSOL is of the whole interconnectedness of all institutions and activities as they stand in relation to each other. Thus it can explain how things hang together and how they work without invoking deterministic, originary or unitary causes, and without implying they are unchanging. It restricts the possibility of there being any autonomous sphere of production, all sectors interacting with each other, though not necessarily in a harmonious or stable manner. The 'organisation' of labour is not 'an' organisation, orchestrated or externally imposed, and the totality of the social organisation of labour is to be conceived not as a pre-given entity or one with outside edges but rather as the overall relational network between the various differentiated sectors that happen to exist at a particular historical conjuncture in a particular society.

Within this framework, clearly, there can be no prior definitions about what constitutes labour nor any preconceptions about socially necessary 'amounts' of labour. What counts as labour will vary according to the social circumstances, and labouring activity may be more or less embedded in or structurally differentiated from other activities. The definition of 'work' would be broad, including all activity involved in the production and reproduction of economic relations and structures in a particular TSOL, irrespective of how and where the labour is carried out. Work might be performed for the state, a capitalist employer, a collective, a feudal lord, a husband, mother-in-law or oneself. It may be paid, unpaid or 'voluntary', and create use or exchange values. And it might be undertaken on a slave plantation, a commune, in the 'public' economy of the market, the 'private' economy of the household, or in the community. Attempting to depart from any essential, intrinsic or categorical definition of work or of what constitutes an economic relation, this is thus a *relational* conception of 'work', activities being understood to be such because they hang together and interdepend in a way that makes it worth thinking of them as forming distinctively economic relations. Finally, the TSOL is a conceptual framework and an approach to analysis, whose value can be demonstrated only through substantive study. It is not 'a theory' or 'an idea' to be 'proved' or 'supported' by examples.

This framework proved fruitful for analysing the changing relationship, and manner of integration, between the household and market economies, in the period before and after the introduction of mass production and consumption. It also offered a new slant on other developments, including the increasing availability of women for standard paid employment, the changing significance and role of the personal wage within the household, and the demise of residential domestic service as an institution.

An aim of the following chapters is to develop further the TSOL perspective. Thus far it has been used for analysis mainly at the macro-level, but now I want to deploy it more at the micro-level, exploring its value in distinguishing between the differing connections between paid employment and household labour for particular people, occupational groups, and local labour markets. In addition, it will need rethinking and refining so as to become capable of taking on board, at this very concrete level of analysis, changes that occur over time between generations, or even within the life course of an individual person, in the interface between or configuration of the different sets of relations and divisions, of home, work and so on. Just as actually existing social organisations of labour all have a spatial dimension, existing in a location and over a certain spatial expanse, so too they have a temporal dimension. The various interfaces and connections occur in temporal sequences, or cycles which repeat each other, rupture, or alter in some other way, that is, they involve temporal orderings that intersect with the passage of historical time but which are distinct from it. So temporality will be more fully developed as an integral aspect of TSOL as part of the overall attempt to introduce spatial, generational and temporal dimensions into the conceptual framework of the total social organisation of labour.

'Relations of knowledge'

Attention to the 'in between stages of research' is another key concern. Discussion of the interpretation and matching of source materials in Chapter 2 engages implicitly with current debates about epistemology, the consequences of postmodern and post-structuralist perspectives for social research, and feminist research methodology. However, these literatures are not referred to explicitly or in detail. Readers familiar with them will recognise how they inform the argument, but this intellectual context is not essential for following the arguments.

The problems of data interpretation have many ramifications. The issue is not simply one of trying to reflect on and bring into the analysis, or to overcome, differences in the social positioning of researcher and researched (Stanley, 1990; Reay, 1996) which has been a central preoccupation of feminist research. I have argued elsewhere (Glucksmann, 1994) that the attempt to equalise the relation between interviewer and interviewee is an impossible and misguided one, given their very different and unequal interests, investment in, and relation to the research process. 'Giving people a voice' does not mean simply repeating what they say and abrogating the role of analysis. Treating people as 'objects' of research, or letting them 'speak for themselves' are not the only alternatives. In oral history and qualitative interviewing it is the researcher who sets the agenda, formulates the questions, takes the initiative. Holding back, at a later stage then, from answering the questions she asked, and restraining herself from analysing and comparing testimonies and life stories, only serves to obscure, in a voluntaristic quest for erasing difference, her own primary and active role in the production of research material. The respective social positioning of researcher and researched are of course crucial to interpretation of the information elicited, as is sensitivity in relation to the more general 'politics of location' affecting who can speak for whom, how, and who to (Mohanty, 1991). But reflexivity is also a larger issue, applicable to all the forms of evidence and documentary sources that are used, whose relations of production are just as much to be scrutinised and taken into account as the role of the researcher in the production of her own data.

Paying close attention to the transcripts, and attempting to verify an interpretation of them by reference to other, independent, sources of evidence is the basic procedure recommended for the kind of research reported here. But sometimes the different sources of data do not fit together or contradict each other. Then one is confronted by the practical problem of what to do, how to respond to inconsistencies, which source to follow, whether any way can be found round the discrepancies, or whether the whole project must be rethought. But there is also a deeper, more epistemologically rooted, question concerning the mismatches and why they should occur, which demonstrates the importance of reflecting on the politics of location and social positioning and production methods of *all* of the sources and evidences used in the triangulation process (whether or not they are corroborative).

These issues are discussed (Chapter 2) in terms of 'knowledge relations' or 'knowledge interactions' (Harvey, 1999a), that is, recognising that all sources of knowledge are produced, on the basis of specific relations between investigator and the object investigated. Whether they are questionnaires, interviews, official statistics, ethnographic observation, and so on, all 'instruments of knowledge' incorporate a particular relation between subject and object of knowledge, researcher and research material. This relation, which differs considerably between the various knowledge instruments, inevitably shapes the nature of the resulting knowledge which could not be produced or thought outside of the knowledge interactions on which it rests. In this sense the research material *is* the interaction between a methodology or mode of investigation and its object.

Themes

Knowledge relations, relational explanation, an 'overall' framework for the study of work constitute central thematic concerns, but they are to be developed through exploration of the research data and in relation to particular occupations, places and people. Just as the experience of individuals can reveal much about social and historical circumstances, so 'little things' often have a significance which extends far beyond themselves. An aim of the ensuing analysis is to move backwards and forwards between differing scales of abstraction and generality, looking at particular people and customs for the bigger story they tell.

The logic underlying the ordering of chapters is to introduce the main characters progressively through Chapters 2, 3 and 4 in such a way that the details of their life histories should be familiar by the time you reach Chapters 5 and 6. But, just as the discussion of time and place is developed in relation to known particular cotton and casual women workers, so too my presentation of their lives, their differently configured economies of home and work and their generational specificity also presuppose the developing analysis of temporality and place and of the TSOL. While the interview grid remains a summary reference point for the whole book you may also want to refer backwards and forwards through the text.

'Research in the making' is the central theme of Chapter 2. It concentrates on the 'in between' stages of research, for which there is the least guidance, ethical or practical, and over which there is little possibility of external surveillance or scrutiny. The challenge of synthesising material from diverse sources, based on distinct 'knowledge interactions', is raised, especially when data are inconsistent. Problems addressed here include those of seaming, jointing, patching and 'slicing the cake', to borrow analogies from sewing, joinery and cookery. Several key characters from the interviews make their first appearance as part of the discussion of the conditions of production and interpretation of oral testimony. And some of the other sources of documentary evidence, from contemporary surveys of the inter-war years to Census statistics, are discussed from a similar perspective.

Chapter 3 is devoted to comparison of 'cottons and casuals', on the basis of a TSOL framework, examining the pattern of connections between divisions in paid work and domestic labour for weavers and casual women workers. Systematic differences are discerned between the two groupings in contrasting configurations of features which include, importantly, the nature of men's employment in addition to their own, and cultural as well as economic characteristics of the localities where they lived and worked. The tradition of married women working was sustained in very different ways, indeed mutually sustaining ways, weavers relying on the ability to buy commodities or services, far beyond the reach of the casual women workers who were more likely to be selling their services. An economic hierarchy and structured inequalities existed, then, *between* working-class women. The two groupings differed also in their perceptions of 'work', in constructions of the home/work division, and in their core identities.

The cake is sliced differently in Chapter 4 where an intergenerational focus comes to the fore, exploring the early lives of the women interviewed. Special attention is given to the links between the labour children performed for wages and the work they contributed to the household, the gendered obligations and reciprocities between successive generations that alter over the life course, and the wide variety of family forms found even within a small sample. Whether poor and unemployed or frequenting cinemas and dance halls, youth were consistently constructed as 'a problem' in contemporary inter-war research, and the evidence for an emergent teenage consumer culture before 1939 and variability in how the slump was experienced by young people are discussed.

Chapter 4 examines also the minority of women in the sample (as in the population at large) who never married, remaining in paid employment until retirement age, and often living with ageing parents for whom they provided financial support. Their pattern of links between work and home, changing parent/child dependencies over the life course, and their distinctive feminine identities provide a counterpoint to the groups of married women workers examined.

Time and space are two co-ordinates framing social relations, understood by social theorists to be always there but traditionally left out of analysis of social processes and phenomena conceived as occurring 'within' them. How far could or should those frames, in fact, be brought into the analysis? What impact would this have on the interpretation of cultural and social processes? And would it signal a positive move towards inter-disciplinarity? These are some of the questions at issue for Chapters 5 and 6 which focus on time and on place respectively, arguing for the importance of a temporal dimension and a spatial perspective.

Temporality is an integral, though often implicit, aspect of social life. Chapter 5 brings it to the foreground to explore the insights to be gained from analysing the temporal organisations and organisations of temporality of the lives of the women interviewed, considering what this might also imply more generally about the value of an analytical focus on gender and temporality. A variety of sociological approaches towards the study of temporality and time use is reviewed, and the framework for an 'economy of time' suggested. This is applied in a return visit to the weavers and casual women workers, who, it is argued, differ systematically with respect to temporality. Three dimensions of temporality are distinguished, relating to the temporal structure of their work/time, the temporal modalities of their life course, and temporality of the division between public and private, seen to be constituted as much temporally as spatially. Similarities between the multiple temporalities negotiated by casual women workers and those signalled as a postmodern feature of 1990s 'new times' prompt a re-evaluation of recent approaches to working time, particularly for their ungendered conceptualisations of industrial or standard time.

The new temporal dimension introduced into the 'total social organisation of labour' is complemented in Chapter 6 by the addition of a spatial dimension. Here new developments in geographical thinking – about the inscription of the social in the spatial, concepts of locality and place and debates concerning their causative properties, the meaning of home, and the rooting of identities in place – are appraised and applied. Salford and Bolton, cottons and casuals, are revisited through a spatial prism, and place and space shown to matter both to the people and their lives, and also (but in a different way) to an interpretation of people and their lives. Two kinds of interconnectivity between people and place are explored. The first centres on 'uneven development' and spatial inequality, especially with respect to housing conditions, and domestic modernisation, within the different parts of Greater Manchester, and also between the North West and South East. Enormous variability and complexity in rounds of housing renewal are discussed in terms of 'patchwork' and 'leapfrogging'. The second spatial aspect centres on locality, localism, and local identity, the varied forms of attachment and identification with place (which may differ between places but not because of places), and the meaning of where they live and of local tradition for the retired weavers and casual women workers I interviewed, especially in their memory of the past.

The final chapter attempts an interweaving of these varied themes, reformulates the TSOL and suggests the value for social analysis of a relational perspective with a focus on intersectionality and configurations. Although these themes are explored throughout the book in relation to a specific research project studying specific historically and geographically situated processes, people and circumstances, I argue that the conclusions, and the questions and implications these in turn raise, and the mode of analysis, are of broader relevance for the analysis of social developments in the twenty-first century.

Notes

1   Details of the decline and discussion of its underlying reasons are to be found in Pollard (1983), Mowat (1955), Buxton and Aldcroft (1979), Branson and Heinemann (1973), Richardson (1967), Saul (1960) and Chandler (1980).

2   See Lewis, (1984, 1992) and Roberts (1995b) for comprehensive accounts of women's work and paid employment during the last century.

3   As a proportion of the total labour force women rose from 29.7 to 30.8 per cent during the same period (Hakim, 1979: 25).

4   I remain extremely grateful to Manchester University Sociology Department for the Hallsworth Senior Research Fellowship. Without it neither the research nor this book would have been possible.

5   The main eventual sources for the research are outlined in the Appendix.

6   The textile industry was traditionally based on many family-owned firms, each specialising in one part of the process or a particular fabric, and in competition with each other. The 'half-time system' of employing school-age girls remained in existence until the 1920s (Frow and Frow, 1970). Spinning and weaving methods had not kept up with the new technology adopted elsewhere, notably in Japan and the USA. These features, internal to the industry, combined with the loss of foreign markets, especially in India, and with increasing competition in the world market to undermine the long-term viability of the British textile industry. For an overview see Glucksmann (1990: 67–71).

7   See Chapter 5 for further discussion along these lines in relation to theories of time.

8   Undoubtedly the women's sense of themselves as English, Lancastrian, Salfordian or whatever was formed in relation and contradistinction to an awareness of Empire and the colonies as peopled by non-English and non-white populations (cf. Hall (1993) and Hall *et al.* (1999), especially Chapter 4). Moreover, discourses of local difference may have 'mimicked' such processes of 'othering' though on a more delimited intra-Lancashire scale. This notwithstanding, race and ethnicity were not the most salient markers of difference between the groupings of women studied here.

9   While indicating the key points of this conceptual approach (all types and forms of labour, the socially specific and constructed character of labour, the connections and organisation between the different forms and their inter-linkage with each other) the term 'total social organisation of labour' could be improved upon. The TSOL is an open, non-essentialist and non-categorical conception and the terms 'total' and 'organisation' were intended to convey this. If I were starting from scratch now I might devise an alternative term but as it has already been used both in my own and in the publications of others (e.g. Crompton, 1997; Levitas, 1998) the time for 'renaming' has passed!

Chapter 2

Seams, cuts and patches

Disparate knowledges

This chapter focuses on the 'in between' stages of the research process. Not the collection of data and not the final narrative and analysis but the long series of processes mediating these two. It aims to unjoint the seams of the apparently seamless web of a completed analysis, and look at some of the problems involved in jointing the seams.

In the last chapter I suggested that this 'in between' is a relatively untheorised phase, with relatively few rules or guidelines. Research methodology handbooks concentrate overwhelmingly on the problems, ethics and practicalities of collecting material but offer much less guidance on what to do with it. Clearly, what goes on in between will depend on the nature of the research problem. In the case of this present project it involves piecing together data of very disparate kinds. There are the interviews that I conducted myself. Then, lumping them together for a moment in one group, there are the numerous reports, surveys and official statistics which were produced at the time about the 1930s and the 1950s containing relevant material. And finally there are the books, theses, novels and films produced in the present about the past, including those based on oral histories similar to mine.

It is difficult to avoid describing the research process other than in terms of temporal sequence homologous to material production or scientific experiment: either raw material worked on by production methods leading to finished product or the 'object, methods, results, conclusion' structure reminiscent of school science experiments. But the notion that qualitative socio-historical research advances by sequential evolution or neat temporal sequence is misleading. It may be both more dialectical and much messier, with constant movement backwards and forwards between the stages of collection, interpretation and writing up, or even within the middle phase itself.

Moreover, it is misleading to conceptualise raw material as being 'raw' in any essential sense. The various data available were all produced for particular purposes, in particular ways, for particular audiences, and at a particular historical time. Their conditions of production are part of what they are, and of what has to be taken on board if they are subsequently to be reused and reinterpreted to throw light on questions different from those posed by their original authors.

Narrowing down then, this chapter concentrates on the issues raised for my research project by deploying diverse sources. Oral testimony and Census occupational statistics represent very different forms of knowledge. So do 1930s social surveys and novels. These sources form the raw material for my study, though they are 'raw' only in the sense of furnishing my starting point. How can these different forms of knowledge be deployed conjointly? Can bits be selected from each and welded together to form a coherent whole? Is is possible, or legitimate, to build up an analysis which bases one point on material taken from one source and the next on a very different one?

So, while later chapters present the results of attempts at such synthesis, in what now follows I outline some of the problems associated with using disparate knowledges, and discuss some of the disparities that have to be confronted. The disparity is twofold: first, sources of knowledge are disparate epistemologically, having been produced by different methods and for distinct purposes. The interactions involved in producing knowledge (the 'knowledge interactions' discussed in Chapter 1) involve 'a dynamic relation between the investigator and the object investigated, deemed to be the "productive engine" of the knowledge produced by the research' (Harvey, 1999a: 187) and result in distinctive forms of knowledge. These may be so different that it is problematic to synthesise or even compare them. Second, they provide disparate, and often contradictory, information. What does the researcher do when sources construe even the 'same' reality very differently? How to avoid the temptation to select out the confirmatory points and keep quiet about those that do not match up? The reasons lying behind such discrepancies are perhaps worth reflecting on, and making explicit, since they may be doubly revealing, both about the representation and what it is representing.

Three portraits

These summaries introduce some of the women interviewed.

Mary Gouden

Mary Gouden lived in the same two-up two-down house in Salford from her birth in 1920 until she was 61. 1980 was a memorable year for her: she was rehoused by the council to a flat where, for the first time, she had a bathroom with running water and an inside toilet. It was also then that she retired after 47 years of continuous full-time work, most of which was for the same firm.

Mary's father worked on the trams and was able to support his relatively small family. Her Scottish mother had come south to work as a maid and gave up waged work on marriage. The public wash-house was too far away so she did the family's wash at home in a boiler with water heated by a coal fire she had to make up, and hung it to dry on a rack in the kitchen. Meals were cooked on a traditional black leaded grate. Mary had one brother, ten years older than herself, who ran an ironmongers shop.

Like all the local youth Mary left school at 14. Her first jobs were in sewing factories and making candlewick bedspreads. She handed over her wage packet to her mother. Her father 'tipped up' all his wages too:

> he was very good ... a stickler for not getting into debt and he wouldn't buy anything on the H.P.[1]

Both father and brother, until he married and left home, gave her 'spends' out of their own spending money.

In 1940, in order to avoid being drafted into war work, Mary started work with some friends at Metropolitan Vickers large engineering factory in nearby

Trafford Park estate. There she remained for the next 40 years, moving from manual work on the shop floor, through rate fixing, to secretarial positions, and ended up as the manager's secretary. Metrovicks had become GEC by then. The skills necessary for such work were acquired on Mary's own initiative and out of working hours. After the war she went to typing classes at night school and also paid to learn shorthand. (And, after retirement, she took courses in public speaking, and had won prizes in competitions.)

Mary's father died in 1942 and her brother was killed in the war the following year. Mary remained living at home and never married. She supported her mother financially, and her mother 'looked after' her. Her mother did all the shopping and cooking and was always waiting with a meal ready on the table when Mary got home from work. She did all the housework on a regular weekly routine and all of Mary's washing.

Their house was rented from a private landlord who would not make any improvements apart from installing a gas fire in the front room. Mary arranged and paid for other internal modernisation herself: during the war she bought two gas rings for cooking to replace the old grate and a gas geyser to supply hot water; around 1950 she had electricity installed. But the problem of the toilet and bathroom remained. She either used a tin bath in front of the fire or went to a friend's house. In her view the Second World War 'did not change that much'. The main changes came:

> when the Corporation built high rise flats ... People thought they were wonderful because they'd got all the facilities.

Slum clearance got underway in Salford in the mid 1960s but Mary still had many more years to wait until she was rehoused. Her mother had died by then and Mary relied on the laundrette to do her washing and on the works canteen for a hot meal.

Before the war Metrovicks had operated an unofficial marriage bar, in common with many of the other local factories and mills. In any case, women comprised only a minority of shop-floor workers there, except during the War when they did both men's and women's work. It was only some years after the War that married women were routinely employed, and then mainly in clerical work.

My comments

When I arrived at Mary Gouden's flat to interview her I was disappointed. It was January, snowing heavily and it had been difficult to find the way. Immediately she corrected my greeting, saying 'I'm Miss Gouden, you know. I'm not married.' After numerous enquiries and many false leads I had finally succeeded in tracking down a woman whose whole working life was at Metrovicks/GEC. And now she wasn't married! As my research project initially concerned the connection between gender inequalities at home and at work for *married* women, many of the questions I had prepared focused on the domestic, parental and financial arrangements between working wife and her husband, and comparison of these with the situation of her mother and father.

Although I went ahead with the interview, adapting the questions to fit Mary's circumstances, at the time I thought the whole thing was probably a waste of time as I had not found the sort of person I was looking for. My notes immediately afterwards centred on what was most striking about what she said: 'able to better herself in employment terms but not in housing... interesting that prepared to pay to learn typing and shorthand to improve career position while still putting up with abysmal living conditions. Hard to imagine secretary to manager in a large engineering firm in the south-east having no loo or bath until retirement.' 'Stresses that change in living conditions not from pre- to post-war but only from 1960s onwards. Implies employment options opened up but changes in living conditions lagged far behind.' On the domestic arrangements I assumed that 'describing her father as "good" meant about money and saving, but presumably also referred to gambling and drink'. And 'the fact that she relied on canteen meals and the laundrette reveal the problems married women with children would have had working full-time at GEC.'

Much later, with the hindsight of more interviews and other material, it became obvious that Mary Gouden's testimony had much to suggest, not least about the significance of the fairly widespread domestic and financial arrangement where one child remained unmarried and (in order to?) cared for elderly parents. But, as will be seen in later discussion, her remarks were also an important ingredient for thinking about uneven change across time, and between the South East and North West; about what is meant by the 'ideal home', its history and ideology; about family organisation in Salford and hence about local culture; about the difference in employment opportunities and patterns for married and unmarried women.

Annie Preston

Annie Preston has also lived in Salford all her life. Like Mary Gouden, Annie endured poor housing in private rented accomodation until she was rehoused in 1971. But, housing apart, their lives took quite different courses. Annie was born in 1917. Her mother died when she was 11; her father was invalided and permanently unemployed following an injury in the timber yard where he worked; and her sister left home early.

When Annie went to work in Dickie Haworth's mill at 14 her wages were the main family income and her father took charge of the housework:

> I left school in 1931 and started in the mill the day after. And I was a weaver and I worked there until I was 22 and got married. I thought 'great, I won't have to work anymore' but I did. [My husband] got a job in the building but I still had to go to work because the money wasn't enough to keep us.

So, after war work, Annie continued to go out to work while raising four children, doing a variety of jobs which she describes as 'all sorts' and which sometimes included several part-time jobs at the same time. She worked in canteens, in factories, and for many years did night cleaning at Salford University from 10 at night until 7 the next morning. In addition she regularly did washing for two other women at the municipal wash-house and received payment for her services.

Annie paid her sister to look after her children:

> She ended up minding all three of them, and I used to push all three of them cramped in a trolley, and if it was raining they would have a big umbrella over them. I would take them every morning and bring them back every night.

The housekeeping money that Annie's husband gave her out of his wages was never sufficient to support the family and her earnings were essential to make ends meet. Money was always very tight. But she implies that this was not discussed. Her husband did no housework, expected his meal to be ready on the table when he came in, and 'hadn't the foggiest how to boil an egg'. Like other traditional Salford men he thought he was 'the king'.

Annie did all the cleaning, according to a strict weekly routine. She baked pies, bread and cakes, and provided only home-cooked meals for the family, sometimes buying ready-peeled potatoes or 'pot herbs' (mixed vegetables) to save a bit of time. She took full responsibility for household financial management including major purchases. And she continued to use the wash-house three times a week until it closed down. The clothes were sorted out the night before, and while she was there 'doing for me sister and another' she also had a bath herself, and did all the flat ironing. The whole operation took three or four hours but the washing went home completely dry and 'gleaming'.

My comments

Annie Preston was now involved in a local history project and had organised for her friends Flo Nuttall and Connie Fowler to take part in the interview along with her. When I turned up all three said they had already seen me before – in the local history library. They had been looking up newspapers from the 1930s on microfilm to find out what films had been showing at the local cinemas as material for a play they were writing about life in Salford before the war to be performed in old people's homes! They were quite at home with the interview situation and more or less ran it themselves, asking each other questions and prompting each other on particular subjects. They talked enthusiastically about the value of preserving the past, particularly the history of Salford.

I came away with a vivid picture of how life had been in Salford: its traditions, the sort of work men and women did, the community spirit and neighbourliness, the poverty, the significance of gambling, the strong division between the sexes, the hard lives of women and so on and so forth. What they had said on tape was all the better for it having been a group interview since collectively they highlighted issues with much greater emphasis than one person could alone. They were also able to discuss family matters in a manner that did not imply personal revelation and so the questions did not seem like prying. For example when explaining traditional male domination and women's response to it, they placed their own experience in the context of others, so providing a more general analysis. Again, all eulogised the municipal wash-house, primarily for its convenience but also for its sociability. It was clear how much they regretted its demise. Flo Nuttall had continued to use it in preference to the washing machine her son bought her.

The session with Annie Preston and her friends suggested new avenues to pursue. One that turned out to be of great importance for the research project as a whole was the contrast between the experience of this group of women and that of married women workers I had interviewed in Bolton and Oldham.

But I was also slightly uneasy, aware that this group had a very definite depiction of Salford to convey. From my notes... 'Unclear how much what they said is to do with their adherence to a historical characterisation of Salford as the "classic slum". Talked as if trying to conform to a stereotype of a (mythical?) past so it's difficult to assess whether what they said was accurate or creating an image of what life was like then.' This was especially so in the case of norms of respectability, neighbourly gossip and moral judgement, in relation to cleanliness and food preparation. So, for instance, despite the existence of numerous pie and chip shops in the vicinity they insisted that their own mothers had never bought chips, and always baked their own pies because this was healthier and cheaper. Their accounts thus confirmed their mothers as having conformed to their models of the 'good mother' to themselves, to each other and to me.

Ever since Engels' *The Condition of the Working Class in England*, a study of Salford in the 1840s, the town has been much written about, and represented in autobiographies, novels, plays and paintings as the archetypical northern industrial working-class town.[2] Annie Preston and her friends were familiar with all this literature, proud to be Salfordians and bearers of the history whose reputation they now upheld in their accounts. Their sense of the past, of place, and of the past of the place made a strong impression. But, as I thought after the interview 'What they say about the history of Salford may in fact tell us more about the present than the past or rather about the significance to them today of a particular image of the past as an aspect of their own and of local identity. Here we get "the past in the present", their own histories mediated both by memory and by Salford's continuing emblematic status.'

Edith Ashworth

Edith Ashworth was a lifetime weaver who lives in Little Hulton, close to Bolton. Her father was a building labourer and her mother a weaver who had continued working until the birth of her seventh child, by which time the oldest was already bringing in a wage.

Edith, born in 1907, was just old enough to work the 'half-time system' in the textile industry before it was abolished. She started work in the cardroom when she was 12, spending three days at school one week and two days the next:

> One day school and go to work another day and when you had any holidays my mother used to have to say to me "ask him to let you work your holidays.' And I did, and I thought I was highly honoured. Stupid idiot, wasn't I? I used to work full time then, 12 year old. Cruel, it was cruel ... and working all the holidays.

At 14 Edith went full time and her wages rose from 11 shillings a week to £1; by 18 she worked four looms and earned £4. She tipped up to her mother, receiving back the customary one shilling in the pound spending money.

> And then she'd borrow it back on a Monday if she had none.
>
> Q: Were you really supporting the rest of the family then?
>
> A: Well, I wouldn't say that but I took more money home than any of them, than me dad or any of them. And if me mother was here she would tell you. But you get no medals for it at all.
>
> Q: Well, you didn't have to do any housework when you were working then?
>
> A: Of course we did.
>
> Q: As well?
>
> A: Sure did. We all had our jobs to do. And on a Sunday I used to do all the baking, all the pies, everybody had pies on a Sunday.

Edith married in 1932, and had two children, in 1933 and 1937. Her husband was a miner, working at the coal face as a coal cutter, one of the most dangerous, skilled, and best paid jobs. During the War, Edith worked in the Ford factory in Trafford Park, together with two of her sisters, but returned to silk weaving full-time afterwards. By then the looms were automatic and she was in charge of 20, earning £14 a week by the mid 1950s.

During the week the children were 'farmed out' with her mother.

> Q: Anyway let me ask, did you have to arrange for someone to pick the children up from school?
>
> A: No, me mother had the children, both of them. She had the children.
>
> Q: And did you pay her?
>
> A: Oh yes, of course. Yes. [Laughs]
>
> Q: Did she have them all the time or just after school?
>
> A: As far as I remember she had them all week. She must have had because I don't remember sending them out to school or anything.
>
> Q: They stayed with her overnight during the week?
>
> A: Yes.
>
> Q: Was that quite a common thing to do? Did you know other people who did it?
>
> A: Oh I had a friend, she was a weaver, Winnie, her mother had hers all week.

With their combined wages, Edith and her husband could afford in 1937 to rent their own house with bath, electricity and Ascot for hot water. She bought her first washing machine as early as 1936, a Canadian made Ecko which lasted years, and a Hoover soon after.

> We always had a washer you know. Practically needed them really.

Edith's husband tipped up his wages and she managed the household finances, though they would take a joint decision about big items like the washing machine. He did the washing up but little other housework.

> Well he always worked shifts. It wasn't very often he was around, he worked nights, he worked afternoons, you know.

My comments

This is a highly selective portrait, using quotations from the transcript of Edith Ashworth's interview, which highlights only certain aspects of her life. They are intended to suggest an obvious contrast to the reader between Edith Ashworth, Mary Gouden and Annie Preston and friends in terms of working life, housing conditions, domestic arrangements and standard of living. The quotes also emphasise Edith's resentment towards her mother for having sent her out to work at such an early age and for what she, and we, might now view as financial exploitation of children and young workers.

These particular quotes were also selected because they draw attention to the brevity of Edith's answers to questions about her life as wife and mother. In fact her interview was more revealing for what she did not say than for what she did. Her answers to virtually all questions around issues of housework, domestic routine and responsibilities, and childcare were pretty monosyllabic, requiring probing and prompting. She was not forthcoming and supplied little detail spontaneously, often responding dismissively as if the questions were dealing only with trivial matters that had been of minor importance to her at the time and continued today to be of little concern. Having realised this, I had to rephrase many questions in such a form that Edith could answer with just a simple 'yes' or 'no'. They would be very boring to reproduce here, serving little purpose than to make this point. She seemed to have no detailed memory, for example, about whether she had a weekly routine for cleaning, washing and cooking. Even her answer about the children boarding with her mother is vague.

On the other hand she became much more expansive and enthusiastic in telling about her work as a weaver, supplying a long list of which firms she had been employed by and when, how many looms she worked and how much she earned. Her description of the different processes in weaving, of what was involved in weaving different kinds of materials, and of the technical developments she had witnessed over the years gave a clear and much more detailed picture of this part of her life.

Did the contrast in how Edith Ashworth talked about these different aspects of her life indicate a failing memory, or a selective memory, or did it reflect the varied and relative significance each held for her, in the past and/or now?

Conditions of production of oral testimony

To say that oral testimonies are produced under certain conditions is a truism. But the problem of knowing whether, how and how much to take these conditions into account when using and interpreting interview material is left entirely to the discretion of each interpreter. There are few commonly acknowledged conventions applying to this phase of research, far fewer certainly than those developed for the collection of data. And interpreters vary enormously in whether and how they treat the testimony as a production. There has been a marked change from the early days of oral history in the 1960s and 1970s when the tendency was to view testimony unproblematically as 'telling it like it is'. Since then much greater scepticism has reigned. Many of the foremost oral historians came to hold the almost opposite view, treating oral testimony about the past as myth, or story, bracketing the question of the relation between the myth and what was being mythologised.[3] Those attempting to develop an explicitly feminist methodology, on the other hand, have been more inclined to view what is produced by an interview as the outcome of negotiation between researcher and researched, a negotiated story produced jointly by the parties involved.[4]

In interviews like the ones I conducted the questions asked are those of today projected onto a past when they may not have been at issue. They reflect the concerns of contemporary feminism and social science such as inequalities of gender, the significance of locality and place, the structure of temporality. Formulation of the questions, and analysis of the response, presuppose terms like identity, culture, subjectivity, sexuality, femininity, all of which derive from today's conceptualisations and vocabulary. Inevitably the researcher views the past through a prism which did not necessarily exist at the time. Furthermore, interviewees in talking about their earlier lives from their present existence may telescope the past and selectively pick out certain memories. And, in this kind of oral history, they are providing answers to the researcher's questions rather than the free-roaming stream of recall of the life story method. The parameters are set by the researcher who defines what is of interest and sets questions accordingly.

The knowledge relations of the interview situation inevitably place the researcher in a position of overall control despite the objective of extracting information about and from the researched. She sets it up; she wants to know; she determines the questions; she analyses the answers; she turns them into the more formal format that is socially recognised as constituting a contribution to knowledge.

But, in so doing, what the interviewees have to say and how they say it may well refine or redefine the project, altering it from its original course. This was certainly true of my project as I have hinted in the comments on the three portraits.

Learning from silences

What is not said may be as indicative as what is. After interviewing several more women it became clear that Edith Ashworth was not alone in suffering from an apparently 'poor memory'; or else many others also shared the same problem. The weavers I interviewed were generally reluctant to talk about housework, unforthcoming and dismissive. They spoke about their mothers' routines in detail but only cursorily of their own. It was immensely frustrating. At first I thought this lack of information doomed the project. I could not get the information I wanted, and yet they were keen to talk about their paid work. Should I just ignore what they said and concentrate on women who did say more about juggling their domestic and paid work? Or should the aims of the research be redrawn so as to capitalise on what was undoubtedly a unique source of information about women's work in cotton textiles?

I had started interviewing retired workers without paying too much attention to the nature of their employment. Gradually, however, it became clear that those who were silent on domestic matters were textile workers, and those who were particularly voluble were multiple part-time casual workers. This contrast eventually became one of the bases for formulating the distinction between weaver and casual workers, and an organising theme for the analysis. Far from having an idea of these as two groups prior to undertaking the research they emerged from the interviews, enabling an advance to be made out of what was for many weeks a setback and source of despair. Evidently weavers did not attribute so much significance to domestic labour; yet their testimony revealed what a sharp distinction they made between home and work, as two separate modes and spheres of life. But this was not so for those women engaged in more casual forms of work: for them work and home, paid and unpaid labour, domestic and other kinds of work were much more interwoven, less distinguishable, not dichotomised.

Particularity revealed by difference

The different configurations of living and working to be detailed in Chapter 3 were formulated as a result of comparison and contrast, by looking at what one woman said and comparing it with another, and postulating distinctions on that basis. This may mean that what I found most significant from the testimony was not necessarily what was of greatest significance to the interviewee. Nor could what was of greatest significance to the eventual argument be gleaned from internal analysis of single transcripts considered in isolation. It was the contrast between them that revealed significance. Comparison exposed numerous differences, and my problem was to ascertain how systematic these were, to analyse and explain them. Thus the specificity of a particular pattern of home/work division stands out by contrast from a different one.

Again, it is the researcher who conceptualises such specificity and difference, and it is possible to achieve this only by working on the various testimonies, taking them as raw material to be dissected and explained. Women in Salford made categorical statements about the absence of work for married women before the war, implying that this was universal. Similarly, women in Bolton made equally categorical and general statments as to the availability of work for married women, or rather the insignificance of marital status. Neither grouping was aware of the mismatches between their statements and others. Both statements were no doubt 'true' but how to account for the difference? Confronting the apparent contradictions and finding ways of understanding and explaining them was my problem, rather than theirs, but one that could have arisen only on the basis of their collective testimony.

Slicing the cake

The material in each of the interviews could be organised in an almost infinite variety of ways, each of which would have a different emphasis or tell a different story. Should the cake be carved up this way or that? How large the slices?

Take for example what Edith Ashworth says about working as a child. Should this be discussed under a heading questioning the mythology of 'happy families'? A central focus then would be the ambivalent relationship of daughters to mothers (Edith Ashworth was not unique in this respect), linked to a discussion of emergent teenage culture, assertiveness and leisure, and the ambiguous situation of young workers in their parental family. The wider context would explore the complexity and non-uniform nature of family structures, given the absence of any standardised nuclear family of origin among a sizeable proportion of the women I interviewed.

Or should her experience be discussed in the context of youth labour, which would probably be in a different chapter, more concerned with economic ties and constraints. In this case I would concentrate on the important contribution of teenagers to household income, as one dimension of the economy of the household unit, using Edith as one example amongst others.

These two aspects of the same situation could be elaborated on in relation to different areas of concern exercising feminists today. The discussion could be oriented to the existing large literature on internal household finance, adding a historical dimension to a field that is mostly about the present day. Or it could be geared to the emerging historical exploration of 'becoming a woman' and the development of feminine subjectivity, undertaken from a psychoanalytically informed perspective.[5]

Evidently these alternatives would involve treating the same material in very different ways, and accentuating different points. A solution could be simply to have a separate section or chapter on mothers, daughters and youth labour which could include both dimensions. But then the precise reference to ongoing debates might get lost as this material would not then feature in the chapters on family form nor on household economy.

Slicing the cake (and there are very many potential cakes) is one of the key decisions to be taken during the 'in between' phase. It affects the entire structure and emphasis of the final product. It has to be done and only the researcher can do it. But again, there is rarely a hint in the final product of why and how the decisions were made and what alternative routes might have been taken. The ordering and transecting of material, over which I (and probably many others) have expended so much head scratching and agonising inevitably will become 'the way the material was ordered', as if this had come easily, suggested by the material itself.

This is enough on problems of 'jointing' for the time being. It is a problematic issue, but once brought into the open could be written about *ad nauseam*. It brings with it the danger of saying more about the research process than about the content of the research, about what goes on in the mind of the researcher than in the patterns she is attempting to analyse. But my aim is to argue for reflexivity as important in helping to 'place' arguments and their basis in evidence, rather than to encourage self-absorption. In practice, though, there may be only a fine line distinguishing reflexivity from self-absorption, and the researcher is probably not in the best position to draw it.

Puzzling numbers

I return now to the process of matching disparate knowledges and utilising sources for purposes other than those for which they were produced. No apparent problem arises if different knowledges about the same subject matter confirm each other despite having been produced under different conditions and for distinct purposes. Collectively they seem to point to something incontrovertible, to have captured something (true?) about how things (really?) were. Thus, most of the other oral history recorded in the Greater Manchester area complements mine, and collectively this kind of material also accords with what has been written in autobiographies and realist novels.

But how does the researcher cope with contradictory information? Privilege one source and treat this as constituting *the* authoritative evidence? Gloss over the differences or act as if she had never come across the mismatch? (After all, it is not very likely that many readers will have encountered it, although there is always the danger of those experts who are familiar with all the sources.)

I came across a host of small and large contradictions. A small one, for example, concerned the state of Trafford Park industrial estate during the Depression. Retired workers interviewed for the 'Bridging the Years' oral history project in Salford repeatedly speak of people being laid off, no work, and lean times. Yet, according to the Metropolitan Borough of Trafford's 1981 *Short History of Trafford Park*:

> *it is significant that during the so-called depression of trade in England in the late 1920s, many of the factories were humming with activity, and extensions were being made to their plants.*
> (Metropolitan Borough of Trafford, 1981; 15)

Maybe some firms were affected and not others; or perhaps prosperity of businesses was at the expense of speed-ups and redundancy for the shop-floor workforce; or possibly the official history, published just after Trafford became an Enterprise Zone in 1980, put the rosiest gloss on a historical period of decline equivalent to that of the 1980s so as not to deter prospective investors.

A rather larger puzzle, and one that was distinctly problematic for my analysis, involved a double set of mismatches: first, discrepancies between what women I interviewed said about the availability of work for married women; and second, inconsistencies between what they had said and what was suggested by Census statistics of women's employment. As already mentioned, some women stated categorically that there were no jobs locally for married women and that married women 'did not work'. Others seemed surprised that the question of jobs for married women should even be at issue; as far as they were concerned married women had always worked.

Such contradictory assertions varied geographically, but this became apparent only as I did more interviews. By and large it was the women in Salford who said that married women 'did not work'. Annie Preston and her friends listed 24 firms near where they lived where women worked before the war but stressed that most left when they married. Some firms operated a marriage bar, although Dickie Haworth's mill and Worralls dyeworks, the largest employers, did not. They, and most of the other women interviewed in Salford, insisted that there was 'no work round here' for married women. I found this odd since Trafford Park was very close and central Manchester also only a bus ride away, and work had been available in both. Moreover, all those who said that married women did not work had in fact themselves engaged more or less permanently in paid work throughout their married life, though not necessarily in formal employment.

However, virtually all of the Bolton women told a different story: married women's employment was the norm. Employers made no distinction between married and single women and neither did they. Work was as available to married as to single women and they had no experience of a marriage bar. All had continued working after marriage; Alice Foster was bored at home and wanted to return to work a few months after her son was born; two who did take time out, at the insistence of their husbands, complained of quarrels since it was husbands who wanted their wives to stay at home against their own wishes.

It could be possible to come to terms with such contradictory testimony simply by taking local variation into account and positing that labour markets were highly localised, geographically circumscribed, and discrete. Linked to this, marked local differences existed both in the traditions of women's work and in the expectations of women about work after marriage.

Hopefully this difference would be confirmed by the official employment statistics in the Census. But no such luck! On the contrary, the Census of 1931 undermines any neat explanation by revealing as practically identical the proportion of women who were occupied in Bolton and in Salford. As against what all the interviewees said the Census suggests little variation between the local towns in those occupied (including the out of work), and in those out of work, as a percentage of the female population aged 14 and over (see Table 4).

Table 4 Percentage of women aged 14 and over, occupied and out of work, in selected Lancashire towns

Town	Occupied women (%)	Out of work (%)
Bolton	47.0	12.4
Manchester	45.5	11.5
Oldham	52.2	21.0
Preston	52.7	20.9
Rochdale	52.8	16.3
Salford	47.1	12.8

Source: Census of Population, *1931, General Tables, Table L: 120–1.*

These figures suggest that the proportions both of those occupied and those out of work were higher in the more exclusively textile towns, but that little difference existed between Bolton and Salford. All, however, had proportions of occupied women much higher than national average for England and Wales of 34.2 per cent and for the whole Census Region North 4 of 41.9 per cent.

Twenty years later, according to the 1951 Census, there had been little alteration to the situation. Now occupied women amounted to 47 per cent of the total female population over 15 in Bolton (the school leaving age had been raised by a year), and 49 per cent in Salford. And, of these, 52 per cent in Bolton and 49 per cent in Salford were married (*Census of Population*, 1951, Occupation Tables, Table 20: 216).

It is in fact quite possible to explain these discrepancies (the fuller account appears in the section on 'Local labour markets and gender divisions of work' in Chapter 3), to show both why the women I interviewed in the two places should have asserted what they did, and also why what both sets of them said was at odds with Census data. But this could not be achieved from within these sources alone, nor from a more detailed scrutiny or contrasting of them. Largely it depended on broadening the perspective so as to bring in other dimensions, and hence further sources of evidence and forms of knowledge, to bear on the two varying factors of married women's work and locality. But it also necessitated ascertaining exactly what was meant by Salford wives' definition of 'not working', and distinguishing between formal standard full-time employment on the one hand and 'all sorts', 'little jobs', on the other, that is, the more casual, informal, and part-time kinds of work. The possibility of a discrepancy existing between the ideal or expectation that 'married women do not work' and a quite different actuality also had to be considered.

Utilising the Census for reliable evidence was doubly problematic. Its limitations as a historical source of information about women's work are well known, notably its failure to break down women's occupations into any detail.[6] This results in women's jobs being classified according only to very broad categories and in many women workers being summarily relegated to residual categories as 'other', 'unskilled', counted as 'unoccupied' or pursuing 'no gainful occupation'. Moreover, standard practice in the 1921 and 1931 Censuses was to enumerate only those engaged in standard full-time employment, thus excluding all those doing casual, seasonal, part-time and informal jobs.[7] Inevitably, these mid twentieth century Censuses underestimate seriously the proportion of women who were (in their terms) 'occupied', especially married women like those in Salford.

I had hoped to get detailed figures from the 1931 and 1951 Censuses so as to be able to compare women workers in the different Lancashire towns according to marital status and age for various occupations. But the gaps and lack of consistency across tables and over time are so great that even these relatively simple demands cannot be met. In 1931 figures are supplied for women's occupations in different local towns but these are not broken down by marital status. When occupations are broken down by the ages of the workers, no details are given for different towns. Thus, while it is possible to compare the age distribution of the female workforce in different occupations, and to get at the employment profile of different towns, it is not possible (at least not straightforwardly) to cross-tabulate.

By 1951 the classification of occupations had been revised, rendering problematic any direct comparison over time. But in contrast to 1931 there was much greater attention to marital status. The data about various Lancashire towns break down gross figures of occupied women into those who are married, and within that those who are married and work part-time. This is the sort of detail I would have wanted for 1931! However the later Census does not perform this detailed breakdown for particular occupations by town, only doing so by region. Even cross-tabulating various tables from the Industry Tables and the Occupation Tables either in 1931 or 1951 would not give me precisely what I want.

Such omissions restrict the value of the Census as a source of information. They also provide an insight into official thinking of the time, and give a hint of how the method of classifying, the extent of detail, what was included and excluded were connected to the purposes for which the Census was undertaken and to its production as a particular form of knowledge. Anyone studying the 1931 and 1951 occupational statistics will notice that the enumerators in 1931 were concerned with the age of women workers, rather than marital status, and with whether they were in work or unemployed. In 1951 this had been replaced by detailed enumeration of marital status and whether they were employed full-time or part-time.

It would be easy to conclude that such concerns merely reflected, as an accurate mirror, developments in employment trends and the transition from an era of economic depression to one of full employment and high demand for labour. But why were they collected and classified in this particular way, and how were they utilised by state agencies? In what way did they inform the formulation of government policy in relation to social welfare, the benefit system and taxation? And how did these purposes affect what information was sought?

Higgs argues (1987, 1991) that the primary concern of nineteenth century Censuses was medical and sanitary research, and that the design of the occupational classification system is to be understood in this light. The General Register Office, strongly influenced by then dominant medical theories, was particularly interested in how work with certain materials, or chemicals, affected mortality. The objective was to construct occupational life tables which would demonstrate the differential life expectancy associated with exposure to different materials. The Censuses are thus to be seen against the background of Victorian scientific beliefs and of social scientists' concern with death rates and sanitation. Their central focus was the health of the population. Hence the interest in the city and urbanisation, migration, and overcrowding as potential contributors to disease and death.

By the end of the century there was pressure for the Census to become more useful as an instrument for economic and social analysis, supplying the sort of information that would permit government departments like the Board of Trade and the Home Office to intervene more effectively in economy and society. Given this history, Higgs warns (1991: 477) that those using the nineteenth century Censuses 'ignore the intellectual history of classification systems at their peril' and cautions against 'mistaking changes in language, or classificatory conventions, for trends in objective reality'.

Viewed from such a perspective Censuses may be read as partial distillations of the ideas and discourses of their time, focused on certain highly selected concerns. This is not a novel argument. Mackenzie (1981) suggested that the development of statistical concepts themselves was to be understood in terms of the purposes for which they were constructed, eugenics for instance being crucial to the emergence of the method of rank ordering. Discussing adaptations and modifications to Census conceptions of 'work', Hakim, to take another example, describes it as 'a social product' (1980: 570). But Censuses are not simply 'reflections', nor simply social constructions. In so far as they also configure and represent to society a picture of itself, they constitute a form of self-surveillance. (The history of official statistics, interestingly, lends itself to a Foucauldian interpretation.) Moreover they supply for the state 'facts' on questions deemed by it to be of concern for the nation (Desrosières, 1991, 1993, 1994), whether the medico-demographic concerns of the mid nineteenth century or those of poverty and income in the early twentieth century. Whilst the maintenance of social order remained the general overriding concern of political thinking throughout this period, there was a transformation in what were believed to constitute the central threats and guarantors of order, from health, disease and sanitation in the mid to late nineteenth century and towards poverty, income distribution, inequality and social class by the mid twentieth century.

No analysis of the mid twentieth century Censuses has been undertaken to parallel that of Higgs for the mid nineteenth century.[8] However, even a cursory overview of the range and detail of the tables reveals shifting areas of interest suggestive of an alteration in the prime concerns of state agencies and social legislators. For example, in 1931 the Census paid detailed attention to the housing density, with numerous tables devoted to enumerating the number of people per room. By 1951 this had given way to what looks to the uninitiated almost like an obsession with the journey to work, with many tables measuring whether people lived and worked in the same place, how far they travelled, how long the journey took and so on. Again, although by 1931 the Industry Tables divided workers according to the status divisions of employment (managerial, operative, own account, out of work) they still continued to classify occupations according to the exact material worked (for example, wool, worsted, silk, artificial silk, jute, hemp, flax, mixed fibres, etc). But by 1951 the classification of manufacturing occupations seemed far more attentive to the nature of job done than to the material worked.

The different modes of classifying women's employment referred to earlier may be recognised as just one element of a much altered representation of society. Configuring the social structure of 1951, the Census responded to postwar change and to the concerns of a new era. Its findings were used as a basis for social and economic intervention during the 1950s. Moreover, by singling out certain trends it contributed to their general recognition and also to their reinforcement. Part-time work would be a good example of this, enumerated for the first time in 1951 (and so drawing the attention of employers to a hitherto untapped source of labour) and a key issue of ideological and policy debate during the subsequent decade.

The Census may thus be seen as constituting a particular type of 'knowledge interaction'. Its questionnaires are distributed through state means, by a government agency, and backed by legal obligation to complete. It acquires information in a specific way and produces knowledge of a particular kind. A historical construction, the Census is by no means an 'objective' or comprehensive record, but nor is it an effect of a societal 'free construal'. Its classification systems react to and interact with the substratum of social and economic realities which they represent. These are then used proactively by the state. So there is an ongoing dynamic in its varied processes of reaction, interaction and proaction.

In moving, thus, from the detailed questions arising out of the research data and the mismatch between the women's testimony and the Census to the larger knowledge relations of official statistics, it becomes evident that the triangulation process is not necessarily a simple or straightforward one of verifying one set of evidence against another.

Class surveys

Not so puzzling as the Census were the numerous social surveys undertaken during the 1930s. Most had clearly stated aims, and were undertaken with specific questions in mind. Utilising them again today involves an appreciation of their original objectives and how these determined the range of issues selected for scrutiny. Here I am thinking not of the vast literature on 'the social condition of Britain' produced by novelists, writers, journalists and political commentators[9], but of rather more formal social investigations. Many attempted to document the extent of poverty, its various dimensions and spiral of effects. Other studies investigated unemployment or health, particularly in relation to women and children.[10] A series of volumes, achieving almost national coverage, surveyed in-depth the social and economic structure of cities or regions, drawing attention to industries and areas of work that were in decline in contrast with those that were expanding.[11]

Research of this nature was widely acknowledged, by government departments and politicians of both left and centre, as a necessary precondition for the rational planning that might solve the economic problems of the time. Many studies were imbued with a belief in the value of impartial study and a faith in planning, their language displaying self confidence in their role in contributing to social amelioration.[12] Charitable foundations, semi-public organisations, universities, and local government authorities were also caught up in the active scientific quest for information about the social, collecting all manner of 'objective facts' for their 'report of an enquiry into the effects of x on y', as so many were titled.

Although surveys of this sort did not provide the systematic picture of women's employment in Manchester and its surrounding area (or indeed of men's) that I had hoped for when embarking on my project, they nevertheless supply valuable information about the changing industrial composition, especially the demise of the Lancashire textile industry and its attendant unemployment.

Some of the surveys that were more specific, and for that reason of greater interest to my project, are all the more telling for their tone, which is often patronising, indicative of the class perspective of their writers and the bounded framework from which they were undertaken. The investigators write as experts, and from the outside, about 'the unemployed', 'slum dwellers' 'adolescent girls', commenting on behaviour in terms that verge on the condescending. Those surveyed are implicitly praised for thrift or for attempting to 'improve' themselves. Ways of conducting life are deemed 'unintelligent' if they do not accord with the researcher's (unstated) definitions of rational activity.

Harley, for example, investigating the leisure pursuits of girl wage earners in Manchester in 1937, comments disapprovingly about how often they frequent the cinema, as opposed to evening classes or girls' clubs. Even so, she concedes that the cinema:

> makes a real contribution to self-respect in the direction of dress and manners ...
> (Harley, 1937: 202)

Having criticised girls' topics of conversation she remarks of newspaper reading that:

> there is very little evidence of intelligent reading ... The newspaper is read more for the passing thrill than from an enlightened interest in world affairs. There appears also to be an inability to link up facts in order to estimate their cause and effect.
> (Harley, 1937: 204)

By contrast, the author of the Manchester University Settlement's 1937 survey of Ancoats, a slum clearance area, is more restrained in offering her own opinion, although it is evident that she views mothers' skills at housekeeping and child rearing as of paramount importance in maintaining family stability and health. On the use of milk by the poor, for example, she merely states that:

> Some of the women held milk as an article of diet in contempt. Its sole use in their opinion was to put into tea. Other mothers who valued fresh milk gave it to their children at those times when money was a little more plentiful.
> (Manchester University Settlement, 1945: 33)

She even defends, but, significantly, on grounds of rationality, women who buy fish and chips against those claiming that 'lazy women resort to the fried fish shop to save themselves trouble.' Thus:

> A widow, with part-time employment in addition to her own domestic work, spent 2 shillings a week on fish and chips for a family of four, serving them on Monday (washing day) and on Friday (cleaning day). This seems to have been a sensible and economical arrangement since there was in those days no British Restaurant ...
> (Manchester University Settlement, 1945: 33)

The contradiction between the 'do-gooding' moralism and self-professed objectivity that permeates many of these surveys reveals the extent to which they were undertaken 'within' the social reformist and scientific rationalist ethos of their time. Like the Census they were produced on the basis of distinctive 'knowledge interactions'. However, sometimes they still provide the sole remaining source of data about their subject matter, whether family budgets of the poor or hobbies of teenage workers. They offer an insight into the role of inter-war social research in Britain, and its publicly acknowledged place in the process of social reform, welfare planning, and formulation and implementation of policies for urban and industrial renewal. In contrast to the Censuses, it was a more straightforward matter for me to directly appropriate the content of such surveys without too much reinterpretation or manipulation, and relatively easy to 'bracket' their moralistic empiricism.

Unobserved observers

A rather different form of knowledge was produced by Mass Observation, again on the basis of distinctive 'knowledge interactions'. Mass Observation intended specifically to give a voice to those who were deprived of effective forms of expression and communication. It also aimed to document, without comment or formal analysis, but in ethnographic detail, the customs and trifles of ordinary life ignored by politicians and policy oriented social researchers, so revealing as 'extraordinary' much that is normally taken for granted as quite ordinary.[13] But these dual aims of some of the earliest 'sociology of everyday life' seem in practice to sit slightly uneasily together. Certainly the women (and it was mostly women) who kept diaries, letters and made personal reports for Mass Observation did 'speak for themselves' in the way that Charles Madge anticipated. But Tom Harrison's background in anthropology and his conviction that behaviour and traditions in his own country were just as extraordinary and worthy of investigation as anything he had encountered in Melanesia meant that a much more 'external' method was required.[14] In his programme, observation was to be undertaken covertly by researchers who remained independent from the people they were studying and who did not participate in the activities they documented. They were not to reveal themselves to their subjects. To privilege 'ordinary life' (by which was meant mainly working class ordinary life) and then engage specially trained (mainly middle class) people to observe it without eliciting any involvement or permission from those being observed seems a bit contradictory. It also places a question mark over the supposed aim for equality between researcher and researched implied in 'giving people a voice'.

Thus Harrison's classic study of the public house as a basic institution of British working life adopted methods which he described in his Preface to *The Pub and the People* (Mass Observation, 1943) as 'reconnaissance', 'penetration', observation, and the study of individuals, as well as statistics and published sources. Based on very many hours spent sitting unobtrusively in pubs, it is an exhaustive and fascinating account of pubs and pub culture in Bolton in the late 1930s even if it does have the (presumably deliberate) effect of making the drinkers seem like wierdos and their various unwritten rules and elaborate games appear strange, not to say freakish. (A good example would be the story about chopping off the heads of tortoises which the researchers overheard one drinker telling another, repeated without comment in *The Pub and the People*.) Yet, that he succeeded in making his own country appear foreign says much about the knowledge relations of such research, the externality of the researcher resulting in objectification of the researched.

These problems aside, I was nevertheless extremely pleased that Bolton had been the subject of intense scrutiny by the Worktown study in 1937–38. Ultimately only one out of four projected volumes was actually published but a mass of information remains available on topics as diverse as shopping habits, the winter sales, the labour exchange, theosophy, holidaying in Blackpool, and clothes washing habits. In addition to the unobserved observations, this material also includes diaries and more formal research reports.

The *Clothes-Washing Report*, published in 1939 and subtitled 'Motives and Methods' was one of the more formal reports, based on 60 interviews with Bolton 'housewives' and on the views of 213 Mass Observation panellists questioned about the pros and cons of sending clothes to the laundry as opposed to washing them at home. Washing clothes was a topic which many of the women I interviewed expounded on spontaneously and at length, and which had been of great significance in their mothers' and their own lives. (They said so much that it would almost have been possible to devote a book to clothes washing alone.) The arduousness of the task was described and the variety of methods used to accomplish it. For some achieving clean, dry and ironed washing was a material symbol of being a successful wife and mother. For others it was a means of earning extra cash, an informal kind of employment.

But, what I was told could not be easily matched with the Mass Observation report. Having gone to the trouble of gathering women's own accounts of what they did (unlike the pub study), the authors (more like the social surveys discussed earlier) filtered this information through their own notions of what was 'sensible'. Even though the report comes over as highly descriptive rather than analytical, we are told in no uncertain terms that some clothes washing habits are more rational and intelligent than others.

> *Washing attitudes* [in Bolton] *contain a large irrational element ...*
> (Mass Observation, 1939: 21)

> *... there is a minority more open-minded either through greater intelligence or through some circumstance which makes them relatively untied-down to the dominant Bolton patterns of behaviour.*
> (Mass Observation, 1939: 23)

... another woman ... with perhaps more energy and horse-sense than average ...
(Mass Observation, 1939: 24)

To understand a further reason for conservatism in washing methods, one has to enter the mentality of the housewife, for whom the idea of making things 'clean' is a very simple and unrationalised one ...
(Mass Observation, 1939: 27)

The report was based on accounts given to an external researcher, that were both observed and judged 'from outside'. The judgmental remarks were influenced, presumably, by the 1930s enthusiasm for applying the techniques of scientific management to the home and obsession with germs and hygiene. They certainly reveal the writer's belief in the superiority of the 'most modern' methods and in the good housewife as an efficient no-nonsense administrator, adaptable and open to change. Thus, those clinging to methods deemed outdated are described as 'unintelligent', and the author derides as 'irrational' the local social rule of Monday as washday. In my interviews, however, women had offered a number of practical reasons as to why Monday should be washday, and it was also quite clear that washing routines varied according to whether or not respondents engaged in waged work, and in the nature of their occupation. This illuminates another problem in the Mass Observation report: all women were referred to simply as 'housewives', even when they were also in full-time employment; sometimes individuals were subtitled as 'a weaver' or other occupation but not systematically enough to be useful. So, although the report does give an idea of washing methods in use at the time, the refraction of information through conventional perceptions of gender, class, and region limit its use now as a corroborative or complementary source. Going back to the 'rawer' data of the original questionnaires might well prove more valuable.

Photo stories

The photograph 'Leaving the Mill' was one of a series taken by Humphrey Spender for the Worktown Project. What can be learned from it? While it tells quite a bit about mill workers it also hints at the position of the photographer.

All the workers are women, and span a variety of ages, including both fairly young and much older women. Some are carrying baskets: was this their lunch are or they going shopping on the way home? They do not seeem to be in a tremendous hurry to get away. Many are walking in groups, arm in arm with each other. All are wearing proper shoes, not clogs. (Many of the Bolton weavers I interviewed said they had only worn clogs until the Second World War. So what to make of this?) Bicycles were a prized possession in the 1930s, especially for women. The two here look quite modern, especially the one with drop handlebars. Were these women perhaps members of a Socialist Clarion group delivering their papers by bike and going for group rides in the countryside? Or did they race for a cycle club? And is it chance that the pram was being pushed past at just this time, or is someone collecting her baby? If the former it looks as if the women may know each other in any case.

But none of the women is looking directly at the camera. It appears that they did not even spot the photographer.

Leaving the Mill, Bolton (Humphrey Spender, 1937)

Washday, Bolton (Humphrey Spender, 1937)

The second photo 'Washday' involves even less interaction between photographer and people, though much is suggested about them from the washing.

Given all the information gathered about washing from various sources I find this a very interesting photograph. It was taken on a Monday, presumably, and perhaps women had done their washing very early before they went out to work? A close scrutiny reveals that pillow cases fill the whole of one washing line, and that pinafores account for most of another. It could be interesting to speculate on the reasons for this. Indeed, a whole story could be woven from this photo. That aside, it gives an unromanticised view of a dark and gloomy street of back-to-back houses on a windy day. The street looks run down and the ground dirty. Although nothing else is shown, the photo is suggestive of those smokey black and white industrial landscapes or even perhaps of the harshness of frontier towns in the far 'Wild West'.

Why is no one about? Did Spender have to wait for the street to be completely empty?

The absence of people reinforces the stark image. Yet this is no innocent photo, fortuitously snapped, simply capturing 'the moment'. On the contrary, it is crafted, constructed and contrived, revealing much about the photographer's relation to his subject matter and what he wanted to achieve. In an interview 40 years after the Worktown project, Spender (1977) discussed the unease that he had felt in his role, at the difference between his own privileged class background and the poverty of those being studied, and the objectives of Mass Observation.

The photograph referred to in the following extract is of men sitting in a pub, perhaps even this one of 'The Vaults' where it is impossible to tell whether

The Vaults, unidentified Bolton pub (Humphrey Spender, 1937)

the sitting man's hand is raised in greeting to the standing man (the eyes of both seated men could be on him) or whether he is objecting to the photograph being taken.

> Q: *Did you talk to those men?*
>
> A: *No. I would have been terrified. The whole difficulty for me, there, was what happens when you talk to them. They are total foreigners, it was acutely embarrassing ...*
>
> Q: *People would probably have been mystified had you tried to explain MO's objectives to them?*
>
> A: *They wouldn't have followed the analogy, they wouldn't have realised this was a kind of social survey. Obviously people accept their own behaviour as being totally logical and unmysterious.*
>
> Q: *Did you find the Bolton environment very stimulating?*
>
> A: *No I didn't. I found the environment really very depressing ... The general atmosphere both climactically and psychologically was depressing.*
>
> Q: *Was that the atmosphere generated by industrial towns?*
>
> A: *Yes, generated by poverty, by my own rather conspicuous function. Of course it was very difficult to conceal oneself.*
>
> Q: *In what way? Because of your accent?*
>
> A: *Yes, for me to go into a North country pub, and really speaking a completely different language, to be a kind of 'hail fellow well met' person was very embarrassing, and for me to be questioned as having taken someone's photograph, 'What the hell are you taking it for?' which often happened ... My main anxiety, purpose was to become invisible and to make my equipment invisible ...*
> (Interview with Spender by Derek Smith, 27 July 1977, unpaginated)

And later, discussing unobserved photography:

> *... there was a feeling that people who are in impoverished circumstances, people who were out of work simply did not like their state being exposed, in many ways the photographs would have been an exploitation. This was something that I felt very keenly.*
> (Interview with Spender by Derek Smith, 27 July 1977, unpaginated)

Spender implicitly criticises Tom Harrison's project. He was uncomfortable with its demand for invisibility and uneasy with the logic of concealment, which inevitably recorded people and their activities externally and hence as alien.

Viewed on their own the photos create a definite image, but one that can be seen, in the light of Spender's comments, as deeply affected by the purpose for which they were taken and their 'conditions of production'. In spite of this, or maybe even because of it, they remain immensely elucidating, complementing other ways of representing the same subject matter.

'Knowing' 'reality'

This chapter has explored a few of the different modes of apprehending reality, and the sorts of questions that arise in utilising them conjointly. Different forms of representation result in different constructions of the same reality. My eventual analysis will have involved reconstructing previously existing constructions. And the reconstructions of mine will inevitably be informed by my own intellectual formation, shaped through the accumulation of previous research experience and trajectories of learning, political perspectives and involvements, and the stock of knowledge and frames of analysis acquired from the sociological tradition. To state the obvious, the ways of thinking that I bring to the material have not surged into my brain just now or from nowhere but result from the long-term intersection of my own intellectual trajectory with its historical context.

I do not believe that the differing constructions which arise out of the different modes of apprehending reality are just texts, nor that they result from free construal on the part of their authors. There was an actually existing reality in 1930s Lancashire and all these different sources apprehend some aspect of it, however partial and however affected by their particular 'method'. Nor does reconstructing mean simply shuffling round pieces of a puzzle into a different arrangement. Rather, reinterpreting disparate forms of knowledge and sources of information on the basis of specific questions produces a new analysis, though necessarily also a partial one affected also by its method.

The researcher can have no independent access to the reality of the 1930s. Rather she/he is totally dependent on existing forms of knowledge and people's memories. Producing new theory from these knowledges involves going beyond the rationality and reality of any one of them, and actively utilising the variety of disparate forms. If she/he believed that each contained its own validity within itself there would be no point in consulting more than one, or interviewing more than one person, as all material would be radically incomparable, yet of equal validity. But each knowledge form is the product of particular knowledge interactions and of its particular location in time and outlook. These are features which can be known and used to inform how each form may now be interpreted and how different forms may be brought into connection with each other. By maximising the use of such disparate knowledges, and actively reinterpreting them, it becomes possible to give a wider frame of reference to the various sources and to produce a new analysis, new social theory.

Just like its sources, the analysis that I develop rests on particular 'knowledge interactions' which are distinct from those of the Census taker, and of the social surveyor, and of the women who speak of their lives. Rather, the standpoint is external to all the sources, including the oral histories collected. While taking the women's testimony as the central data to be understood, the analysis deploys the various sources to make sense of each other, informed by a TSOL perspective. 'Theorisation' of the women's lives thus reflects my own 'knowledge relation' to the material.

The effect of history also enters actively into the reinterpretation of the various forms of knowledge. Not only is their meaning different now from when they were produced, but historical change also places today's analyst in a quite different relation to the subject matter than existed for those writing about it at the time. Our new social realities provide a tool for reinterpretation. New categories of thought are deployed, analysis of the past and of writing from the past being undertaken through the prism of today's concepts and questions, as part of an inevitable and continual process.

My aim in drawing on diverse knowledges is not to develop a theory about other theories or an interpretation of already-existing interpretations. Rather, it is to utilise all of these as the basis for developing an interpretation or theory of what happened, of social reality, of how people's lives were made, and how social structure hung together. Each of these sources attempted to 'grasp reality' in its own way and using its own instruments of knowledge, whether by enumerating and classifying as in the Census, by questionnaires and observation as in the various surveys, or by people recounting their own memories of the past. Reinterpreting these interpretations is a necessary step to reinterpreting the reality that they were interpreting, not to dissolving it away.

Notes

1   This and all subsequent quotations are taken from the transcripts of the interviews I conducted unless indicated otherwise. All names are pseudonymised.

2   For example Robert Roberts' autobiographies (1971, 1976); Walter Greenwood's 1933 novel *Love on the Dole*; Shelagh Delaney's play *A Taste of Honey*, filmed by Tony Richardson in 1962; the paintings of L.S. Lowry; not to mention *Coronation Street*, Britain's longest running soap opera. See Chapter 6 for a fuller discussion.

3   Contrast for example Thompson (1978) with Samuel and Thompson (1990) or Tonkin (1992), or contributions to the journal *Oral History* at the beginning of the 1980s with those of a decade later.

4   See for example Stanley (1990). The different approaches, their problems and implications are discussed in Glucksmann (1994).

5   These alternative directions might pursue the pioneering work of Pahl (1989) or of Alexander (1994) respectively.

6   Higgs (1987: 63) provides a useful summary of nineteenth century omissions and their effects. Nissell (1980) overviews a more contemporary situation.

7   The official statistics collected by the Ministry of Labour covered only those in jobs insured against unemployment, excluded certain insured occupations and, until 1934, young people under the age of 16. For my purposes they do not represent a very useful source of employment statistics since so many of the women I interviewed worked in uninsured occupations.

8   But see Szreter (1984, 1991) for analysis of the Registrar General's social classification of occupations along similar lines.

9   See for example the works of Brockway (1932), Cole and Cole (1937), Greenwood (n.d.), Hutt (1933), Orwell (1937), and Priestley (1934).

10 Examples include Rice (1931), Orr (1936), M'Gonigle and Kirby (1936), Gollan (1937), Caradog Jones (1937), Pilgrim Trust (1938), Jewkes and Winterbottom (1933a).

11 The most comprehensive was that of London (Smith, 1930–35), followed by Merseyside (Caradog Jones, 1934). In addition to Lancashire (Daniels and Jewkes, 1932), surveys were also conducted of South Wales (Marquand, 1932), Bristol (Tout, 1938), Southampton (Ford, 1934), York (Rowntree, 1941), Tyneside (Mess, 1928), Brynmawr (Jennings, 1934), and Cumberland and Furness (Jewkes and Winterbottom, 1933b).

12 This was particularly evident in the publications of Political and Economic Planning (PEP) and its journal *Planning*. Founded in 1931 by a group of civil servants, businessmen, and academics for 'the impartial study of the problems of industry', it devoted many reports and pamphlets to the question of how best to solve contemporary problems. For discussion of the faith in planning see Mowat (1955: 462), Samuel (1986: 25–9), Pollard (1983: 104), and Glucksmann (1990: 78).

13 For an account of Mass Observation see Calder and Sheridan (1984), and Madge and Harrison (1938, 1939).

14 On returning from Melanesia in 1936 Tom Harrison went to Bolton, birthplace of the founder of Unilever, the only fragment of western life to have 'impacted into those cannibals on their Melanesian mountain' (quoted in *Worktown*, 1977).

Chapter 3

Gendered economies of home and work

What connection existed between the gender divisions of paid employment experienced by the women I interviewed and the gender divisions of domestic labour in their own household? This question represents the starting point for this chapter. It is a question that may be explored at different levels of analysis and generality. At the most concrete, it is concerned with how working women coped with domestic labour and childcare while also engaging in paid employment. How did they manage the 'dual roles' of worker and wife in an epoch prior to the mass employment of married women and prior also to the mass availability of consumer durables, 'labour-saving' devices, and other commodities that were associated with the expansion of married women's employment in the post-war period? Did they do everything themselves, working ten or twelve hours a day for pay, then going home and doing all the the cooking, cleaning, and washing for their husband and children? Or were they accustomed to men helping at home and so view domestic labour as a relatively non-gendered activity?

Shifting perspective from the experience of individuals to a more general level, the question relates to the characteristics of the gender divisions of paid employment and of unpaid domestic labour and the nature of the links between them. If husbands took part in domestic labour when their wives took part in waged work did this depend on the sort of work the husband did, or on the occupation of the wife, or on both? Could any systematic patterns be discerned, and, if so, how are we to explain variations in the allocation of men's and women's labour between waged and unwaged work, between labour undertaken 'at work' and 'at home'?

And what would answers to such questions indicate more schematically at a societal level about the interlinkage between market economy and household economy in Lancashire between the 1930s and 1960s? What circuits connected these two sectors, and what exchanges of commodities, labour and wages occurred between them? Did women workers purchase ready-made commodities and were households involved in market-type exchanges with the formal economy? Were market and household economies more or less insulated from each other than in the period before mass production?

Micro-TSOLs: configurations of labour

This line of enquiry will be pursued from the perspective of the 'total social organisation of labour' (as outlined in Chapter 1). An advantage of this framework is that its umbrella notion of work permits consideration of labour of all kinds, irrespective of the social and economic relations within which it is conducted and regardless of how 'labour' may be embedded in non-work activities and relationships. Since the TSOL is not tied to a conception of work defined solely as formal paid employment it is possible to analyse connections and exchanges occurring between different forms of labour. There may be a systematic connection between work conducted in the commodity sector and non-commodity work; activity that is officially, or popularly, considered 'real work' may be underpinned by labour that is 'hidden' and performed under very different conditions. The TSOL framework is designed specifically to explore work that crosses the divide between commodity and non-commodity sectors and to analyse the pattern of exchanges, reciprocities, dependencies and inequalities that straddle the multiplicity of forms and relations of work.

All the women I interviewed came from the same areas of Lancashire; they were in the same age bracket; all would count as 'working class', and most engaged in manual work. Yet, it was clear from the outset of the research, that, despite these similarities, significant variations existed between their configurations of home and work. The TSOL approach – here used as a micro-level working concept – provides a means to tease out such differences and to identify patterns of interface between home and work, whether the micro-level in focus is particular households, specific occupational groups, or local labour markets.

The chapter begins by delineating two groups of women workers and then analysing the patterns of home/work that distinguish them. It moves on to their use of domestic commodities and personal services, exploring inequalities and reciprocities that divide and unite them. Introducing a spatial dimension, the final sections examine the significance of local labour markets and local traditions.

Defining identities: weavers and casual women workers

Discussion centres on two groups of married women: weavers or spinners employed in the cotton industry and those more casually employed in a variety of jobs from cleaning, through canteen work, and serving in a pub, to childminding and doing other people's washing. All left school and started work at 14 or earlier and most married in their early twenties. It was after they had children that differences between their home/work configurations became pronounced. Textile and casual workers seemed to vary from then along a range of dimensions in addition to their actual employment, including relation to their husbands, household division of labour, involvement in community and family networks, and, not least, their identities.

The differences between the two groups are exemplified by two women introduced in Chapter 2, Edith Ashworth, the life long weaver from Little Hulton, and Annie Preston, the office cleaner and part-time washer from Salford. But, as can be seen from the interview grid, their examples are multiplied by others. Edith Ashworth's experience was echoed, amongst others, by Alice Foster and Lily Hunt, weavers from Bolton and Oldham respectively, and Annie Preston's by Flo Nuttall and Vera Rogers, both from Salford, and by Alice Foster's friend Nellie Lynch.[1]

However, to identify the women as particular kinds of worker often necessitated going beyond their own definitions. Many women who undertook casual work did not talk much about it, if at all, appearing not to identify themselves as having been employed. In interview they tended to remain silent unless prompted. The session with Nellie Lynch, for example, looked as if it would never get going. Alice Foster had already talked about herself and when Nellie Lynch's turn came she kept repeating that she had nothing to say about her work:

> Nellie Lynch: Well mine's not a lot ... There's not a lot to tell ... You'll only be ten minutes with me.
>
> Alice Foster: Give over, Nellie. Your life's as interesting as mine.
>
> Nellie Lynch: Give over, Alice. She'll only be ten minutes.

Such reluctance occurred too consistently to be interpreted merely as interview nerves. Other women started by denying that they had anything, or, significantly, anything 'interesting', to say about their work. Nevertheless they were apparently quite at ease in talking as mothers and wives. The identities they expressed were clearly as mothers rather than as workers, despite having engaged in paid employment over many years. This suggested that their notion of 'worker' was something which they did not see themselves as conforming to. Gaining information about their work was thus mediated, or obstructed, by their own adherence to a dichotomous construction of worker versus wife/mother. The way they spoke implied these were mutually exclusive categories, two sides of a dualism, in which they had no hesitation about their own location. All the dualisms of home/private/unpaid/informal versus work/public/paid/formal contested by recent feminist thinking were evident in how they talked about their lives. They downplayed their own paid work and did not expound on it, insofar as it fell short of official definitions of standard wage labour, full-time work, contractual employment relations and so forth. When talking to an outsider, they appeared to follow traditional valorisation by treating one series as serious enough to warrant discussion under the label of 'work' but not the other. They themselves were not 'real' workers, because they were not doing a 'proper' job. Their identity was as wives and mothers, their self-esteem linked to their skills in discharging domestic responsibilities, and their pride tied to success in keeping home and family clean, fed and clothed.

According to official employment statistics and Census categories these wives and mothers would probably not appear as workers since they did not conform to the standard definitions of 'gainful employment' or 'economic activity' that confer official recognition of 'occupied' status. There are few histories of casual work, in contrast to the volumes devoted to the textile industry. Pervasive popular conceptions of what counts as a 'proper job' and 'real work' have altered little over the century and compound the official picture. Many of the jobs that casual workers were doing in the 1930s and into the postwar period were pejoratively constructed by the 1950s and 1960s as 'little jobs' done for 'pin money'. No wonder the women did not or, more accurately, *could not* identify themselves as workers, or even as working mothers.

No such problem existed with the weavers. In interview they immediately identified themselves as such when asked about their work history. Both at the time and now in retirement their work identity was first and foremost as weavers or spinners, their self-esteem and pride associated with the skills of their paid employment. They spoke fluently about this aspect of their lives, confident in their expertise with industrial processes and familiarity with formal employment relations. Their reticence was restricted to questions concerning domestic labour.

Clearly, the work/home division was conceived[2] as a dualism by both groups of women, each placing themselves at opposite ends of the divide. Access to information about their jobs was thus mediated by their own identities. For textile workers everything worked in the same direction to define them unequivocally as workers, from official statistics through trade union organisation to popular beliefs. There is no problem for the researcher straightforwardly accepting their own definitions, regardless of the constructions of worker/mother implied.

But the term 'casual women workers' is mine rather than theirs. They comprise a distinctive occupational group on account of their shared work relations and kinds of job. Since they are not in a position to claim for themselves the title of 'worker', analytical ascription from within a theoretical framework is required if they are to be acknowledged as workers and the significance of their paid employment recognised. In contrast to the textile workers, everything conspires against casually employed women being seen socially, economically, ideologically or culturally as workers, even to the extent that they do not see themselves in this way. And if 'casual women workers' is a clumsy phrase that sounds odd this too is an effect of the absence of generally accepted terminology to denote their work.

Despite describing themselves as mothers rather than workers many casually employed women nevertheless worked 'full-time' for pay. It was normal for them to be permanently engaged in this way. Many engaged in numerous forms of work, often combining multiple part-time jobs, like night-cleaning and childminding, or canteen and laundry work. In hours, such work usually amounted to the equivalent of a full-time job, and to the equivalent of a textile worker's hours, even if not undertaken over a continuous nine hour day.

Thus, it is my contention that women who engaged in the various kinds of casual work are to be viewed as workers just as those working in standard forms of employment. However, since the meaning they accord to 'work' is mediated by their own identity as mothers and not as workers, viewing them in this way is possible only on condition of putting in question their own self-definition. If rejecting a 'separate spheres' paradigm is the precondition for analysing interconnections between gender divisions and inequalities of home and work, this may necessitate also going beyond any version of the paradigm held by the actors themselves.

Casual women workers

Annie Preston's history of paid work reveals just how busy she was kept. After the birth of her first child:

> *... I still had to go to work because the money wasn't enough to keep us. And I went to work, making purses at a leather place. And then [after more children were born] ... we decided to go to University to clean at night and we worked all night then. From 10 o'clock till 7 o'clock the next morning.*

In addition, there was the washing Mrs Preston did at the municipal wash-house for two other women:

> *I was always on the last hour at the wash-house because I worked ten o'clock till eight so I had to rush but I used to go for myself and then me cousin, she had a bad foot. I went for her and another one, three times a week.*

Annie Preston's friend Flo Nuttall did regular shifts in factory canteens for many years in addition to night cleaning, and she also took 'out' washing. Nellie Lynch did part-time cleaning and worked in a pub. Vera Rogers did office work during the week and occasional shop work at weekends.

All these jobs were poorly paid but the casual women's wages were nevertheless essential to household income, contributing to the maintenance of a basic standard of living, especially when supplementing a low or unreliable male wage. The women's husbands were typically engaged in unskilled manual work, also for long hours (when they could get the work), earning wages that were below average when they were in work but none when they were laid off. Annie Preston's husband worked in the building industry after he came out of the army, and later as a crane driver. Flo Nuttall's was a lorry driver. Vera Rogers' worked in a warehouse. Many husbands of casual women workers were thus in insecure employment themselves, in the building industry where they often were unable to earn a regular income in winter, as lorry drivers, or on Salford docks. Here conditions were so casualised that they could not be sure of working from one day to the next or from one shift to the next. In the following discussion between Agnes Brown and her friend Hilda Walker about the insecurity of dock work they were talking about their fathers. For the next generation things had improved a bit but dock work, one of the main employers of male labour in Salford, remained irregular and the pay low, until the docks eventually closed down.

Hilda Walker:	*They used to have what they called 'the blue eyed boys' on the docks didn't they. If you weren't in the clique you couldn't get work at all.*
Q:	*Did the dockers have to get work tickets?*
Hilda Walker:	*They used to queue up for what they called 'a tally' and they used to hand them out. It was like a lot of animals going round a pen, weren't they?*
Agnes Brown:	*And a lot of religion played a part on the docks. If there was a C of E[3] foreman he would only start C of E men. If there was a Roman Catholic one, then he would only start his own and all that.*
Hilda Walker:	*If you wasn't in the clique you didn't get work.*

> *Agnes Brown:* No, they all stood in a place [to get the tally]. My father was fortunate, my father would do half a night and he thought he was lucky if he got half a night. He come home at 5 o'clock and me mam would have his tea ready and he'd say 'hurry up, I'm going back. I've got half a night', and he used to go back. Got a tally and he worked till gone 10 and it was called 'half a night'. He got that at Christmas and he used to jump for it because it was more money to buy kids Christmas toys. Orange boats used to come up from Spain, he used to go on the orange boats to get them out for Christmas in the shops. 'Half a night' it was called.

Most husbands gave their wives a set amount of housekeeping money every week, retaining the remainder of their wage for personal spending. Very few casual women workers, and few of the women I interviewed in Salford generally, had husbands who 'tipped up' their whole wage for household use, even though many of their fathers had. The experience of Annie Preston and Flo Nuttall was probably typical:

> *Q:* I'll ask you about money now and your arrangements at home. Did your husbands hand over all their wages to you or give you housekeeping?
>
> *Flo Nuttall:* Just give you so much.
>
> *Annie Preston:* We only got housekeeping money.
>
> *Q:* Was that the same as your mothers or don't you know?
>
> *Annie Preston:* Well me father used to tip all his up.
>
> *Flo Nuttall:* My stepfather used to take it.
>
> *Annie Preston:* No, me father he used to tip it all up, because like at Christmas time he used to be coming home from work and there was a shop where they sold toys and he used to lay things up like a doll and pram for me sister, a shilling a week, and cups and saucers for me, a shilling a week, and that was out of his spends.
>
> *Q:* But your own husbands gave you housekeeping?
>
> *Annie Preston:* Yes, housekeeping off your own husband was different.
>
> *Q:* Were you responsible for paying all the bills?
>
> *Annie Preston:* Yes, the rent, the insurances, tick if you got tick[4], clothes. In fact I used to buy my husband's clothes until I thought I'm a fool. And I said to him, I'm not buying you any, mind you, they was only 30 bob, 30 bob tailors for a suit. But it was a lot of money out of your wages. I said you'll have to start buying your own so after that I never bought them. I used to buy him shirts, pullovers, shoes, everything and you couldn't do it, you couldn't do it really.

Many husbands did not disclose their wages to their wives and many wives, like Agnes Brown (see below), did not expect them to. Women were in the dark as to the balance between what their husbands handed over and what was kept for 'spends'. Household income could therefore be unreliable not only through irregular male earnings but also as a result of husbands keeping back a high proportion of their wages.[5]

The women's attitude was to accept what they were given and not ask for more even if it was insufficient to cover costs, as evidenced by Vera Rogers' response to an unexpected financial outlay:

> Vera Rogers: I thought where am I going to find the money? It never occurred to me to ask for more. I just went out and earned it. I think its probably you are indoctrinated that way because that's how it was with my parents. You inherit that attitude.
>
> Q: Your husband gave you a certain amount of housekeeping?
>
> Vera Rogers: Yes, and you didn't ask for any more ... it would have been better I think, if I had said to him I need some extra money for ... But I don't think ... he was probably not aware then that more money was needed and it never occurred to me to tell him that I want some more money. So I talked it over with me mum and she said 'well, go and see if you can get a bit of work to pay for it.'

It was up to the women to manage as best they could on what was made available, by providing the extra income themselves through their own earnings, by making savings wherever possible, or by resorting to the pawnshop and buying groceries 'on tick'. That their pride was at stake in asking their husband for more money suggested that it would shame them to do so. It is problematic now to reconstruct the exact proportion of household income provided by casual women workers but it seems that many supplied at least one-third of the total, their contribution varying between a quarter and a half.

Whatever the exact proportion, the women allocated all their earnings to common household use. Their wages went on basics, particularly food and clothing for children, not on personal spending money for themselves or for luxuries.

Vera Rogers had five children to feed and clothe:

> Q: What were your wages used for? Was your money still for necessities or did you ever buy anything special for yourself?
>
> Vera Rogers: I could have managed to feed them on the housekeeping money but I couldn't afford to buy them the clothes I wanted for them.

When asked what their earnings were spent on, Annie Preston and Flo Nuttall were unequivocal:

> Annie Preston: It went back on the food.
>
> Flo Nuttall: It went on food for the table.

Annie Preston: You got nothing out of it, it all went back on food.

Q: So you didn't have any spending money, but your husbands did?

Flo Nuttall: Oh no, no.

Annie Preston: Oh yes, he used to go out for a drink with his mates, Friday and Saturday, Sunday. He always had, and he asked for more money. I'd say 'oh aye, you don't like me to have anything, do you', but you didn't have it.

Flo Nuttall: You didn't spend it unwisely. You had to budget things, like the kids started staying to school dinners, well I used to have to put the dinner money away on a Friday and put it on top of the cupboards until they could take it to school and it was a penny bank, a couple of coppers[6] to put in the school bank but if I didn't do that I wouldn't have had it on the Monday.

Q: So you're saying your own wages really went for basics, the necessities, it wasn't for buying any luxuries?

Flo Nuttall: It went on the children's back when they wanted a school uniform.

Annie Preston: We never had luxuries.

Flo Nuttall: No, you never got any.

Despite effectively working full-time and earning a significant proportion of family finances, they took pride primarily in their housework and expressed highly developed notions of domesticity. They talked in greater detail, with more feeling and confidence about their role as managers of the household than about their paid work, so creating the definite impression that their own self-worth was more rooted in their domestic than their employed status.

All gave detailed accounts of their weekly routines and methods of cleaning, cooking, washing and childcare, expressing satisfaction and pleasure in how they had succeeded in keeping house, linen, and children clean and fed in the constant battle against dirt and poverty. It mattered to them all, as to Annie Preston (Chapter 2), that they baked their own pies and bread and that the washing smelled fresh. Annie Preston used the wash-house so often that her husband accused her of 'having a fella' there. Flo Nuttall took pride in bringing home clean washing that she described as 'gleaming':

> I used to come home dead proud of my washing, all smooth and dry and you could put it away.

She used the wash-house in the evening after work:

> You used to book about 6 o'clock. You'd go home and get your washing the night before all ready in bundles, didn't we, your woollens, your whites, your coloureds. Especially when it was all hot in summer and you'd come out and you'd be stinking. Mind you if say I was with Annie, we used to go in the bath and one would watch the washing because they used to nick it if you didn't watch it. And you watched my washing

*while I'd go and have a bath and we used to watch their washing while
they went to have a bath.*

In their memory, a rigid gender division of labour reigned in the homes of
casual women workers with men going out to work and doing absolutely nothing
in the house. Women undertook all domestic labour, on a fairly labour intensive
basis, and all financial management:

Q:	*Do you think men did less work over all?*
Annie Preston:	*Oh they did. Mine never did anything in the house.*
Flo Nuttall:	*It would finish when they left the factory.*
Annie Preston:	*I think it was beneath them to wash pots or do things like that. The man's place was in the work and the woman's was in the home. It was supposed to be all done by the time he came in from work and all he did was come in, have a wash, sit down and his meal would be put in front of him and that was it, wasn't it?*
Q:	*Even if the wife was working as well?*
Flo Nuttall:	*Oh yes. You always had a neighbour to come in if you wasn't well. You'd go in to them or they would come in to you. No, they never did a thing, the men.*

That husbands appeared unaware that their wives' contribution was basic
to household income was a strong source of resentment:

Annie Preston: *Me husband, he never ever coughed up for anything. Say
I got a new three-piece suite, I used to get it on tick, on
the hire purchase. He used to come home and say 'oh
that's nice'. I said 'yeah, but you don't ask how you've
got it.' Never thought how I paid it. They lived in a world
of their own, didn't they?*

Although they seemed to willingly assume responsibility for everything
domestic these women were also, in retrospect at least, scathing about the local
tradition of male-supremacist thinking, extremely resentful of husbands'
domination, and contemptuous of men's inability to cope with even the simplest
domestic chore as the following quotations show. Annie Preston again was
particularly vehement about domestic incompetence:

*I remember when I had one of me children, and I had all me children at
home, and I remember saying to me husband, 'now put those potatoes
on'. I was upstairs in bed, and he comes upstairs with a pan of potatoes.
'Test these, see if they are done' and things like that. But he couldn't tell
when potatoes was done. And that's when he had to do things then, but
it was beneath him really to do it, he hadn't the foggiest idea how to boil
an egg or anything. You couldn't have left him in charge of the kids or
'owt like that and say 'I'm going in hospital for a month, look after them',
he couldn't cope. Mind you I blame ourselves really, we are too soft.*

Discussion between Annie Preston and her friends about how men thought
and acted as bosses displayed an explicit gender consciousness:

> Annie Preston: Like when they used to say a man's home is his castle, my god it was, and he was the king and all, wan't he? Oh yes, he was still the boss.

> Flo Nuttall: We used to have a saying 'is your master in?'. Even the other day I heard Mrs. Burgess say 'oh your master was a nice man'.

> Ivy Turner: They used to all call them 'the master'. Now the younger age groups won't have it, thank goodness.

> Annie Preston: No I don't blame them, there are not as daft as us. If you'd have kept arguing, you would have been fighting all your married life. Because you had to fight for whatever you got really. But you have just got to let them go.

Annie Preston's final comment reveals much about relations between wives and husbands. Women could have stood up to their husbands and she could have argued with hers; they were at odds over numerous issues. But what would be the point? She implies that this would open the flood gates: once started, there would be no end to arguments. Everything could be challenged and fought over. Nowadays things are different but in those days you did not expect to discuss everything, to bring into the open all the disagreements, or even the agreements. Men were like that, married life was like that, and you just got on with it. Like the other women in Salford, most of her working and leisure time was spent in the company of women rather than with her husband. She and he did not seem to do much in common. Many issues were just not talked about but marriage was not brought into question by the absence of discussion or agreement.

A conclusion to be drawn from this outline of the casual women workers is that the nature of their paid work, its gendered divisions and inequalities did indeed interlock with those of their domestic labour. There was a definite interaction between the two. The labour of husbands and wives differed systematically, and in both areas. In their paid employment casual women worked in gender-segregated single-sex occupations, as also did most of their husbands. Only women did office or night cleaning; only men worked on the docks, in construction or as lorry drivers. Their households, and many other aspects of family and community life, were also characterised by strict gender division. Women took virtually sole responsibility for the home, children and for managing household finances. Men spent much of their leisure time with other men, and women with other women.

It was evident that the low earning capacity of casual women workers reinforced their arduous domestic labour: they did not earn enough to buy ready-made food or clothes, laundry services, domestic appliances or other consumer durables. Their jobs were badly paid, and all the work they undertook was labour intensive, whether at home or for pay. They could not buy the goods or services to alleviate domestic chores which might in turn have released time to engage in better paid work.

Thus, a dual vicious circle connected women's work in both areas and gender inequalities in both areas. Women were in a weak position in the labour market and in the home: while they contributed income and labour to the household, men contributed wages but appropriated labour, and also time. Gender inequality for women in the two areas was thus mutually reinforcing. Women's invidious position in relation to men both in paid work and in domestic labour was reflected in their strong perception of gender difference and inequality.

But the relation between money and authority within the family was more complex than a simple case of who brought in more. Women negotiated around their husbands, aware that little was to be gained by actively putting male authority to the test. At the same time they implied that the traditional notion of 'the man is boss' was just that, a leftover from a byegone era. It had not disappeared in the period that they were talking about but no one seriously accepted it now. For women in Salford this traditonal notion was integral to their portrayal of 'life as it was'. Retaining the opaque power of a myth, it remained a threat in the background, hinted at in the apparently disparaging jokes women made about men.

Women weavers

By contrast, the nexus of relations linking gender and work was quite different for women weavers, spinners and other cotton workers. There was a tradition in the textile industry of married women and mothers continuing permanently in full-time and 'standard' employment.[7] Many of the women interviewed were themselves daughters of weavers, whom they described as having given up paid work only after the birth of their fourth (in some cases, seventh) child. Their mothers had not expected the arrival of children to put an end to their paid employment and neither did they. Although they had far fewer children themselves, mostly one or two, most had also returned to work fairly soon after childbirth and continued as weavers until the sheds closed down or they reached retirement age. Of the cotton workers on the interview grid Alice Foster, Nellie Lynch, Edith Ashworth, Lily Hunt, Clarice Holmes, Doreen Baker and Marjorie Fisher all had mothers who had worked in the same industry. But whereas Edith Ashworth, Clarice Holmes and Marjorie Fisher came from families of five, seven and eight respectively they themselves had two, one and two children. (From a family of 14, Nellie Lynch went on to have four.)

Weaving was possibly unique amongst traditional industries for its relative absence of gender segregation. Both men and women were employed in weaving sheds, in the same occupations and for identical rates of pay per loom. This does not mean that both sexes were to be found in all weaving sheds, or even in all sections of the weaving industry, or in all towns where weaving employment existed (Home Office, 1930: 8–10; Savage, 1988, see also note 22 below). Nor does it imply that take-home pay was the same for men and women (Lewis, 1984: 164), since men often worked more looms than women and were employed as overlookers.[8] But it does follow that women weavers were doing work which was not constructed purely as 'women's work', and that they might be used to working alongside men as well as women, and on a relatively equal basis. Pay rates in weaving, as in the cotton industry generally, although relatively low for men, were relatively high for women in relation to women's wages at the time, both locally and nationally.[9]

The earnings of the women weavers I interviewed were thus higher than those of the casual women workers and relatively stable, equivalent to men's wages for similar work and often on a par with that of their husbands, some of whom also worked in cotton. The casual women, by contrast, did 'women's work' with other women and for 'women's wages'.[10]

The employment profile of weavers' husbands also differed considerably from that of the casual workers, few working in construction, on the docks or driving. Apart from those who also worked in the textile industry there were miners, foundry workers, and engineers. A proportion were skilled workers who had undergone apprenticeship. Generally their conditions of employment were less casualised and seasonal, their rates of pay likely to be more standardised, regular and higher than those of the 'casual husbands'.

Women weavers bought ready-made meals and clothes, laundry services[11] and domestic appliances. They readily admitted to having bought pie dinners from the chippy which the casual women consistently denied. They 'farmed out' their children with relatives or neighbours whom they paid, sometimes collecting them every night but more often bringing them home only for the weekend. Many bought labour-saving consumer durables as soon as they became available, and the proportion who had electric irons, vacuum cleaners, and especially washing machines in the 1930s was remarkable. Most had bought a washing machine by the mid 1950s even if they did not have a bath at home or inside toilet. None had used the municipal wash-house.

Edith Ashworth (Chapter 2) exemplifies all these features. She paid her mother to look after her two children while she remained in continuous full-time employment. Her husband was a coal cutter who earned high wages relative to many other male manual workers (including weavers). Their combined income enabled them to rent a house with all mod cons before the Second World War, and she was also in a position to buy a washing machine and vacuum cleaner when her children were very young.

The experiences of other weavers was similar. Born in 1917, Alice Foster of Bolton was ten years younger than Edith Ashworth. Having started work as a spinner in 1931, she later switched to weaving. She married a foundry worker, had one child in 1945, and remained in continuous full-time employment. Mrs Foster boarded her son with her older sister during the week, paying her up to half of her wages in return:

> I went back [to work] a few weeks after he [her son] were born. Oh, I couldn't stop at home. I shouldn't know what to do with myself ...

She described her son as having grown up with his cousins 'as brothers and sisters'.

Greater similarity with men in pay and manner of employment was matched by a more equal domestic division of labour where, according to their wives at least, many husbands took some responsibility for housework, cooking and childcare. Several echoed Alice Foster's brisk summing-up:

> Housework were done at weekend. Bill was good ... he helped out with cleaning and washing.

Many women weavers appeared to accord so little significance to housework that they were reluctant even to discuss it in interview, and they were not as spontaneously forthcoming about cleaning, cooking or washing as the 'casual' women had been. They certainly did not talk in glowing terms about donkeying the steps or the satisfaction of sweetly smelling clean washing. Rather they gave the impression of taking domestic labour very much in their stride.

Moreover, there was no mention of husbands getting a better deal or the unfairness of having to do 'two shifts'. Most husbands, including Mrs Foster's and Mrs Ashworth's, tipped up all their wages, and others had a 'one purse' arrangement. Very few followed the casual workers' husbands in the housekeeping allowance system.[12] Couples were likely to discuss household purchases involving a large outlay. Even if money was tight it did not seem to be such a cause of conflict or recrimination, but a problem to be confronted jointly. There was little evidence of the hostility between the sexes over domestic labour so strongly expressed by the casual workers, and little suggestion that men made hard lives even harder.

Many weavers spoke of going out for a drink with their husbands and gave the impression of spending some of their leisure time as a couple. But then, compared with the casual women workers weavers had a much clearer demarcation between working time and not working time, and more of the time that they were not working for pay was ear-marked for leisure.

Lily Hunt's testimony on such questions was typical. A weaver from Oldham, she was born in 1911, married in 1939, to another mill worker, and had two children. Note the very different tone and emphasis of her depiction of housework and husband from that of Annie Preston, the night cleaner:

Q: How did you manage doing housework and cooking when you were working full-time?

Lily Hunt: It didn't seem to be any problem. No, you just had a routine. We just had to do it at night. I used to make my dinner at night for the day after. And whoever was home first of the two of us would set the tea going. I used to make meat puddings one night for the day after, and all sorts of things. You had to have a routine to do your work at night.

Q: And did your husband help at all?

Lily Hunt: Mine did. He helped with the housework. He washed up. I didn't wash up. He saw to the boy while I saw to the girl.

Q: Did he tip up? Did you deal with all the money matters?

Lily Hunt: Well we used to join it, we had a joint account and everything used to be joint. We worked together like that. It was none of 'this was mine and that's yours'.

Lily Hunt's brief, almost throwaway, statement about childcare is particularly noteworthy.[13]

From the collective testimony of the weavers the picture emerged, on the surface at least, of a more 'companionate' marriage of partners than that experienced by the casual women workers. Yet it differed in significant ways from the conventional model because of the absence of an explicit ideology of the home.[14]

Weavers' understanding of what constituted 'work' was quite different from the casual workers. So too was their construction of the division between home and work, and their self-positioning in that division. Their self-esteem was as weavers, and they took pride in the number of looms they managed, their speed of work, and level of earnings. Unlike the casual women workers, the weavers' identity was very much as skilled workers, and not as housewives, which explains their lack of expansiveness about domestic labour. But then the worth of their paid work was socially recognised, in a way that that of the casual workers' was not, conferring on weavers the status of valued workers doing 'proper' jobs. The self-reputation of the casual workers, in contrast, was tied up with making ends meet and their achievement was judged by how successfully they kept the family fed and clothed on very meagre resources.

Thus, paid work interlocked with domestic labour for weavers as for casual women workers but in a quite distinct manner. Their different patterns of home/ work were connected with differences between their husbands' occupations as well as their own. The patterns are therefore to be understood as crystallising a triple inter-connection between men's work, women's work and domestic labour.

At the risk of being overly schematic, a contrast could be drawn between the casual women workers and the weavers on almost every dimension that I have examined: gender-segregated versus gender-unsegregated work; higher versus lower wage rates; more versus less labour intensive domestic labour; husbands working in insecure, low paid work which was exclusively 'men's work' versus husbands in more secure employment, probably better paid and sometimes unsegregated; husbands who tended to give a portion of their wages as housekeeping allowance, did no housework or childcare, and took little part in financial management versus husbands who 'tipped up' all their wages, some also taking part in domestic labour and family finances; relatively gender-segregated versus relatively gender-unsegregated home life and leisure activities.

Economically, the difference between the two groups of women was marked. For weavers there was a ratchet effect whereby their higher earning capacity enabled them to reduce the time and labour devoted to domestic chores. Their greater financial independence gave them more control over their own lives. Women were not so financially dependent on men and men did not expect to be serviced so extensively by women. This resulted in weavers' household relationships being structured by gender in distinct ways from the casual workers. For weavers greater gender equality in employment and in the home were mutually self-reinforcing, as was inequality for the casual workers.

These patterns also throw light on the very different identities of the women which were so startling at the outset of the research. They bring into relief the varied ways and meanings of 'being a woman' even amongst such a small and restricted 'sample' of manual working-class women in Lancashire in the mid twentieth century. What it meant to be a woman was different for a weaver than for a casual woman worker, evidence of what feminist analysis theorises as distinct femininities, that are both constitutive of and constituted by gendered subjectivities.

Aside: patterns, groups and configurations

The analysis so far has suggested a connection between structured inequalities in the home and in paid employment such that different patterns of wage earning interlocked with different patterns of domestic labour. But these are not to be understood as rigid or pre-given categories into which people could be neatly slotted. Rather there were different constellations of being and acting around which weavers and casual workers clustered in response to different circumstances of possibilities and constraints. No simple correlation existed between the employment characteristics of a couple and their household arrangements. It would be overly simplistic, as we shall see, to infer any unmediated direct causal link between husband's and wife's waged work and domestic labour.

The patterns of home/work interface exemplified by the two groups by no means exhaust the range of interfaces existing in the area at the time (those for single women and young workers will be explored in Chapter 4). Distinguishing between patterns is in part a heuristic exercise, a means by which to single out the factors that predispose households to a particular connection between home and work or to a particular linkage with the market economy. The aim in identifying patterns is to demonstrate how the various aspects 'fit' together, both the points of tension and the ways they mutually reinforce and reproduce each other. The patterns thus represent archetypes exemplifying particular connections within the much greater complexity of individuals' actual lives and households' actual connection to their context. However, in order to be of use the patterns do not need to 'fit' all cases under consideration. By indicating some parameters that are crucial to the analysis of particular configurations of home/work they provide a framework which may illuminate also the many instances that do not approximate to either pattern or which are mixtures of the two.

As for 'groups', weavers and casual women workers constituted 'groups' only insofar as distinct patterns of economic interconnections existed between their gender divisions of work in paid employment and domestic labour. They were not actively, or socially constituted as groups, and no one 'belonged' to them as to a precise or identical model.

Not only was there variation within the two groupings but many individuals also differed considerably at different stages of the life course. This was particularly evident in the mothers of the women interviewed, a large proportion of the older generation of cotton workers having ended up by taking in washing (Lily Hunt; Marjorie Fisher), and/or going out cleaning (Vera Rogers; Hilda Walker), and/or looking after children (Agnes Brown; Edith Ashworth; Vera Rogers) after many years spent as spinners or weavers. Some daughters, like Nellie Lynch, could also be seen as shifting between the patterns. She had started work as a weaver in 1932 but her later life was closer to that of the casual women workers. After the birth of her first child, her husband, a miner, 'wouldn't allow' her to go out to work. Eventually she went cleaning part-time. Widowed young and with sole financial responsibilty for four children, she took whatever work she could get, combining multiple part-time jobs. Agnes Brown also straddled both patterns but simultaneously rather than sequentially: like the weavers she remained in continuous standard full-time employment as a bus conductress but other features of her life were closer to the casual women workers. Others, like Marjorie Fisher and Doreen Baker, ended up in a variety of different occupations having started out as cotton workers.

Many changes occurred during the historical period spanned by these women's working lives, and this is another factor militating against any neat one-to-one correspondence of women and 'groups'. One of the most significant is the secular decline of the textile industry from the 1920s, and the eventual virtual disappearance of jobs in spinning and weaving by the 1970s. Another is the introduction of part-time work for married women, unknown before the Second World War, but expanding rapidly from the 1950s.

The experiences of many of the women interviewed reflect these changes. Some weavers were already retired by the time this work dried up, but others had to seek alternative employment. Edith Ashworth spent several years as a cleaner and general help in hospitals and social services between Tootals closing down in 1958 and her eventual retirement. Hilda Walker approximated more closely to the national postwar pattern, returning part-time in 1950 to clerical work at Metropolitan Vickers similar to that which she had done full-time between 1930 and 1941. During severe unemployment in the early 1930s, Marjorie Fisher had supported her family as a young spinner; she took time out when her children were young before returning to full-time work in engineering factories.

That the experience of particular individuals cannot be slotted neatly into 'a pattern' does not undermine the attempt to analyse configurations of home/work. The challenge for TSOL analysis is to broaden the framework, and take into consideration other factors that may elucidate both the 'departures' from the patterns and the approximations, so enabling a more nuanced and differentiated understanding of the various interconnections. Variations in local labour markets and the employment circumstances for men and women specific to different places are one such factor to be considered.

Housework, husbands and commodities

Bearing these complexities in mind, this section explores the question of how women's full-time employment could be combined with the exigencies of domestic labour and childrearing in the period before mass production.

Edith Ashworth and Annie Preston were very different from each other, exemplifying all the differences outlined earlier. One was the weaver from Little Hulton, the other the night cleaner from Salford. However they had in common that neither of their husbands lifted a finger in the home. But the husbands too were very different, at opposite ends of the spectrum of manual work, one a highly skilled and highly paid coal cutter, the other a lower skilled, lower paid and seasonally employed building labourer. Nevertheless, both worked in exclusively male occupations in heavy industries with a strong tradition of masculinism. The domestic division of labour (or, more accurately, lack of it) appeared in the cases of Mrs Ashworth and Mrs Preston to be more closely associated with the nature of the men's occupations than with the employment status of either husband or wife. The women's waged work did not determine or explain their husbands' behaviour.

Despite this common feature of their husbands' lack of involvement, Edith Ashworth and Annie Preston managed their responsibility for the household in very different ways. Mrs Ashworth bought commodities to substitute or aid her own domestic labour and also purchased services from other women. She had bought a washing machine and vacuum cleaner before the war and a fridge soon after. She paid her mother for minding her two children during the week and had no hesitation in buying ready-made meals when they were more convenient. But apart from 'pot herbs' for making stew (Chapter 2) Mrs Preston bought no commodities, undertaking all housework herself on the basis of her own labour. She used the wash-house until she was rehoused in 1971, acquired a vacuum cleaner in the 1960s and a fridge in the 1970s. While working in a standard day-time job Annie Preston had paid her sister for looking after three of her children, but later her sister paid Annie for doing her washing. She was proud to have done all her own cooking and baking rather than relying on the pie shop or chippy.

While few casually employed women's husbands helped, weavers' husbands were much more likely to, though to a variable extent. The nature of their sharing also varied, sometimes amounting to little more than helping (with washing up or dusting), frequently involving responsibility for outside tasks alone (chopping wood or bringing in coal), and only more occasionally assuming full responsibility for indoor household jobs or childcare. Similarity in employment status and engaging in similar work to their wives, in occupations that were relatively unsegregated, seemed to be the most important factors predisposing husbands to share domestic labour.

Here the experience of the weavers who spoke to me confirms existing research. Abendstern (1986)[15] and Gittins (1982), amongst other historians, have drawn attention to the greater extent of task sharing in the home where both women and men were employed in weaving, in the same jobs and for the same wages, as they were in some, but by no means all, cotton towns. While such wives were relatively highly paid for women, their husbands would have been relatively low paid for skilled manual work. In towns where employment opportunities for men were more varied and weaving remained primarily a female occupation, this situation did not obtain. Sociological evidence from the 1970s and 1980s, also emphasises that the greater the equivalence in contribution to household income of husband and wife, the more likely the husband is to take part in domestic labour.[16] Thus, it is not possible to draw direct conclusions about domestic divisions of labour from wives' and husbands' paid employment. Although a clear connection existed between the degree of gender division in waged work and in domestic labour, these factors were themselves framed by others.

However, that husbands helped cannot alone explain how women coped with domestic labour when they worked full-time, as the example of Mrs Ashworth suggests. An alternative, or additional, possibility was to buy either labour-replacing commodities, or services from other women, or both.[17] These involved the purchaser in economic interchange with either the market and/or with a network of women in the community, or with both.

The situation of casual workers with respect to these possibilities was simpler than that of the weavers and more homogeneous. Most husbands, including

Annie Preston's, did not share in domestic labour and few wives had sufficient resources to purchase substitutes for their own labour. On the contrary, they were more likely to be selling their own labour services.

Amongst the weavers there was far greater variation, a range of different balances being struck by different individuals between the different possibilities. Some whose husbands shared household tasks and childcare, also bought both commodities and services in addition. Others just bought goods or services. Whereas the 'casual' women were usually on the minus side of all three dimensions, the weavers were usually on the plus side in two out of three, and in a few cases in all three.

Looking at this in terms of the linkage between household and market economy the weavers' situation was in some ways transitional between the epochs of pre- and post-mass production and consumption: they prefigured postwar women workers in the extent of commoditisation of domestic labour, but unlike their later counterparts, also relied to a greater extent on buying services from other women in their local community. The circuits linking the weavers' household economy with the market sector were both more numerous and more dense than those of the casual women, again placing them more on a par with a norm which became widespread only after the consolidation of mass consumption.

The tradition of married women working was thus sustained, or made viable, in different ways. That it relied in part on facilities that were external to the household demonstrates the necessity of broadening analysis from an exclusive focus on its internal dynamics to a consideration of the relation of households to both commodity sector and family/neighbourhood networks. The domestic division of labour was not the only significant factor, although this is the one most often singled out for attention in sociological and historical accounts of employment and household relations.

Divisions between women: inequality and reciprocity

Part of the explanation of the different modes of managing household responsibility of weavers and casual workers obviously lay in their different financial circumstances. The weavers were better off, in a position to afford things far beyond the reach of the casual women. An evident effect of their higher wages was to directly purchase the labour of others. Even though paying kin or neighbours was frequently described as a means of redistributing the wage between women in an extended family or close-knit community, it did nevertheless result in a hierarchy of employment, and hence structured inequalities, *between* working class women. Around the higher waged employment of married women grew a number of informal jobs performed by other women on a casual basis within the community. So long as they remained in work, the weavers were in a stronger economic position than those whose services they bought. And of course it was precisely the 'casual' type of women who were selling their services.

The position of Agnes Brown of Salford was similar to that of the weavers. She was in continuous full-time employment as a bus conductress. She had started as a spinner, and also worked in engineering and cable factories before going on the buses. She paid her mother to look after her son while she was at work.

> Q: How did you manage for childcare?
>
> A: Well I had my mother next door. She looked after him. I knew I couldn't leave him with anybody better. Well I've done shift work, I've done evenings and late duties and so one week I was with him the afternoon, I used to bring him home from school and the following week I was on lates you see.
>
> Q: Did you pay your mother for looking after him?
>
> A: Oh yes. I said to her I'll pay your rent every week. My father had died, you see, and I paid her rent and I used to pay her electric bill.
>
> Q: What proportion of your wage was that?
>
> A: When I started on the buses the wages was £5 a week. You see why I stuck the buses was because I got the same rate as the men guards. I paid the rent and I paid the electric bill and I started with £5 a week. I give her a £1 a week. Yes, every week, well she deserved it, I gave her a £1 a week. Well it helped her and it helped me.

Although some described it as a simple economic transaction, many women echoed the sentiment of Mrs Brown's final sentence in emphasising the mutual benefit to both parties when they paid sisters, cousins or neighbours for labour services.

Those providing the service also spoke in terms of 'helping', as Annie Preston and Flo Nuttall did about taking other people's laundry to the wash-house. When analysed in greater detail, however, the nature of these two women's 'help' was actually different, at least in terms of economic relations. Annie Preston was paid for doing other people's laundry and so it represented part of her income, and one of her part-time jobs. By contrast, Mrs Nuttall did her neighbour's washing and ironing in the municipal wash-house in exchange for the neighbour looking after her son while Mrs Nuttall engaged in other part-time paid employment.[18] This situation conformed more to a traditional definition of reciprocity, being a non-monetary exchange of labour.

Speaking from the perspective of a purchaser rather than provider of labour services, Kath Hinton made clear that for her paying for childcare represented a straightforward economic exchange rather than kin or community-based reciprocity. In discussion, she was more concerned to outline her work trajectory than expand on how she managed for childcare.

> Kath Hinton: We got the council house. So we came up this way. And I put the youngest out with a neighbour while I went out to work.
>
> Q: When you paid for the neighbour to look after your daughter was it a large part of your wages that went on it?
>
> Kath Hinton: I can't remember. I dont think she charged me a lot. No, I can't remember. But it wouldn't have been worth going

> *out for, for just half a wage ... Then I went to Ferrantis in Moston in 1957. And there they trained me to do soldering.*

Q: *What did they make there?*

Kath Hinton: *I was doing radar for the ground to air missiles called the Bloodhound. So I was doing the radar on that... In between I was leaving Ferrantis because in 1959 I had my youngest child then. When she was about four years old I farmed her out again while I went back.*

Q: *Who did you farm her out with?*

Kath Hinton: *A neighbour, I think it was the same one that had the other one. So then I went back from 1963 to 65 – that was making computers when they first started to come in. But not the small computers, the big ones, the very big ones.*

Although none of these transactions amounted to market exchanges as conventionally understood, those involving payment nevertheless constituted a particular form of economic relationship, and notably one between women who were economic unequals. That the transactions were usually embedded in, and inextricable from, other, non-economic, family and community relationships should not obscure their economic character.[19] Although all reciprocal work is of economic effect, it is still important to distinguish between situations where payment is and is not involved. The economic relationship between people who buy or sell services between themselves differs qualitatively from one where people undertake reciprocal labour services with no exchange of money; in the latter case they are on a more equal footing with each other, whereas in the former they are not, and one person is, to all intents and purposes, employing the other. What significance, if any, this economic difference has for any other aspect of their relationship is an open question to be investigated. It may be that it has no greater significance than this economic one. But even if not, recognition of economic inequalities like this between women in close community settings helps to dispel romanticised portrayals of 'communities of women' as if they all were performing reciprocal services for each other on an equal basis. The 'ties that bind' may, in some cases but not others, be more of necessity or multi-dimensional. Reciprocity between neighbours who were all in the same boat differed from the ties of economic need and support when weavers employed other women and casual women workers performed services for pay.

Domestic service-type relations of employment may be seen as a distinctive form of inequality existing between working class women and dividing them from each other, a hierarchy separate from but interlinked with the class inequalities of waged work, and the gender inequalities of both paid work and domestic labour. While these different series of inequalities could be expected to compound each other, they are nevertheless distinct in type and quality, and hence incommensurable. Attempting to add them up or flattening them so as to fit on a common quantifiable scale would be a fruitless exercise that seriously missed the point.

Local labour markets and gender divisions of work

The discussion of weavers and casual workers so far has only alluded to locality. But in fact there was a marked spatial dimension to the different pattern connecting gender division at home and at work in towns that were geographically very close to each other.

No single pattern of female employment was common to the Greater Manchester area as a whole; large differences existed between central Manchester itself, Rochdale, Salford, Eccles, Oldham and Bolton, in married women's participation rates and especially in occupational concentration. In 1931, women workers were highly concentrated in cotton manufacture in Bolton and Oldham where they comprised 56 per cent and 62 per cent respectively of all females aged 14 and above in employment (*Census of Population*, 1931, Industry Tables, Table 2: 62–71). (These figures exclude those out of work, and would be considerably higher if they were included.) By contrast, cotton manufacture accounted for only 11.5 per cent and 7.5 per cent of women workers in Salford and Manchester respectively. In Salford women were spread through a larger range of industries than in Bolton, being most highly concentrated at 21.4 per cent in clothing manufacture.

By 1951, the differences remained, in a slightly attenuated form. In Bolton women were still heavily concentrated as textile workers (37 per cent). A long way behind textiles came the broad category of personal service which accounted for 15.9 per cent of women workers. There was still less bunching of women workers in Salford. Here they were most heavily concentrated, at 21.3 per cent, as 'makers of textile goods and articles of dress', but textile manufacture itself accounted for only 7.4 per cent of occupied women. Women were more likely to be clerks and typists in Salford than in Bolton, and the percentage who worked as charwomen and office cleaners was almost double (*Census of Population*, 1951, Occupation Tables, Table A: 628–31). Table 5 compares the industrial concentration of women workers in 1931 in Bolton, Manchester, Oldham and Salford, while Table 6 shows the broad occupational groups accounting for the highest proportions of women workers in the same towns in 1951.

Table 5 Industrial concentration of women workers in selected industries in Bolton, Manchester, Oldham and Salford, 1931

	Bolton		Manchester		Oldham		Salford	
	Total	%	Total	%	Total	%	Total	%
Cotton manufacture	17632	55.9	9673	7.5	15506	62.1	4342	11.5
Clothing manufacture	873	2.8	31627	24.4	444	1.8	8071	21.4
Manufacture of metals etc.	442	1.4	4693	3.6	861	3.4	2002	5.3
Commerce and finance	3256	10.3	24695	19.1	2527	10.1	6465	17.2
Personal service	3340	10.6	21283	16.5	2362	9.5	5728	15.2
Total numbers employed	31518		129378		24991		37660	

All females 14 and above in employment, excluding those out of work.
Source: Census of Population, 1931, Industry Tables, Table 2: 62–71.

Table 6 Principal occupations of women in Bolton, Manchester, Oldham and
Salford, 1951. Percentage of all occupied women

	Bolton	Manchester	Oldham	Salford
Textile workers	36.9	5.2	42.1	7.4
Makers of textile goods	7.3	20.3	3.2	21.3
Personal service	15.9	19.6	12.4	18.9
Clerks, typists	9.9	19.3	9.9	14.3
Commerce, finance	10.4	10.4	8.7	8.5

Source: Calculated from Census of Population, 1951, Occupation Tables, Table A:
628–31.

In fact, the difference between Bolton and Salford was so pronounced that
instead of distinguishing between the two patterns as characteristic of weavers
and casual workers I could almost have referred to them as characterising
married women workers in Bolton and Salford respectively. A far greater
proportion of those interviewed in Salford conformed to the 'casual' workers'
pattern and a far greater proportion of those encountered in Bolton
approximated to the weavers' pattern. The Oldham women were more similar
to those of Bolton than Salford, and this too was strongly reflected in the
employment statistics.

The structure of local labour markets, both for men and women, especially
for married women, could be anticipated to have an important effect in shaping
the patterns of paid work/domestic labour/commoditisation under analysis.[20]
And significantly the greatest difference in the range and nature of work available
for married women in the places I conducted interviews was between Salford
and the cotton towns as a group.

Although there was some weaving and spinning in Salford it was not
primarily a cotton town. Only women were employed in textiles there and
opportunities for married women to engage in standard forms of employment,
outside of textiles, were highly restricted since many firms operated a marriage
bar before the Second World War. As for the cotton towns, experts on
Lancashire[21] provide evidence of the many and criss-crossing differences that
differentiate between Oldham, Rochdale, Preston, Burnley, Nelson and Bolton.
Despite all being textile towns with discrete and geographically circumscribed
labour markets, there were significant variations both in the proportion of
women engaged in waged work and in the degree and nature of gender
segregation in employment. Much of this literature suggests that the labour
market for men was crucial in differentiating between the different places. Men
and women were more often employed in similar jobs at similar levels of pay in
cotton towns where there were few alternative or better job opportunities for
men outside of weaving.[22] In such 'one trade' towns considerable overlap existed
between men's and women's jobs and rates of pay, although even here those in
supervisory positions in charge of male and female weavers would be men.
Burnley and Nelson were the best examples of this. But in Preston and other
towns where other higher paid work was available to men, men and women
were less likely to be engaged in similar work, the gender division of labour
was more pronounced and pay rates less equal.

Historians of the area have pursued the implications of such differences for variations in the politics between the towns and in the political involvement of women in suffrage, industrial and political organisation (e.g. Liddington and Norris, 1978; Liddington, 1984; Mark-Lawson *et al.*, 1985; Bruley, 1993). But it is evident that there was also a connection between the nature and degree of gender division in paid employment and in domestic labour such as I have suggested.

In Salford as a whole a high proportion of both women and men were engaged in poorly paid casual work. The labour market was rigidly and unequally divided along lines of gender, women being in a worse position than men, engaging in even lower paid and equally or more casual work. While dock and building work, important forms of male employment in Salford, had exclusively male workforces, the reverse held in cleaning where the workforce was overwhelmingly female. So the particular form of sexual division that characterised casual workers was also especially prevalent in Salford. In Bolton, by contrast, the labour market for men was not only more heterogeneous in range and skill level but also included some occupations and workplaces that were relatively unsegregated along lines of gender. (See Tables 7 and 8 for differences in male employment between Bolton, Salford, Manchester and Oldham, for 1931 and 1951.) In 1931, 25.7 per cent of all men were employed in cotton manufacture in Bolton but only 3.2 per cent in Salford (*Census of Population*, 1931, Industry Tables, Table 2: 62–71). The co-variation between men and women in both towns is noteworthy, both sexes in Bolton being heavily concentrated in textiles, while no occupation in Salford accounted for nearly such a high proportion of the total workforce. This provides confirmatory evidence of the link between domestic sharing, gendering of occupations and locality.

Table 7 Industrial concentration of male workers in selected industries in Bolton, Manchester, Oldham and Salford, 1931

	Bolton		Manchester		Oldham		Salford	
	Total	%	Total	%	Total	%	Total	%
Cotton manufacture	12975	25.7	5796	2.72	11903	31.6	2019	3.21
Transport and commun.	3285	6.5	23580	11.1	1741	4.6	9054	14.4
Building and contracting	3072	6.0	11587	5.4	1756	4.7	2938	4.7
Engineering	3890	7.7	11730	5.5	5592	14.8	2953	4.7
Commerce and finance*	7531	14.9	51276	24.0	5095	13.5	12859	20.4
Total numbers employed	50493		213352		37714		62884	

All males 14 and above in employment, excluding those out of work.
* To demonstrate the problems of assuming categories to be equivalent across historical periods, the occupations included here are not what we might today describe as the 'financial services economy', as the occupations include dealing in livestock and goods, as well as retail and wholesale markets in addition to banking and finance.
Source: Census of Population, 1931, Industry Tables, Table 2: 62–71.

Table 8 Principal occupations of men in Bolton, Manchester, Oldham and Salford, 1951. Percentage of all occupied men

	Bolton	Manchester	Oldham	Salford
Textile workers	12.9	1.7	13.0	2.7
Transport etc.	7.2	11.5	6.2	15.1
Building and contracting	4.9	5.3	4.5	4.4
Metal and engineering	18.8	18.2	21.2	18.4
Commerce, finance, excluding clerks	8.8	10.6	7.6	8.1

Source: Calculated from Census of Population, 1951, Occupation Tables, Table A: 628–31.

It would be possible to rewrite my earlier analysis of how different patterns of wage earning interlocked with different patterns of domestic labour for weavers and casual workers so as to take into account the extra dimension of locality. In so far as gender division in paid work coexisted with gender division in domestic labour, the nature of the domestic division rested not simply on low pay, nor on gender division in paid work as such, but rather on the particular nature and degree of segregation that characteristised the local labour market. In towns where men and women were more frequently employed in similar work for similar rates of pay a pattern of domestic sharing could be expected to be more common than where this was not the case. Although household arrangements were not caused by, and could not be 'read off' from, local labour markets, the character of the labour market was clearly important.

Associated with variations in employment structure were the different histories, traditions and customs which also marked off one town from another. Local cultures of work, gender relations and household arrangements affected both expectations and practices. Again the different traditions of Bolton and Salford overlapped with the weaver/casual women variation. Notably, it was women living in Salford who emphasised the ideal of men's role as breadwinner, understated the extent of married women's waged work, and described family life in gender-segregated terms. Although some Salford fathers and husbands did earn enough for their wives not to work, for many this was impossible. Yet this remained the ideal against which all were measured. And, despite their criticisms, the Salford women presented male dominance as central to 'what life's like round here'.

Men should have earned enough but they did not. Married women should not have to go out to work but they did. Such notions of what 'should be' throw light on the apparent contradiction when Salford women simultaneously downplayed their own paid work while at the same time emphasising the necessity of their financial contribution to family income. Similarly, for husbands to acknowledge wives' financial contribution would have involved admitting their own inability to live up to the breadwinner ideal. Local custom discouraged wives from telling their husband they could not manage on his money. To do so would bring into the open the discrepancy between actual circumstances and the ideal. All seemed to skirt around this in a spiral of double binds of failed expectations and unspoken resentments. Thus, women's reputation amongst other women locally (as well as their own self-pride) was judged by success in coping with whatever their husbands provided.

Such variations in local discourse elucidate the mismatch (to which attention was drawn in Chapter 2) between what women said and the Census statistics about married women's employment. If Salford women were prone to underplay the extent of married women's paid employment then actual rates would be higher than those acknowledged (as the Census suggests), even if many of the jobs were unlikely to be classed as 'proper work'.

Different patterns of home/work interconnect with differences both in employment structure and in culture and tradition. But, rather than being conceptualised as independently existing or exogenously causal variables, local labour markets and local discourses are part and parcel of the different configurations of home/work. Questions of locality and 'what its like round here' will be explored further in Chapter 6.

Agnes Brown

If particular notions of family life enjoyed widespread local currency then it is not surprising that Salford women should express them even when their own working life was closer to that of the weavers than the casual women. Agnes Brown is the bus conductress who straddles both patterns. She was the daughter of a Salford docker and a mill worker, and the eldest of 12 siblings who had one son herself. In working life and family pattern she resembled the weavers. Mrs Brown started work as a cotton spinner, moved on to engineering at Metrovicks, and then to Glovers cable factory before going on the buses. A shop steward, she worked actively for equal pay. Unlike the casual women workers, her employment was continuous and full-time. She talked at length about industrial processes, working conditions, wage discrimination and trade union politics. But in terms of husband and home she was more similar to them. Significantly, she was much more tolerant of inequality in domestic labour than in waged work, where her militancy had led to victimisation and being sacked. Her husband was a bricklayer with relatively insecure employment and income. He took no part in housework, belonging as Mrs Brown put it 'to the old brigade'. She did all her washing and prepared her husband's meal before she went out to work, presenting her responsibilities for domestic labour as entirely normal, in accord with local tradition and family practice.

> Q: When you were on the buses, what did you do for cooking, how did you arrange your housework?
>
> A: Well in the morning when I got up and just before I went out, I made a meal for my hubby or left it in casseroles in the oven. My mother came in. She watched it. When he came in at 5 o'clock he got his meal on then.
>
> Q: So you can't have had much leisure time at all?
>
> A: No I didn't have a lot of leisure time no, but I worked Saturdays and Sundays. I worked holidays times, as you know they do on the buses. And I used to get up in morning and go to wash-house for 7 o'clock and I'd take my mother's bedding. I used to do all the big things she had, and I've done all mine and I used to take it home and then that was done then for the week. Because it was more convenient, the

wash-house. It was quicker, that's why I liked the wash-house. They had what you called callenders, the ironers, you shoved them through and they'd be all dried and ironed when I come home.

Q: Did you ever get a washing machine?

A: Yes I got a washing machine when I come over here.

Q: When was that?

A: Sixteen years I've only had a washing machine. But before that I always went to communal wash-house. It was more convenient.

Q: Did your husband help at all in the house?

A: No, men didn't, no. My husband belongs to the old brigade.

Q: Did you think it was fair, because you must have been working much longer hours than him?

A: Well I resented it but tradition, you see. You'd been brought up in an atmosphere when the man was the boss, like me mam always had the meal on the table when he walked in. And it was accepted that it should be there when he came in, a northern tradition. And you sort of followed your mother, what your mother had done.

Mrs Brown also recognised explicitly the impact of local tradition on her household finances:

Q: And going back to your mother's generation, did your father hand over his wages?

A: Oh no, no.

Q: He didn't?

A: Oh no nobody did. He gave my mother so much to manage on and if she didn't manage it was just too bad. They had their spends.

Q: And what about your husband and you?

A: Well he was the same. I never asked my husband for anything, I just accepted his wages. But if I bought anything in the house, if I went out and bought something which I did, he would say how much had that cost and when I told him he would give me half ... My husband doesn't know the price of a loaf. He just says 'the gas bill's there', or 'your telephone bill has come'. I run all the lot. I do all the bills and run everything.

Q: So did the housekeeping depend on your money then? Did you put all your wages in?

A: Well it subsidised their [i.e. men's] money because I couldn't have gone on holiday on his money. He was a building worker so the winter, you don't know what the winter was going to be like. If it was a long winter he could be rained off, or frosted off, and that was it. So I stuck it you see, we couldn't have had the standard of living that we had without. It subsidised his money, it was necessary.

Notes

1   These are groups only in the analytical sense discussed below. They are not mutually exclusive, nor are these two the only 'groups'.

2   I am drawing here on the analytical frame used by Pringle (1989: Chapter 10) to highlight differences in the construction of 'work and home' by the secretaries she interviewed. In her study these varied according to occupational level, marital status and stage in the life-cycle.

3   Church of England.

4   Hire purchase.

5   Whether or not men held back wages was independent of the size of income. Davies (1992a) uses similar findings to reject the suggestion of any 'rough/respectable' division existing between husbands who withheld more or less of their wages. Indeed, one history contained in the *Growing Up in Bolton* collection tells of a mill worker on £9 a week (a high wage) who failed to hand over sufficient wages and whose family relied on his daughter's earnings.

6   Coppers were coins of small denomination such as halfpennies and pennies which were made of copper.

7   The interview material on which this section relies confirms much existing research on women cotton workers, including that of Roberts (1984, 1995b), Abendstern (1986), and the large oral history project *Growing Up in Bolton* (1981–83). However, unlike Roberts' findings, the weavers who spoke to me gave no indication that they would have wanted or expected to give up paid work on marriage or motherhood. Rather, the reverse was the case and in this they contrasted markedly with the casual women workers.

8   In spinning, however, there was considerable occupational segregation by gender. Both men and women worked in mills but on different processes, men doing more skilled worked as mule spinners, and mechanical repair, while women were concentrated as ring spinners on machinery that was more automated.

9   'In 1924, out of 84 industries, 77 had hourly earnings for all males above, and six earnings below, those in the cotton industry. For all females, out of 84 industries, 12 had earnings above, and 71 earnings below, those in cotton. The wages of women workers in the cotton industry, therefore, compare very favourably with the wages for women in other industries; but for men the comparison is unfavourable to the cotton industry' (Jewkes and Gray, 1935: 15–16).

10   The prosperity of weavers was relative to casual women workers. It should be borne in mind throughout the following discussion that weavers worked long hours, and were increasingly subject over the years to work intensification (the 'more looms' policy) and unemployment. They could not be considered well paid or prosperous in any absolute sense but only relatively so in comparison with other female manual workers.

11   Beauchamp (1937: 17) noted the practice of buying dinners and laundry services was common among married women weavers in the early years of the twentieth century.

12   See Pahl (1989) on money in marriage. Many of the women I interviewed described their patterns of money management in very similar terms to the housekeeping allocative systems she outlines (Chapter 5). Pahl's historical account suggests tipping up occurred where there was less income overall and was replaced by the housekeeping system as male wages grew. However, I found tipping up to be more prevalent amongst weavers where more income entered the household overall and the housekeeping system to be more characteristic of the relatively poorer casual workers' households.

13   It also echoes the testimony of some Preston women reported by Roberts (1984: especially 118).

14 Again, weavers appear to be 'ahead' of their time in the relatively companionate nature of their marriages. Finch and Summerfield (1991) suggest that this form of marriage emerged in the years of postwar reconstruction during the 1950s and view it as the most distinctive feature of domestic life of that period. My findings resonate with Gittins' account (1982: 185) of textile workers in Burnley. Where both partners did similar work in the same or similar workplaces they tended to an equal 'role relationship' where domestic tasks were shared. Gittins associates the absence of domestic ideology in such households with women spending so little time at home. The impression arising from my interviews was that it had more to do with weavers' identity as workers.

15 In her oral history of Rochdale, Abendstern (1986: 185) cautions against accepting at face value wives' accounts of the extent to which husbands helped. She suggests that they may have exaggerated, finding actual 'lack of help and support ... difficult to admit'. But why this should be so was not clear.

16 More contemporary evidence suggests that men take on domestic labour only when wives bring equivalent levels of income into the household and/or work similar hours as their husbands (Pahl, 1984: 275–6; Yeandle, 1984; Gershuny et al., 1986: 33; Morris, 1990: 90). Kiernan and Wicks (1991) report that the greater the extent of a woman's employment, the greater the extent of domestic tasks undertaken by a male partner.

17 Having few children was probably the greatest labour saving 'device' of all. Most weavers had two, or only one, in contrast to the casual women workers' four or five. While this imposed greater costs for the casual women it also brought more pay packets into the home when the children left school and started work. See Chapter 4 for detailed discussion of the contribution of children to household labour and income.

18 'The woman next door used to mind my son and I'd take her some washing ... she used to be pleased seeing the towels nice and the sheets.'

19 The embeddedness of work in non-work and non-economic relationships is explored further in the context of reconceptualising 'work' in Glucksmann (1995). On the embeddedness of economic action more generally see the classic writings of Polanyi et al., (1955) on instituted economic process and of Granovetter (1985).

20 Focusing on the intra-economic determinations, as I am here, does not imply that economic 'localism' is determined only by the economic (e.g., labour markets).

21 See Savage (1985, 1988), Murgatroyd et al. (1985), and Roberts (1984) on Preston, Barrow and Lancaster; Higgs (1986) on Rochdale; Gittins (1982) on Burnley, Anderson (1971) on the history of the family in Lancashire; Davies (1992a) on Salford.

22 For details of the many variations in the gender division of labour existing between the different cotton towns and different sectors of the weaving trade see Jewkes and Gray (1935), Daniels and Jewkes (1932), Home Office (1930). Savage (1988) explains how the difference between towns concentrating on weaving (Preston, Blackburn and Burnley) as opposed to spinning (Oldham, Bolton and the towns surrounding Manchester) was transected by a broad west–east divide of the fine trade dealing in high quality cotton (Bolton, Chorley and Preston) as against the coarse trade (Blackburn, Oldham and Burnley) which complicated matters considerably. The spatial/sexual pattern was further overlaid by distinct patterns of recruitment, modes of skill acquisition, and job loss specific to particular towns.

Chapter 4
'We were also daughters once'

This chapter slices the cake a different way, exploring the relationship between children and parents, particularly those of daughters and mothers, from the perspective of the younger generation. The focus is still on work but young workers now occupy centre stage. Again the main players are the women I interviewed but they appear as daughters in their parental home rather than as the adult workers and wives they were to become. As young women all had engaged in waged work and contributed income to their family of origin for a period of ten or fifteen years from the time they left school. All also undertook domestic labour at home in their 'out of work' hours.

Most married and left home during their twenties, but a sizeable minority did not, and attention will be devoted also to the particular circumstances of single women. Those who did not marry tended to remain living at home with their parents, and, as both generations grew older, the pattern of who did what for whom was gradually transposed.

Analysis will thus concentrate on exchanges, reciprocities, and obligations between successive generations rather than between husbands and wives. The counterpoints are young workers and 'single' women rather than weavers and casual women workers. As with casual women workers and weavers, the labour that children performed for wages was linked to the work they contributed to the household. The various aspects of this linkage and the differing modes of interconnection represent a central theme of this chapter, particularly the first part which focuses on young women and their families and households of widely varying forms.[1] The second part discusses research and discourses about young people in the 1930s, especially relating to their experiences of unemployment and leisure, the construction of a 'youth problem', and the emergence of 'teenagers'. The final part turns to the single women interviewed and suggests the distinctiveness of their circumstances and identities.

Families and work

Putting youth in their place

The labouring activity of young people in the first three decades of the twentieth century was of crucial importance to their families. But to appreciate its full significance depends on recognising the historically specific character of the household economy at that time. This was the period before the state provided a safety net through welfare provision. Few state benefits of any kind were available to assist those in need or in extreme poverty; insurance against unemployment was highly restricted; free health care was unknown. Families could rely therefore only on what their members brought in, and for many the wages of children were crucial to survival.

This was also an epoch prior to the mass production of household commodities and to the availability of consumer durables and labour-saving appliances. Most goods and services used in the household had also to be produced there, and on the basis of intensive labour. While middle class families employed domestic servants to process raw materials into finished clothes and meals as well as washing and cleaning by hand, working class women did it themselves.

In circumstances where such extensive demands were made on household finances and production the work of children assumed special significance. Domestic organisation imposed constraints and obligations which affected all generations. So it was not up to girls to choose whether or not to do housework or to go to work. Nor should they be interpreted as merely 'helping out'. Their inputs of both wages and labour were integral to the household economy as a whole and were anticipated as normal by parents and children alike. At a certain stage in their life course households relied on the income of children: for most families their earnings comprised a normal component of the 'family wage', and in some it was indispensable. Children expected to contribute from the time they left school as a matter of course, and may have felt they were letting their parents down if they failed to find work. Later I shall suggest that variability of family form during this period placed some young workers in a particularly responsible position for maintaining home and family, their input far exceeding even the 'normal' contribution.

Although there was an evident economic dimension to the relation between young workers and their parents this was not differentiated out in practice from the totality of the child/parent relationship. Rather, the economic dimension was embedded in all other aspects of that relationship in particular families. While it may be abstracted out for analytical purposes, to do so would not suggest the existence of a 'pure' economic relationship. Such an exercise might also draw attention away from how the relationship was actually experienced by participants at the time and also from what remains most distinctive about it in their memory. For many this was precisely the overlapping and cross-cutting of the economic with other dimensions, notably love, authority and power. Once children started to bring home a wage the parameters of parental authority came under scrutiny, although they were not usually up for renegotiation. Considerable tension also surrounded the newly gained rights of wage-earning children *vis-à-vis* pre-existing obligations, especially in relation to fathers and siblings. Simultaneously a child in one context and an adult in another, the status of the young worker was felt to be ambiguous.

Looking at young workers through the prism of the family demonstrates again the value of a total social organisation of labour (TSOL) framework which encourages analysis of the interconnectedness of different kinds of labour performed by different people in different contexts. The working-class family in early twentieth century Lancashire was constituted as a multi-generational household economy which intersected with wage-earning work in a distinctive manner. Whether one looks at the individual household or at the total social organisation of labour, youth labour straddled both spheres. When children reached the age of 14 it made a difference to particular families; it also made a difference at the societal level since each cohort represented an addition of hundreds of thousands to the labour force. As 'juveniles' school leavers were often deliberately recruited by employers in preference to their elders. They could be paid less and were thought to be more biddable and nimble-fingered. But they also represented extra competition for adult workers during high unemployment in the 1920s and 1930s, and themselves added to the dole queues.

However, it was within the power of the state to alter this situation through interventionist policy. Changing the school leaving age represented one of the policy instruments available to the state to regulate the entry of young people to the labour market. Raising it (as occurred in 1939) would remove in one fell swoop a whole annual cohort of juvenile workers, and slow down considerably over following years the expansion of the total labour force. At a societal level such intervention would enable governments to redraw the connection between the education system and employment, provide the possibility of raising the skill level of new entrants to the labour market, as well as the politically desirable effect of removing millions from the unemployment figures. The effects would also be felt, necessarily but possibly not as an intended consequence of the policy change, by all those families reliant on young workers' wages whose income would be dramatically affected. For hundreds of thousands of children to remain at school even for one extra year posed problems of a societal scale that required eventual resolution by government action. They could not have been overcome by all families with 14 year old children scrimping and saving and finding their own individual means of making up the shortfall for a year. And, as it happened, the extension of compulsory education in the postwar period and its attendant decline in the supply of youth labour comprised one dimension only of a much larger restructuring of the labour force. Soon after the youngest workers disappeared, married women began to enter the labour market on a mass scale for the first time, recruited especially to part-time work, and not long afterwards migrant workers from British colonies and former colonies were encouraged to enter as workers.[2]

Whichever part of the overall picture is in focus there was an 'organisation' to the labour which carried with it constraints and possibilities. Altering one element at one level could reverberate through all the rest.

'Mine, thine, and ours'

The families of origin of the women interviewed took a variety of forms, defying definition as either 'extended' or 'nuclear'. Many described compound families where parents had separated or died (maternal mortality was still quite high) and the remaining spouse had remarried so that groups of step-siblings were common. Some daughters left the parental home to live with an older sister because they could not get on with their step-parent. Others were effectively brought up by an older sibling or acted as mother themselves while still very young to even younger siblings. Part of this was due to demographic factors. Lower life expectancy, poor medical services, and continuing high rates of maternal mortality meant widows and widowers were relatively commonplace. So too were the 'unclaimed treasures' whose potential husbands were killed in the First World War. But demographic considerations aside, the notion of a standard family unit just did not seem to apply. A high proportion of the women came from what are known now as 'single parent families'; other households included an unmarried or widowed aunt and her children; many were 'mixed' families of step-children.

Nellie Lynch saw nothing out of the ordinary about the structure of her family of origin:

> As I say ours was a mixed family. Ours, thine and mine ... My dad had three lads, my mother had two boys and two girls when they married and then they had me and I was the eldest of five of us. Then my mother died [in childbirth] when I was ten and my youngest brother was only two. Of course I had to be the mother to them because the others were grown up and courting and getting ready for marriage.

Nellie Lynch goes on to describe conflicts between family members and the burden of her childhood responsibilities for housekeeping and wage earning. Her friend Alice Foster also came from a mixed family. After her mother 'deserted' them when Alice was 11, her father married a much younger woman who was the same age as Alice's older sister. Alice was more or less brought up by her sister from whom she learned cooking and housework.

Others had similar experiences. Annie Preston's mother died when she was 11 and her father was invalided by a work injury. Flo Nuttall had a stepfather she hated, and step-siblings. Kath Hinton's 'workshy' father effectively left her mother as a single parent, absenting himself from family life by going to his mother 'for his feeds'.

And Connie Mitchell brought the only regular wage into her home when she reached 14:

> Q: And what did your father do?
>
> A: Well I'm not interested in him really because he was in the Navy you see and he left my mother with five children. So we had a hard life really.
>
> Q: How did she manage?
>
> A: Well she had to do because there was no family allowance then. Until I left school, no them days was hard. And if you was married you couldn't work. [N.B. They lived in Trafford Park.] Because when I was at Brooke Bonds I was there from 14 till I was 25, that's like 10 years, I got married but I had to leave.

Before Connie started work her mother had to make ends meet by taking in washing at two shillings and sixpence a time. Financial circumstances improved as one child after another reached school leaving age.

Childhood and life in the family of origin were rarely idealised as carefree, happy or 'the best days of my life', even at a distance of 60 or 70 years. Quite apart from economic hardship, many still spoke with bitterness about unfair treatment and conflictual relationships. Clarice Holmes (born in 1895) remembered her mother hitting her with the frying pan to teach her how to cook for the whole family while she was laid up ill in bed. Several hinted at domestic violence on the part of drunken fathers.

Despite the absence of a standard family or household form, social and economic life was reproduced both on a daily basis and over generations. Men went out to work, children were raised, clothes were washed, in families with varied structures. But it is also clear that in some families the labour of children could assume a particular significance far in excess of adding their income at 14 to a collective 'family wage'. Children's role in household labour and their wage earning capacity were often vital to survival in a period before the existence of the welfare state. In the absence of other provisions (bar the work house) children frequently assumed responsibility for the care, or financial support, of other children and adults. The structure of some households, notably those formed around a single parent or a compound step-family where people did not get on, made the labour of children particularly crucial. In a later period the equivalent of their contribution might be resourced by the welfare state.[3]

The absence of a standard form renders problematic any easy definition of the household or family as an economic unit. Neither conventionally 'nuclear' nor 'extended', different families had economic ties with different ranges of relatives, inter- and intra-generational. Some sisters retained continuous relations of economic reciprocity after they formed their own families, but others did not. And what of the location of the household/family unit within the wider network of kin, neighbourhood and community, and the role of women's networks of support and reciprocity? Again the women's testimonies suggested considerable variation, some families linked more closely into a local network than others, and some women more rooted than others in informal mutual support groupings of women. The picture emerges of a unit with no fixed boundaries, blurring with kin relations extending both within and across generations and with neighbours in a local community.[4]

Girls' work

Q: *Can you tell me a bit about when you started work? In the cotton mill, what job you did and ...*

A: *Yes, when I went in the cotton mill in the first place I was what they called a 'setter on'. That is, there were frames that made bobbins and one woman would be called the 'tenter' and you that helped was called the 'setter on'. What you had to do was when they were, they called it 'slipping', that was when the bobbin was full, you had to take them off and put empty bobbins on to start again so I used to help to take all the bobbins off and put the others on and then they'd set it on, it went going.*

Q: *Were there certain days for different sorts of household duties?*

A: *Oh yes, washing at Monday. Washing and ironing Monday and Tuesday. At Wednesday in them days it weren't stainless steel, you had to clean your knives, forks and spoons. We used to have to whitning, metal polish, and there were one night when we had to sit down and do all the cutlery and all that. We had a fender, it were steel, a long fender and we used to have to emery paper it and then put whitning on it and shine it with a duster and then on another night we'd have to do the black leading. Black leading the grate and all that and then on another night we'd scrub all the floors. We'd something to do every day.*

Q: This was after you'd finished school or work was it?

A: Yes, yes, after we'd finished work.

Q: Did the boys do it as well or just ... ?

A: No, the lads didn't do owt. They got away with it. It were us as had to do it.
(*Growing Up in Bolton*, 1981–83, 34 JP/SS/1B/009 Transcript: 12)

So speaks 'JP', a Bolton weaver born in 1908, about her early days as a 'setter on'. She had gone into the mill on the 'half-time' system at the age of 12 knotting quilts. Her mother took in washing. As 'JP' started work at six o'clock in the morning the household duties she catalogues were probably performed after completing a 12 hour day in waged work.

Her testimony (it is echoed by many others in the *Growing Up in Bolton* collection) is quoted to signal two linked points. First, that 'work' for young women encompassed both paid employment and domestic labour as a matter of course. They worked at 'work' and at 'home', paid and unpaid, formal and informal, under the supervision of an employer and of their mother. The second point, implied in the first, is the highly gendered nature of both forms of youth labour. Boys were rarely asked to undertake domestic labour and never the kind or amount of basic work contributing to daily reproduction that was regularly and automatically expected of their sisters. They might chop wood, bring in coal or perform other such 'outdoor' duties that were relatively discrete and did not take up much time or they undertook larger but less frequent one-off jobs like decorating (Abendstern, 1986: 163–4).

While becoming workers, girls were thus also becoming women, and all that entailed. They were expected to learn all the domestic skills needed to be wives and mothers. Variations between young men and women in household duties were undoubtedly formative of adult gendered identity, girls learning what it was to be a woman, and boys identifying which activities were involved in being a man and which responsibilities were excluded.

But, while highlighting the importance of domestic labour for the formation of femininity and masculinity, it is important not to downplay the domestic labour input of young women for what it was. At a time when a far greater proportion of productive and broadly economic tasks were undertaken within the household the significance of young women's contribution to such household work, on top of their waged work, should not be underestimated, especially when contrasted with the relatively minor input of young men.

In paid employment young workers worked similar hours but usually for unequal rates of pay, boys earning more than girls. At home both tipped up their wages, receiving back a percentage for their personal spending. If there was a discrepancy in this respect boys received more spending money, increasing in amount as they grew older. Thus, in addition to their labour, girls appear to have contributed a relatively greater proportion of their wages to household use. Consequently they had less time for leisure activities than their brothers, and less money to spend on them.

Such differential expectations for boys and girls come over strongly in oral histories of the time and area (Roberts, 1984, 1995a; Abendstern, 1986; Fowler, 1988, 1992; Davies, 1992a, 1992b), suggesting interviewees' keen awareness of unequal treatment and their continuing sense of having had a raw deal. But, as suggested below, it would be hardly possible to guess either of these important dimensions of youth labour from social research devoted to the subject at the time.

'A little drudge'

Let's return to Nellie Lynch to illustrate the argument so far. Coming from a compound 'mixed' family, with no mother from the age of ten, Nellie Lynch had no choice but to assume major responsibility for the household as well as looking after her younger siblings. No one else was there to do it and there were no external sources of support to which her father could apply.

This was no happy family. Her older sisters quarrelled with her father and had left home. Clearly, though, they felt obliged to give Nellie some assistance. Her father helped in the house and she attempted to enlist her younger brothers in limited domestic duties. The older ones took no part.

When she started paid work she automatically handed her wages to her father for household use as well as continuing to perform many domestic and caring duties. I find her account of what she spent her own pennies on quite poignant, indicative of the time when even children needed to insure against the cost of future illness and also clear evidence that she was still a child. Her words are equally striking for what they tell of family conflict and break-up, the tensions and constraints for those who remained, and Nellie's feelings about blame, and of having been simultaneously a bully and 'a little drudge'.

Nellie Lynch: So I was brought up with a lot of blame, you know, my father used to say 'if anything is wrong they will blame you'. And I was brought up under like a threat. And my two sisters and me two brothers used to say that I was a bully, but only because I was frightened of them coming into any trouble and that.

Q: Did you have to do the cooking then, and the cleaning?

Nellie Lynch: Well me sisters, older than me did it at first, but you see it was their step-father and they couldn't get on so they left home. And then I was left with me three half brothers belonging to my father, the others left home because they couldn't get on with their step-father so they left home ... Then when I was 14 I left school and I went working in like a warehouse, they called it Shoddies, a kind of a warehouse. And then when I was 15 I started in the mill as a dorfer. To learn dorfing we got no wages, we got no wages for two weeks and then when you learned the dorfing my wage was fourteen and three ha'pence. And I had to give that fourteen, tip it up and the three ha'pence, we had to give a penny to the infirmary, that's the hospital, and with the halfpenny I used to buy Wrigley's spearmint and that was my spending money. Clothes, we used to have hand-me-downs and second-hand clothes.

Q: What happened with looking after the house and other children when you were at work? Did you do it when you came home?

Nellie Lynch:	Yes when I came home, because the big lads didn't do it. So it was left to me. You see me father used to say 'you can't go out tonight you've got this to do, you've got that to do'. And then again I had to see to the little 'un, but the little 'un, he was only two, me older sister looked after him. Of course me dad paid her for looking after him.
Q:	Did you do the cooking then?
Nellie Lynch:	Yes, I helped me father when he came in. He worked in a foundry, my father, and when he came home from work I used to help him.
Q:	So he did some of the housework as well and the cooking?
Nellie Lynch:	Oh yes. And I had a sister two years younger than me, well she kind of helped me wash up. But there was always squabbles because they wanted to go out and play and I used to bully them saying they had to do this and they had to do that, but it were only for their own benefit.
Q:	Did you get the younger boys to help as well?
Nellie Lynch:	Yes. And you know we used to have peg rugs, we used to sit and make our own peg rugs and I used to have the lads shaking them rugs, you know, you shook them. And we'd no hot water, we used to have hot water boiling kettles, but I'm talking about when my mother died but when my mother were alive she used to do all the baking, all the washing and everything.
Q:	And what did you do about the washing after she'd died. Who did the washing, washing the clothes?
Nellie Lynch:	We all used to do it.
Q:	You still did it at home?
Nellie Lynch:	Yes. And then me eldest sister used to come down and see to us, but she couldn't get on with me father you see, she did it for like our sake. Then I think I was 20 I left home, because I couldn't stand it no more because I was a little drudge so I went living with my eldest sister. And I were working in the mill, I worked in the mill all the time from being 15, all the time, dorfing until I got me own frames. And there was always squabbles. Me sisters we never got on, it were kind of jealousy, telling tales on one another.

'Super-exploited' youth?

Having noted the necessity for youth labour, and its gendering, it is worth reflecting on the multiple subordination experienced by girls, as both female and young. The historically distinctive character of family economy and formal economy entailed a particular form of 'double shift' for women, which was redoubled for the young.

The oldest women I interviewed, like Edith Ashworth and Clarice Holmes had worked under the half-time system (see Chapter 1, note 6) from the age of 12. By the 1930s Clarice was a main organiser in Bolton of unemployed workers' marches and acted as a 'two pence a week lawyer' in support of claims for unemployment benefit. Her daughter, Doreen Baker, attended dole school. Whether the younger women of her generation were in or out of work, and for how long, depended on their occupation and where they came from.

As young workers, all the women had handed their wage packets intact to their mother right up to the time they left home on marriage. They received back their small amount of spending money for stockings and the cinema while their mothers bought their clothes out of the girls' own earnings. All continued to have domestic duties after they started waged work, and these appear more onerous and time consuming than the customary 'bucket' or 'hellfire' night (Friday in Bolton, Thursday in Rochdale) which remains in popular memory as the night when all young women in the town stayed in to do domestic chores. Like 'JP' from Bolton many had daily duties, or baked at the weekend, saw to their younger siblings and cared for sick parents.

What of the young women's response to the double shift? Did starting work alter their status at home? Did their parents start treating them like grown ups? Answers to such questions are revealing of internalised obligations to the family. Becoming a wage contributor might disrupt the apparent naturalness of these felt constraints. It could also bring into question the previously accepted articulation of the various aspects of child/parent relationships, especially those connecting economic resources and parental authority. Yet, as we shall see, ties between a wage-earning daughter and her parents that from the outside look almost identical in structural terms were in fact experienced very differently depending on the nature of relationships in particular families. Thus, one daughter's memory of having financially supported her family during the depression was bitter and resentful, while another was fond and happy.

For many, the best remembered privilege gained at home on attaining wage-earning status concerned food. They were allowed to sit at table for their meals rather than stand, sometimes to eat with their father. They received more protein and larger portions. Now they would get a whole egg to themselves when as children they had to share it with siblings or hope that their father would give them the top off his.

In the 1930s entry to the world of paid work was the time from when many children expected to start 'paying back' their parents. Pearl Jephcott recounts the agony of one 14 year old whose difficulty in finding a first job caused extreme anxiety about her inability to 'pay back':

> By 7.30 a.m. I was out looking for work but all in vain, and for three whole weeks I haunted factories and the Unemployment Exchange, and every teatime I could hardly eat my tea for crying.
>
> 'But everybody can find a job, except me!' I used to cry till finally my father used to order me from the table, and get real impatient with me, while my mother used to console me with: 'There is plenty of time, so stop worrying!'

> *I did worry nevertheless, and what did worry me was, my father and mother had to keep me on nothing, and I thought that they had kept me for 14 years without me giving them any money, it was going to be dreadful if they had to keep me for the rest of my life.'*
> ('One Girl's Story' quoted in Jephcott, 1942: 19)

Finding work, tipping up and domestic duties were not questioned by the women I interviewed. Arguments with parents were more likely to centre on how many evenings they were allowed to go out and how late they could stay. In retrospect a number expressed resentment against their brothers who endured fewer restrictions, and against over-bearing fathers who were felt to assert unjustified authority as if they were still children.[5]

Some daughters resented, some resisted, and others accepted as normal demands made by parents that would now be regarded as excessive. In families where money was already a contentious issue young earners were more inclined to view their own financial contribution as conferring the right to take part in family disputes. Daughters also felt legitimate in overtly challenging parental authority when they earned more than a father whom they thought to be unfair to the family.

'AB' was one such daughter who saw her own economic weight as justifying her to rebuke the father she thought irresponsible and male supremacist. A weaver from Bolton, she was born in 1916 to a family of eight girls. Both parents had worked in the mill but her mother found it hard to make ends meet. Her father drank away most of his wages and contributed little to housekeeping despite making good money as a spinner:

> *... it was a case of robbing Peter to pay Paul all the time, because with him drinking and spending all his money like he did, I mean my mother couldn't really save anything. She said the bit she did save to buy that house eventually was out of what we earned by tipping our wages up. She never got a proper wage off him, but he always wanted the best of anything and he wouldn't sit at the table with us. She always had to set one corner of the table specially for him and we all had to keep away while he was eating. It was a case of he ate first and if there was chance of any meat, he had it and we had to do without.*
> (*Growing Up in Bolton*, 1981–83, 28 AB/JW/1a/009 Transcript: 15)

AB's mother took in washing and went cleaning. She wanted AB to learn a trade and was not pleased when she went into weaving. Soon however AB and her younger sisters were earning more in weaving than their older sisters and father in the mill. 'AB' tipped up her whole wage 'right from leaving school up to the Friday as I was getting married on the Saturday'. And high earnings gave her courage to confront her father:

> *At that time he was on about £12 or £14 a week which was a good wage at that time, and she was lucky if she got £3 you see, so when I was tipping £5 up which was by the time I was getting married it had gone up to about £8 or £9 [in 1938] I just turned round and said 'Look. I'm bringing in more money than you and when I go you will have to pull your socks up because the younger ones are all coming up and they will want more.' And of course he turned round and said I was being cheeky and all that and he was a bit nasty with me for some time and apart from that he still*

carried on right up to just before I got married. He didn't only used to go on at me – used to get nasty with with my mother as well, oh yes, he used to knock my mother about ... So really when he changed in the last three years, it was something I was proud of. At least he died before her and its given her three happy years to look back on.
(*Growing Up in Bolton*, 1981–83, 28 AB/JW/1a/009 Transcript: 15)

The ironic tone suffusing Edith Ashworth's entire account of her early life is quite evident from the excerpt in Chapter 2. She felt that she had been exploited by a mother who did not have her best interests at heart. Edith's wages were so high that:

no wonder me mother didn't want me to get married, was it?

In addition to going out to work and tipping up wages from the age of 12, the housework and baking, Edith also had to make clothes for the family. Her sister (who sat in on my interview with her) remarked dryly that:

Mother got a sewing machine when Edith was 15 with a definite object in mind. She was the sewer in the family. Not so much a luxury as ... she showed an inclination that way. And she's sewn ever since, poor thing.

Nowadays girl workers like Edith Ashworth would certainly be viewed as extremely hard done by. They represented cheap labour to employers. Parents pocketed their earnings, and on top of that appropriated additional work and time in the form of the unpaid domestic labour that was not required of their brothers or fathers. But whether or not daughters experienced this as exploitation, or felt that parents appreciated their wage-earning status seemed to depend very much on particular family relationships. In this respect Marjorie Fisher is a counter example to Edith Ashworth. Their circumstances were not dissimilar, the normal pattern of the time. Yet Marjorie willingly supported her large family out of her wages from mill work when her father was unemployed. Indeed she was even sympathetic to the reasons underlying his drinking habit and has not a bad word to say about him. She did not seem to feel she had a raw deal either at the time or 60 years later.

Q: Was your father's wage too small to support the whole family really?

A: Well yes, you know and in them days he liked to drink so there wasn't much money for my mother.

Q: Do you know if he handed it all over or did he give her housekeeping?

A: Well I think when they first got married he did but as time went on I think she got what was left sometimes when he'd been to the pub. He was teetotal for a right long time when he didn't drink and he was a different person then. But I think it was the same with a lot of working men, they drank. Whether they'd lost companionship with their wives and when you think of the house, the washing was there, the baking you know. And my mother was pretty good really.

Q: So did your mother manage all the finances?

A: My mother managed the finances, a very good manager. I mean we'd have roast beef on a Sunday when I know other people didn't have it and they'd got more money coming in than my mother had. She was very good, she was a very good manager. To say that we were poor we had reasonably good food. We'd make potato pies, potato hash. She'd buy chops, you know, pork chops, pork steak and steak and onions. We had all that so you know, our mam looked after us. We never had a posh house but it was always clean and comfortable.

Marjorie's family included eight surviving children. At 14 she went into the cardroom as a back tenter, worked in many different mills, and had graduated to being an intermediate tenter by the time her father lost his job in the depression.

Q: And when your father was unemployed were you the only one bringing in a wage?

A: I was for a while, yes. We went through a period in the '30s when my sister was married and her husband came out of work and she'd two children, she came to live with us – we hadn't enough. And I had two brothers at home at the time. They was a little bit older than us. We were the three youngest ... And when they was out of work and my father couldn't get a job and my brother-in-law couldn't get a job there was only my wage going in. And dad got a bit [of dole] for him and me mother. I just forget how much dole it was for my sister. I know he only used to get a shilling or two shilling for each child. Fancy that to keep a child. And my sister, she had one baby while she was with us and that baby died. And I remember you had to pay to go in hospital, I think it were two guineas or something like that – I don't know how much it was. You had to pay for maternity before the health came. And me mother hadn't the money, nobody had the money.

Supporting the rest of the family virtually single-handedly, Marjorie had no spending money of her own until she was 20. But unlike Edith Ashworth she has only warm memories of her mother and of harmonious family life.

During the period when the women I interviewed were young, reciprocal exchange between children and parents within the family of origin was still the norm. A decade or two later the more dominant pattern was for each generation to 'give back' only to the succeeding one rather than also to the preceding one. Thus, by the time Edith Ashworth, Marjorie Fisher and the others were themselves mothers of wage-earning teenagers the situation for youth labour had changed considerably. They had smaller families than their mothers and the age of leaving school and entering paid work had been raised. Their children did not appear to represent an economic resource in the same way as they had. If they did talk about children's contribution it seemed more like a gift than essential to family income, as when Annie Preston and Flo Nuttall detailed the consumer durables their sons had bought them. At the very most children 'helping out' was optional rather than expected. Overall, there was little mention of teenage income, especially not from weavers. However, despite the altered economic circumstances separating the two generations, it is impossible to know whether reliance on children's wages might have been more difficult to admit to an interviewer than having been a child contributor themselves.

Unemployed youth and teenage leisure

Out of work youth ...

Not only did contemporary literature substantially ignore the double shift of young women workers, it also thematised youth in general as 'a problem' to such an extent that it could be accused of reinforcing their subordination. Nowhere was this more evident than in writings about youth unemployment and culture.

Research on young workers at the time revolved around two apparently contradictory worries, one relating to unemployment and the disaffection that might result from it, the other to the emergence of new forms of leisure activity and what these suggested about the spending power and outlook of youth. Obviously such worries were closely connected to economic and social developments of the time which affected young people in different ways. All, however, were constructed as causes for public concern, providing fuel for a series of moral panics in which young people figured as the possible source of political and social unrest. Whether in work or unemployed, young people just could not win.

The literature about youth labour focused exclusively on paid employment and especially on the twin problems of 'blind alley jobs' and juvenile unemployment. Liberal minded social researchers, like John and Sylvia Jewkes, Allen Winterbottom, and Pearl Jephcott, as well as communist politicians like John Gollan, all drew attention to the consequences for young workers of the erosion of industries which in the past had offered opportunities for skilled work, and the expansion of unskilled work in others that required little training and led 'nowhere'. Their discussions highlighted the contradictory tendencies that led to increased unemployment in certain regions and industries while the retail sector and 'new' mechanised industries simultaneously stimulated the 'scramble for little fingers'. Although Gollan did acknowledge that the 'little fingers' in special demand were those of girls, and that 'boy labour' was worse affected by transformation of the skill structure (which so drastically reduced the number of apprenticeships), no concerted attention was devoted to gender differences in youth employment and unemployment, nor to the double burden of labour shouldered exclusively by girls.[6]

> *Responses to juvenile unemployment were both moral and economic. Enforced idleness would waste the nation's resources and failure to provide vocational training would weaken the labour force of the future. But some commentators (e.g. Meara, 1936) singled out as cause for greater concern 'demoralisation' of the young unemployed, a development to be feared as a potential source of social disorder or political extremism, as it had been in Victorian times. Prolonged periods out of work were thought to undermine the employability of young people through a 'literal deterioration in their physical capacities, but more fundamentally by preventing the inculcation of the stability and disciplines of the work ethic and by stifling the growth of appropriate aspirations ...'.*
> (Rees and Rees, 1982: 17)

Government policies were designed to overcome the problem thus defined.

The education offered by Junior Instruction Centres clearly reflected worries about the effects of 'demoralisation'.[7] The curriculum was practical rather than vocational (Morgan, 1939), a central objective to:

> give the boys and girls a real interest in life, to keep their minds and fingers active and alert and their bodies fit ...
> (Ministry of Labour, 1934: 4)

Boys were instructed in woodwork, boot repairing and leatherwork, girls only in the domestic skills of cookery, dress-making and home nursing, much to the resentment of many who attended 'dole school'.

As one affected by short-time working in 1934, Doreen Baker was not impressed by the conditions imposed on her right to unemployment benefit; nor was her experience of 'dole school' particularly positive:

> Doreen Baker: ... it was short time. Sometimes we'd be working a week, playing a week, working a week, off two weeks and then you'd have to go to the Labour Exchange. And then if you wasn't 18 you had to go to what they called Dole School, half a day, and if you didn't go you didn't get any money.
>
> Q: What did they teach you there?
>
> Doreen Baker: Well at first I went to Chelfont Street and I wasn't a bit impressed. Because they wanted PT and housewifery, things like cleaning sculleries out and cookery and I didn't want to do that. And then there was another class and I arrived, making gloves, leather gloves home made. I could have spent all day making gloves, I made gloves for everybody. Anyway as I say, me dad died when I were 18 and we was on very short time so I literally walked Bolton to try and get another job.

The school leaving age represented a second prong of policy. The labour movement supported the recommendations of the Hadow Report of 1927 to raise the age to 15 as did many employers. But while they viewed it primarily as a means of combating unemployment, the former also stressed educational and skill objectives. In a supreme example of hedge-betting, the eventual Education Act (1936) raised the school leaving age to 15 as from September 1939 but:

> subject to the provision that a child may leave school at any time after attaining the age of 14 years provided 'beneficial' employment has been obtained.
> (Jewkes and Jewkes, 1938: 147)

Such a blatant attempt to satisfy all interested constituencies aroused only opposition from the educational authorities.

Sizeable regional variations in youth unemployment were also to be addressed by means of the Industrial Transference Scheme which arranged for migration out of depressed areas to those where work was available. Thousands of young women were pressured by this scheme into working as maids since the main channel of employment for girl transferees was domestic service. Girls in Manchester and the North West were less badly affected by such measures, however, than those from the areas of highest unemployment in Wales, Scotland and the North East.

Looking back at inter-war youth unemployment in the 1970s at a time when it was again high on the political agenda, economic historians (e.g., Garside, 1977, 1979; Benjamin and Kochin, 1979) renewed controversy as to its actual extent and the efficacy of public policy. Whether or not juvenile unemployment was as serious as many had believed at the time, all later experts agreed on its patchy incidence such that young workers were in high demand and short supply in some places while in others they could find no work however hard they looked. These variations were closely associated with economic restructuring and the spatial location of declining and expanding industries so that towns close to each other experienced widely differing rates of unemployment, depending on their industrial structure.

Manchester, like London, with its expanding retail, administrative and financial sectors experienced relatively low rates overall (despite considerable losses in textile occupations). Yet in neighbouring cotton towns or those with higher proportions of unskilled labouring jobs young people were severely affected. Although inadequacies in the collection and collation of official statistics make any definitive assessment problematic, it is nevertheless possible to discern quite significant variations between Manchester and the other towns from which my interviewees came.[8] Young women aged from 14 to 20 suffered higher rates of unemployment in Oldham (11.3 per cent) and Salford (8 per cent) than in Bolton (5.3 per cent) and Manchester (6.4 per cent) (calculated from *Census of Population*, 1931, Occupation Tables, Table 18: 606–9). Within this certain occupations were worse affected, notably textile workers and undefined unskilled workers. Moreover, the same occupational group experienced variable rates in different towns. For instance 13.4 per cent of young female textile workers in Oldham, but 6.6 per cent in Bolton were out of work (*Census of Population*, 1931, Occupation Tables, Table 18: 606–9).

Comparing the young women who were worst affected with all women is also revealing: in Bolton 12.4 per cent of all women workers but 15.4 per cent of cotton workers were unemployed, and in Oldham 21 per cent of all women workers and 26.5 per cent of cotton workers (calculated from *Census of Population*, 1931, Occupation Tables, Table 16: 234–5), suggesting that older women suffered higher unemployment than young women.

In Salford the situation for young workers remained serious throughout the course of the depression, and affected a wide range of occupations. According to an index devised by the Ministry of Labour, unemployment rates in Salford exceeded 10 per cent in seven of the ten years between 1927 and 1936, only dipping in 1936. Yet in adjacent Manchester they never reached this level. The contrast with London is even more striking. Here the highest level reached was 3.7 per cent in 1932 (Ministry of Labour figures tabulated in Fowler, 1988: 371).

Like Doreen Baker in Bolton, many of the other women interviewed had been out of work. However their experiences differed, and reflected certain variations captured by the official statistics. Those from Oldham reported having tramped the streets looking for work, Kath Hinton claiming to have worn out several pairs of shoes in the process. Lily Hunt eventually gave up the search and moved to pub work in Blackpool. The Salford women experienced less difficulty, finding it possible to move from job to job. And cotton workers Edith Ashworth and Marjorie Fisher remained in employment throughout, in Little Hulton and Rochdale respectively, becoming the mainstay of their families' finances.

... and youth out of work

Appreciation of the spatial variations in employment and unemployment helps throw light on the second, and ostensibly quite opposite, area of concern, namely the consumption patterns and leisure activities of young people. This issue too aroused vigorous debate both at the time and more recently. When did teenagers and teenage culture make their first appearance? Was it after the Second World War in the relatively more affluent 1950s, as popular wisdom suggests, following Abrams (1961)? Or do recent social and oral historians have a point in dating the the emergence of 'postwar' adolescent culture in the 1930s?

While some researchers (e.g. Roberts, 1984: 42–3, 1995a: 45–6; to some extent also Davies, 1992a: 83) emphasise the continuing childlike dependence and submission of young workers within the family, others (e.g. Fowler, 1988: 206–16, 1992; echoing Harley, 1937; James and Moore, 1940; Jephcott, 1942) emphasise their relative affluence and autonomy, and argue that leisure activities and spending patterns evident in the 1930s were precursors of the 1950s.

Young Mancunians certainly enjoyed high rates of economic activity and correspondingly high levels of disposable income.[9] Their leisure pursuits were the object of considerable scrutiny at the time and appear to have been a popular topic for MA students' dissertations at Manchester University (Fielder, 1932; Middleton, 1931; Harley, 1937; Thompson, 1937). Their comments frequently assume the 'do-gooding' tone common to contemporary social surveys (noted in Chapter 2), implying that young people's time and money could be better spent on more edifying activity. Harley was particularly critical of the cinema, having discovered that 90 per cent of her sample of girl workers attended at least once a week and that some went as many as six times, and this was in addition to dance halls. Her criticism extended further, to the girls' supposedly undiscriminating consumption of magazines and the 'glorification of materialism' to which they exposed themselves.

Jephcott was less censorious, her criticisms reserved for cinema and film. Nevertheless, she was equally concerned with how to improve girls and their lot.

> *Veronica Lake and Lana Turner do more for the girl of fourteen than merely set her hairstyle ... young people ... are forming their tastes ... and basing their conception both of worthwhile entertainment and of a life that is worth living on the standards set by the film corporations. On the whole these are standards which exhalt violence, vulgarity, sentimentality and false psychology.'*
> (Jephcott, 1942: 119)[10]

The passion for dancing came in for less condemnation because Jephcott judged its socially and physically active character to be beneficial to young women:

> *Dancing provides one solution to this urgent need for movement and it is a solution that requires much less mental alertness than, for example, a keep-fit class ... psychologists tell us that rhythmical movement is a recognized means by which relief is afforded to anxiety.*
> (Jephcott, 1942: 122)

Moreover:

> *Girls also appreciate the sociability of a dance hall and the company of their contemporaries ... she can wear a smart frock and good stockings and try to look really glamorous before her equals. She is in honourable competition with her contemporaries. Dancing is one of the recognized ways, particularly now that churchgoing has declined, in which boys and girls expect to find their future partner. Magazines advise their readers that this is so.*
> (Jephcott, 1942: 123)

In Manchester, though not necessarily in nearby Oldham or Bolton, older teenagers came to expect more than the very basic spending money 14 year olds received from their mothers. And it was such older urban young people who formed the chief market for the rapidly expanding commercialised leisure pursuits of cinema and the dance hall. In Manchester, Salford and similar towns thousands of cinemas and dance halls sprang up during the 1930s. Evidently a burgeoning youth market for consumer products and leisure activities and energetic entrepreneurial activity in this field were mutually reinforcing developments. The proliferation of magazines for young people and their popularity even in areas of high unemployement ensured extensive advertising access for the new and expanding manufacturers of fashion clothing, cosmetics, motorcycles and soft drinks which were all specifically targeted at the youth market.

Oral histories of Lancashire (especially those of Abendstern, Davies, Fowler, Power, E. Roberts and D. Thompson), confirm contemporary impressions since they also offer contradictory accounts of adolescents. However, a close reading of the unemployment statistics reveals the arguments of these authors to be partly at cross purposes. The towns they researched experienced rates of youth unemployment sufficiently different to explain their varied conclusions about the existence of 'teenagers'. It would be quite reasonable, therefore, to see teenagers as an emergent group in Manchester, less obviously so in Salford, and more definitely not in Barrow-in-Furness, Lancaster or Preston.

Thus Fowler is probably justified in asserting that:

> *a distinctive teenage culture based on access to commercialized leisure and conspicuous consumption of leisure products and services aimed at the young were clearly evident in Manchester in the 1920s and 1930s.*
> (Fowler, 1988: 244)

In Salford young people who enjoyed the new commercial pursuits of cinema and dance hall continued to participate in the more traditional and informal 'monkey parade' (taking over the main streets on Sunday evenings) and to belong to corner gangs (Roberts, 1971: 146–85; Davies, 1992a: 103–16). No doubt Salford was not unique: older and newer forms of adolescent culture co-existed in all towns but assumed a differential significance in each.

If the relatively affluent are in prime focus then young people may plausibly be viewed as 'teenagers' in all but name. But the well-off were only one grouping of many. Even so, moral panic over the supposed unruly consequences of 'independent' youth undoubtedly contributed to the construction both of a distinct category of 'youth' and of 'a problem'. Yet warnings about the deleterious effects of cinema-going and of 'independent' youth promoting a crime wave were voiced almost in the same breath as fears of the unrest and crime that might be fomented by the 'demoralised' young unemployed who hung around street corners. This scale of inconsistency suggests that youth as such was the object of opposition and fear, and 'idleness' the condition for criticism. It did not seem to matter much for the purposes of such blame or scapegoating whether the young people were in or out of work, in the cinema or on the street corner. It is in this sense that contemporary studies both participated in and culturally complemented the economically entrenched subordination of youth, especially female youth.

'Single' women

Daughters who did not marry

The pattern of a daughter who did not marry but remained living with ageing parents has been quite common historically, certainly much more so until the mid twentieth century in Britain than today. In terms of the exchanges examined in this and the previous chapter, daughters co-residing long-term with parents represent a grouping that was distinctive in a number of ways, and a very special case of 'youth' labour. Outside the home the single women I interviewed shared a characteristic pattern of paid employment. Their household economies were also structured around a characteristic set of exchanges, obligations, and reciprocities linking family members. In short, the single women interviewed shared, in the terms used earlier, a particular pattern of home/work interface, which was historically specific and differed from those of both groups of married women worker. In the postwar period demographic change (the decline in family size and increase in life expectancy), together with transformation of family forms and of women's patterns of employment, have brought changes to both sides in such partnerships. Combined with extension of state welfare provision for the elderly, they make co-residence and inter-dependency between elderly parents and an ageing child less frequent.

Historians and sociologists (e.g. Finch and Groves, 1983; Graham, 1983; Gittins, 1982, 1993; Lewis and Meredith, 1988; Finch, 1989) have drawn attention to the crucial role of daughters (married and unmarried) as unpaid carers of the elderly in studies of ageing, dependency and welfare, and family and kinship obligations. The tendency for unmarried female relatives to 'stand in' and perform domestic labour where no wife is present is also noted (e.g. Delphy and Leonard, 1992). But far less attention has focused on single women as such, and there is little to draw on which deals specifically with working-class single women in twentieth century Britain.[11]

In the absence of such a literature, and of a concerted challenge to dominant discourses of marriage and the heterosexual couple, it is difficult to avoid writing about single women except in contrast to married women, and so effectively categorising women in terms of a dominant cultural dualism of marital status. In a much quoted essay, Scott (1988: 175) wrote that the category 'worker' is an already gendered one, 'established through a contrast between the presumably natural qualities of men and women.' Attempts to redress the balance by writing the history of 'women workers' 'start the story ... too late' since they leave in place the naturalised contrast and reify 'a fixed categorical difference'. An analogous argument could well be made for the category 'single', also a solidified repository of already constituted meaning and valuation where unmarried contrasts negatively with married, and marital status is elevated to be constitutive of woman's identity. If 'meanings are constructed through exclusions' (Scott, 1988: 7), then (at the level of meaning) being married is certainly constructed by contrast with being unmarried, 'on the shelf', 'an old maid', or 'spinster'. In order to refuse such a fixed dualism and its implied hierarchy of valuation, the task for feminist analysis (begun by Holden, 1996; Davidoff *et al.*, 1999) is to show that neither 'married' nor 'single' is an internally homogeneous grouping and that both are part of a wider pattern of relationships.

Daughters co-residing with elderly parents represent one of the multiplicity of family forms outlined earlier, now to be explored in more detail, keeping firmly in mind these cautions about singleness. For working class children the norm was to live with and contribute financially to the family of origin until marriage. For women who did not marry, the options to leave home and live differently were highly restricted. Cultural and economic constraints would have predisposed a significant proportion of women from poor families in Salford or Oldham who did not marry to remain in the parental home. (There were probably more options open to men who did not marry, although many also co-resided with parents, married siblings or other kin.)

As a social pattern, single women remaining 'at home' is straightforward to comprehend. It 'works' as an economic household unit, and there is a rationale to the co-residence, caring and mutual support that had advantages for both parties concerned. For such a household form to 'work' need not presuppose a good relationship or emotional dependency between parents and daughters.[12]

Yet when particular women are in mind the question always seems to be asked as to *why* they remained at home, suggesting both that a reason is needed and that a personal choice was made. Usually the answers are couched in terms of marriage: X stayed at home *because* she had not married or X did not marry *because* she stayed at home to look after parents. So it was significant that all the single women I interviewed gave different reasons for having remained at home. For all it just happened rather than being the result of an explicit decision. Moreover, it was treated as nothing out of the ordinary, requiring no more explanation than any other way of living. None implied they had 'not met the right person' nor that they had 'failed' to marry.[13] This is a salutory reminder that present-day questions about choice, emotionality and sexuality may make anachronistic assumptions that hold little meaning for the women themselves, especially in view of the prevalence of households like theirs and of 'mixed' families in general.

'Godforsaken spinsters'

Although only a very small number were interviewed (no claims are being made here for representativeness) their lives reveal much about the circumstances of single women of their class, time and place. Since my efforts had been strenuously geared towards finding married women it is noteworthy that as many as three should have passed through all the filtering devices for potential respondents. A possible explanation relates to my initial concern to find women who had worked throughout their lives in industry, preferably on the Trafford Park estate. As I later discovered, and as the women in Salford repeatedly stressed, there was little work for married women in Trafford Park or in local industry. The three women I did manage to find who had been employed long term in this way were all unmarried, and all their friends who had also worked in Trafford Park were single as well!

We have already met Mary Gouden in Chapter 2. She worked for Metropolitan Vickers for 40 years, first on the shop floor and later as a clerical worker and personal assistant. One of two siblings from what sounded like a highly respectable family, her father and brother both died within two years of Mary starting work, leaving her with responsibility for her mother.

Ivy Turner was born in 1914, the youngest of eight children whose parents had migrated from Derbyshire to Salford in search of work.

> My name is Ivy Turner. I'm not married so I've no family to talk about but I was the youngest of eight, four girls and four boys. I left school in 1928, when I was 14 and I went to work at the Co-op, at the Co-op Tea Factory which was then at Castlefield. I was there two years and they built a new warehouse at the bottom near Trafford Bridge and I was there for the rest of my working days. Yes, I worked there until I was 62. Forty-eight years I was there. And then the place closed.

Ivy's father was a lorry driver and dock worker and her mother had been cook in a stately home before she married. Jobs at the Co-operative tea factory in Trafford Park where teas were blended and packed were hard to come by.

Ivy Turner: ... if you got in the Co-op you were made. Well my mother had a friend and she was a chargehand. When I was 14 this lady asked for me and I had to have two references, you know one from school and one from church. Oh I hated it the first two years. 'Ooh' I said 'I'm not going any more', I said 'I don't like it.' 'You're going, that lady asked for you, and you're going!' [her mother]

Q: Do you think there were better conditions or was it better paid at the Co-op?

Ivy Turner: Well the pay was quite good. It was 10 shillings to start with a week. You worked from 8 o'clock til 5. Then as time went on, you got to 22 and you got two guineas. And you got a week's holiday and then you got a fortnight later on. It was a very good firm to work for, sick pay as well yes.

Over the 48 years the factory expanded, many work processes were mechanised, and Ivy progressed from packing and blending to the position of forelady, earning a moderately higher rate than the women she was in charge of. Women were still excluded from supervisory positions.

Her father died in 1934 and although many of her siblings remained working locally, it seems that she became responsible for her mother until the latter's death in 1951.

Ivy Turner:	*I had four brothers. Of course intermittently they were out of work and as they all grew up they got married and I was left at home.*
Q:	*And you stayed at home?*
Ivy Turner:	*Me mother tied me to her apron strings you see. I don't grumble, you know, quite alright. [Laughs] ... So really I was left at home for quite a while.*

Ivy's family seemed thus to conform to the tradition, if such existed, of the youngest daughter remaining at home to look after the mother. It was just Ivy's bad luck to have been the youngest. Rather than 'failing to marry' she was subject to a form of intergenerational constraint (cf. Duquenin, 1984) which was integral to family form and marriage rather than an alternative to them. Ivy talked with great enthusiasm about her paid employment, stressing repeatedly what 'interesting' work she had done. But her account of having stayed at home was told with muted regret, suggesting that she had not been in a position to refuse what she saw as an obligation. And fulfilling this obligation foreclosed other opportunities and wider experience. As she explained it was not just her mother who tied her to her apron strings: when the war came her supervisor thought he was doing her a good turn by taking her home circumstances into consideration. She would have preferred to join the forces if the choice had been up to her.

Ivy Turner:	*But at the Co-op when they got married, they stopped the married ladies.*
Q:	*A marriage bar?*
Ivy Turner:	*Until the war, and then they brought them back you see. Because they did move quite a lot to war work from there, but I was put on a man's job. It did me a favour really because he knew I was the only one at home. But I would rather have gone in the forces, but I couldn't, you see.*

Amy Fowler is the third 'single' woman. Unlike the others she married in her mid fifties. Both she and her husband had cared for elderly mothers and married only after both had died. Amy was the eldest of five surviving children (putting paid to any assumption that supporting parents always befell the youngest). At 14 she started at a box works but moved after two years to Glovers cable factory where she remained for the next 35 years. She worked on the shop floor, becoming a planning controller and transferring to staff status in 1958. From 1970 Amy entered a succession of other factory jobs until retirement age.

What was distinctive about these three women was their common pattern of exchange with parents at a certain stage in the life course. The daughters all engaged in continuous full-time employment. They provided financial support for their widowed mothers, and took responsibility for major financial decisions. Their mothers 'looked after' them, performing domestic labour, doing the shopping, cooking their meals and washing their clothes. This contrasts with the 'caring' role of unmarried daughters that might have been assumed from a reading of the available literature. None of the three spoke of caring for their mothers in a domestic or physical sense except right at the very end of their lives. Rather, what they did was to bring in the money, and to arrange (and pay) for electricity to be laid on, a bath to be installed, or a fireplace to be modernised. Far from 'standing in' for wives, these women thus assumed the position of breadwinner more usually associated with husbands. And their mothers supplied the domestic servicing that accrued to their status as provider.

As young workers Mary and Amy had conformed to the norm for girls, tipping up to their mothers and doing housework in addition to paid labour. Ivy Turner got off lightly in this respect but from her account this sounds almost like recompense in advance. Her siblings spared her from housework but seemed almost to have predestined her to 'look after' their mother in the future:

> Well I didn't do any work really until they'd all got married. I mean I had three sisters and they used to do it so all my evenings were free. Yes I was in the GFS at the time. The Girls Friendly Society. They used to call it 'the Godforsaken Spinsters'. That's why I'm not married. [14] And I used to go Tuesday, Wednesday there, Monday we used to go to the pictures, Thursday we used to go dancing, Friday was choir practice, Saturday night was dancing at night and Sunday was church three times in the choir. So it was only really till I was left with me mother that I started with work.

At a certain point however there was a renegotiation of who did what for whom. Presumably this occurred in their mid to late twenties when it became clear that they would not be leaving home. (By this time all their fathers had died.) From then the tables began to turn: they, rather than their mothers, decided what proportion of their wages to allocate to household income; they dropped the domestic duties they had performed until then. In terms of dependency too the relative positions began to reverse, the mother now more exclusively dependent for her livelihood on the daughter who effectively became head of household as her father had previously been.

Mary Gouden seemed almost to have taken the place of her father:

> Mary Gouden: ... it was funny after my brother died she was hopeless with money, I had to take over everything to do it. Mind you she was getting older then but I did it then.
>
> Q: How did you manage with doing all your cleaning and cooking when you were working full time?
>
> Mary Gouden: Well its amazing, you see my mother did everything for me and she used to be standing at the window waiting for me to come down the street and the meal was there

> on the table. I didn't cook much while my mother was
> alive.

As Amy Fowler's mother grew older she also 'took charge' of housing and money matters while her mother 'looked after' her. Note that Amy does not acknowledge domestic labour as 'work'. Her attitude towards washing differs markedly from the Salford casual workers who might well have been her neighbours.

Q: Can we just finish with your home life. You lived at home
                while your mother was still alive?

Amy Fowler: But in 1966 we moved from Robert Hall Street into a
                council flat, due to the fact that I had a brush with the
                Landlord. My father had died in 1957. And the law said
                you could only change the tenancy once, and of course
                my mother became the tenant. Well I knew that if there
                was any trouble he could say to me 'you've got no home'.
                That would be his rights. So by the time we moved into a
                council property and my mother became the tenant but I
                also became a secondary tenant you see, and that was
                in 1966.

Q: So did she look after you or did you look after her? Who
                did the washing and the cooking and the shopping?

Amy Fowler: Oh she did. And it was up to probably 1970.

Q: And did you give her housekeeping money then, or did
                you still tip it all up?

Amy Fowler: No. I used to give her the housekeeping money and I
                also paid the difference in rent because the rents were
                higher. Plus I would say to her I will pay the electricity
                bills because they were all electric at that time.

Q: And how did she do the washing or did you do the
                washing; when was the copper replaced?

Amy Fowler: The copper was replaced in 1966 ... she used to go to the
                launderettes which were not very far from where we lived,
                and she didn't work. I think it was a social gathering really.

Although it would be inappropriate to make any general claims about single women's relation to home/work, these three particular women do appear to have shared a distinctive pattern of intergenerational reciprocities and exchange with their parents at a certain stage in the life course. As they became adults and their parents grew older the flows of support between generations were gradually transformed from a pattern of servicing and dependency characteristic of households containing young workers to one with quite different obligations and forms of caring and dependence. And there is no reason to doubt that these patterns were repeated many times over by other women whose circumstances were similar to theirs in Salford, with its particular employment structure and poor housing conditions.

Cottons, casuals and singles

The pattern of intra-household exchange and home/work configuration of Ivy Turner, Amy Fowler and Mary Gouden differed systematically from those of both the cotton and casual married women workers analysed in Chapter 3.

Like the weavers the single women engaged in standard full-time and permanent employment. But like the casual women theirs too was 'women's work', paid according to women's rates of pay. Their jobs were strictly sex-typed as either male or female and the workforce was segregated by gender. Only women did clerical work like Mary Gouden; the cable jointing machines operated by Amy Fowler were all operated by women while male workers operated different machinery; tea blending and packing was done exclusively by women and no supervisors were women. In their 40 or so years of service, these women had probably progressed close to the top of the female career hierarchy but the ladder was a very short one.

The three firms where they worked were also all of a particular kind, with conditions distinct from weaving sheds and mills. They occupied a particular place in the local employment structure and also recruited from a particular niche in the labour market, seeking the best qualified and 'respectable' young women so as to foster a reliable workforce and low labour turnover. Metrovicks and the Co-op were known as good places to work and it was hard to get a job there: you had to be 'spoken for' and supply good references. In return recruits received training, higher pay and better conditions (including holiday and sick pay) than in many other Salford factories and mills.

All three firms had also operated a marriage bar before the Second World War, their managements pursuing traditional paternalistic practices which construed men/husbands as breadwinner and women/wives as domestic dependants. However, the exclusion of married women by no means implied the absence of older women since such workplaces continued to employ single women in characteristic positions over the long term. Single and married women were thus complementary to each other in the workplace as in the family, assuming a distinctive but equally crucial role in maintaining both institutions. In firms which operated a marriage bar the female workforce consisted mostly of young women between the ages of 14 and 24, with a minority of older unmarried women and some widows. Amy's shop at Glovers contained a surprisingly high proportion of widows but to her mind they were really single:

> Young and widows, widowed from the First World War. Yes there were quite a lot of widows. In fact the section where I worked in, let me see ... there was about six or seven widows in that department out of the 14 ... yes, that was quite a lot. Some of them they called themselves 'unclaimed treasures'... they said they lost their boyfriends in the First World War so they were spinsters really.

Clearly, it was no accident that I could not find married women who had worked in Trafford Park factories over a lifetime and no accident either that the single women I came across all worked in this type of firm. From the firms' perspective Mary, Ivy and Amy were ideal employees: loyal, conscientious, repaying many times over any investment in their training.

Wages were sufficient for all three women to support themselves and their mothers, their rates probably in between those earned by the two groups of married women, but more stable than either. Like the casual women workers the single women all lived in substandard housing in Salford, owned by private landlords, until they were rehoused from the 1970s. They paid for improvements in infrastructural facilities but, unlike the weavers, did not purchase consumer durables or the services of other women. Indeed, the single women were quite dismissive when discussing domestic labour and, unlike the other groups, took no responsibility for it while their mothers were alive. Their mothers had to rely on their own labour to do the housework.

After the death of their mothers the single women had to fend for themselves. It was now after the Second World War and more married women were employed in the various factories. However, their comments made clear that it would still have been hard to combine full-time work with caring for a family and, significantly, most of the married women worked part-time. Even for one person Ivy relied on the laundry for her washing and Mary on the works canteen for her main meal. Amy married. Mary and Ivy lived on in their parental homes, eventually moving, decades later, to new council accommodation. But it was an adjustment to arrange for their own cooking and washing.

> Mary Gouden: Quite a few of my friends said I wouldn't be able to manage on my own but I managed alright. You've got to cope if it happens. Because a lot of people said 'she'll never live on her own because she's too dependent on her mother' but I coped eventually. And it was OK, because what was good about it, I could have a hot meal at work. They had a canteen ... we could get a hot meal at work so you could cope with perhaps a snack in the evenings.

And:

> Ivy Turner: Well after me mother died I thought 'what am I going to do with this stuff' and I used to take it to, there used to be a little shop round the corner of the next street that took laundry in. It was a Co-op and I used to take the big stuff there and collect it every Friday.

> Q: Did that cost more [than bagwash or laundrette]?

> Ivy Turner: Oh yes because it was already ironed and nice. You could just take it out of the parcel and it was the easiest way for me.

The home/work configuration of the single women was as interlocking and distinctive as both the other patterns outlined. In terms of paid employment single women occupied a particular position in the labour market and worked under conditions that were specific to them. Their domestic role and the structure of their household economies were also particular to them. And there was a clear interconnection between the two sides of the equation: their input into each sphere both presupposed and was the condition of their situation in the other. The lives of the single women were perhaps characterised by a greater degree of gender segregation than cotton or casual women workers since they experienced work, home and leisure overwhelmingly in the company of other women.

The distinctive experience of the single women provides further support for thinking of femininities, whether single or married, in the plural. Although they too were manual (at the outset), working-class, living in the same localised part of Lancashire as the weavers and casual workers, their experience of womanhood was different and distinctive. They did not engage with men in the domestic arena but in the wider world, including that of work, they were equally subject to male dominance as all other women. But it would be completely misleading to extrapolate from the financial responsibility they had for their mothers or from the domestic servicing they received that they 'assumed a man's role'. Theirs was a different way of being a woman, subjectively experienced and positively described as such.

The relationship between mothers and daughters has been integral to the discussion of young women workers and of single women even though not signalled as an explicit theme. I hope to have given some indication of the ambivalence of daughters to mothers. Idealisation of mothers' trojan-like efforts in caring for them as children was frequently expressed in almost the same breath as resentment at what was felt to be unjustified parental control and exploitation. With hindsight they might look differently at the dual position of still being a child subject to maternal authority in the home while being an independent earning agent in the adult world of work. The ambivalence did not diminish with the passage of time. Indeed, in hindsight, some now thought they had been unwittingly 'used' by their mothers although at the time they had just accepted it. Conflicts then about growing up revolved around going out at night, how often and how late, and to a lesser extent around rights over labour and earnings. A generation later it would probably have been more explicitly over sex and sexuality and possibly privacy. But these were not verbalised as of paramount concern to the women as teenagers in the 1920s and 1930s.

Their own later lives displayed continuities and discontinuities with those of their mothers. Reflecting retrospectively, the women I interviewed took their mothers as the definitive reference point for estimating how much things had changed in their own lives. They discussed whether they had reproduced their mothers' lives and followed in their footsteps, and the ways in which they had broken away and changed. This chapter gives some clues. Other aspects will emerge from the discussion of time, a theme central to their way of differentiating between the two generations.

Notes

1   From a distinct perspective, the discussion will thus touch on themes that have been the subject of disparate, long-standing and often extensive, literatures in sociology, social policy and history. These include the family, family history, youth and adolescence, generations and the life course, kin relations and obligations, dependency and caring. Although these diverse literatures inform the discussion the intention is to develop analysis on the basis of the source material.

2   Significantly too free education was introduced as the school leaving age was raised.

3   In terms of the TSOL this is further evidence of broad interconnections between the extension of educational provision, the declining significance of youth labour and the decreasing salience of children's contribution to family reproduction associated with the introduction of the welfare state in the postwar period.

4   It would no doubt be possible, by detailed analysis of particular households within their local contexts, to identify and account for patterns of connection and structures of networks. From the testimonies I collected the distinction between textile and casual workers appeared to come into play, the latter's friendship and social networks apparently more strongly linked to a community base of women living nearby. See Chapters 5 and 6 for further discussion of questions of place.

5   Interestingly, this resentment of fathers by some women was voiced in far stronger terms than their later criticisms of husbands not sharing domestic labour.

6   Jephcott's *Girls Growing Up* (1942), published a bit later than the period under consideration, is a rare exception which did concentrate on girls, though not on gender comparison.

7   The Junior Instruction Centres were a revamped version of the older Juvenile Unemployment Centres. When the age of entry to unemployment insurance was lowered from 16 to 14 they were compelled to provide educational provision and young people were obliged to attend (Garside, 1977).

8   Inadequacies arise since the relevant Census data aggregates 14 to 20 year olds into one grouping. It also relates to 1931 when rates were not at their highest. The Ministry of Labour supplied annual figures for all under 18s. But these were not broken down by sex, and since not all young people registered as unemployed can represent only estimates.

9   That young workers enjoyed significant amounts of disposable income was also noted in the *New London Survey*, and those of Merseyside, Southampton and York.

10 And: 'The intelligent girl of fifteen who spends from 8 a.m. to 5 p.m. in hammering three nails into a cardboard box cannot be satisfied by such a life. She searches for a vicarious satisfaction and she finds it in the diamond stealing, blackmail and breath taking adventures of the gangster film; in the side-splitting humour of the *Hold That Ghost* variety, and in the good times, lovely clothes, and "kisses that thrill" which pour out of Hollywood and Denham ...' (Jephcott, 1942: 119).

11 In addition to the growing literature on lesbians, most historical research relates to middle class single women, especially those in the teaching profession, and to the eighteenth and nineteenth centuries. See Oram (1985), Jeffreys, (1985), Vicinus, (1985), Anderson, (1984), Hufton, (1984) and Sharpe, (1991). Katherine Holden's PhD thesis 1996 fills an important gap in the literature. See also Davidoff *et al.* (1999).

12 Indeed some daughters who cared for their mothers, interviewed by Lewis and Meredith (1988) spoke of the poor or problematic relationships they had with their mothers (especially 57–65). See also Finch's discussion (1989: 205–10) of the relationship between the development of family obligations and emotions.

13 Duquenin (1984) emphasises that only or last daughters were in a special position of both privilege and responsibility in relation to their parents in contrast to older siblings. Most of the non-marrying women in the early twentieth century Devon textile town she studied came from this category. As younger children they experienced a more favourable situation 'in terms of material comforts, education, job opportunities and finance' (Duquenin, 1984: 42) but simultaneously greater demands were placed on them for care and companionship in impending old age. Duquenin makes the point that the options of marrying versus caring that now seem like self-sacrifice 'seem not to have presented themselves as immediate alternatives, or else the issue did not seem so important' (Duquenin, 1984: 44).

14 Note Ivy Turner's wording here and reference to 'Godforsaken Spinsters'. This may suqqest that even though she felt no need to explain her single state there may well have been community pity for or criticism of the unmarried state to which she is responding by using her membership of the GFS as a reason for being unmarried. Thanks to Katherine Holden for this insight.

Chapter 5
Time for women

The mutual obligations and exchanges of labour and money that were the focus of Chapter 4 involved a generational time-lag. They occurred between generations, affecting young women in particular sets of relationships with their mothers and parental families at a certain point in time, and with their own daughters and husbands in other ways at a later stage. Temporality was an essential, though implicit, dimension of all these exchanges and equally essential to an interpretation of them. More widely, the total social organisation of labour is also to be understood as a temporal organisation. The time dimension is central to any particular organisation of labour: labour is organised across time and it may also change over time.

Temporality is an element of all social relationships, processes and structures, an integral aspect that is both constitutive of them and constituted by them. The aim of this chapter is to bring some of that implicit temporality to the foreground. The perspective thus shifts again from the successive intergenerational cycle of relationships between daughter and mother, and mother and daughter, to the temporal organisations and organisations of temporality of the lives of the women interviewed. What insights are to be gained from exploring differences and similarities in relation to temporality between them? And what might this suggest more generally about the value of an analytical focus on gender and temporality?

A few initial points may help guide the discussion. First, to clarify definitions, the term 'temporality' will be used to denote the distinctive structuring of time, of which chronometric or standard linear time is just one instance amongst many. Because time can be ordered and regulated, and enter social processes, in myriad different ways, the possible structurings of time, or temporalities, are almost infinite. The character and form of different temporalities are to be specified. Clock time, though privileged as the dominant mode of temporal control in modern or industrial society, still represents only one of these. People's lives, even at a particular 'point in time', frequently involve many different temporalities, including clock time, that intersect or collide with each other. We are usually not aware of the coincidence of these different temporalities, so accustomed that we do not need consciously to integrate them. Nevertheless we are all aware of time, and everyone experiences temporality.

The second point is that although different temporalities could be expected to be accompanied by different experiences of time, differences in temporality cannot be reduced to how they are experienced. It might be possible to gain knowledge of temporal structurings only from people's empirical experience of them, but the experience is not all there is to temporality. Even if it is actually constituted through and by social process, temporality is also constitutive of social process.

At a general level the central question is to what extent an analytical focus on temporality might offer a systematic means of pinpointing variation both within and between genders. At the level of concrete material, analysis has to confront the probability of multiple temporalities in relation to multiple femininities (and masculinities). But it is only on the basis of substantive knowledge of the temporalities specific to particular groups of women and men that a more general framework for conceptualising gender and temporality could be developed. So, although this chapter concentrates on exploring the temporalities of weavers and casual women workers in their own right and for their own significance, the ensuing analysis is intended to be relevant also to feminist and social theory more broadly.

Time has been reproblematised in recent years, both in practice and as a question for theory (Harvey, 1999b). It seems to be at a premium as never before, to be protected, managed, and above all, not wasted. There is never enough of it. Patterns of working that had prevailed as 'standard' for over half a century have been disrupted by new production regimes and by patterns of 'flexible' employment (e.g. 'just in time' manufacture, 'zero-hours' contracts, 'hot desking', tele-homeworking). New terminologies of time have emerged ('quality time', 'time management') indicating just how precious it has become. In Britain public policy think tanks and political parties (e.g. Hewitt, 1993; Demos Quarterly, 1995) canvassed for new ways of organising working time, as did the Equal Opportunities Commission, and the European Union instituted the Working Time Directive. What amounts to a virtual 'temporal' turn may be discerned from the deluge of publications about time issuing from many social science disciplines (for example Adam, 1990, 1995; Osborne, 1995; the journal Time and Society).

Temporality thus represents a theme of contemporary analysis which I am using as a tool to reinterpret the past. In this sense the framework is imposed on the material from the outside. A temporal perspective did not emerge spontaneously from the oral testimony I collected. It was not an issue raised by the women. Yet time and temporality were evident in all of their accounts. Many varied forms of temporality and regulations of time were dispersed and intersected in their day-to-day activity and across their whole lifespan. For the most part these remained unspoken and implicit, though it was possible to reconstruct them from clues given in what was said about diverse other matters. But once explicitly thought about, temporality also became a conceptual tool for the women themselves, which they used actively to rethink their memories. In this way the research instrument also provided a lever for the women to question their own pasts and to reflect on how they think now about how things were then.

Looking back at the multiple temporalities negotiated apparently unproblematically by working mothers in the 1930s may be instructive too for contemporary debates, suggesting that standard abstract chronometric time may never have had the overriding dominance that has been ascribed to it, at least not for women. In that case the presumed current 'destabilisation' of standard time, a cause for such widespread concern, would also be a fiction. Looking behind that fiction could reveal not only a lack of historical awareness but also the dominance of a male-defined conception of time.

Sociology, time, theory, gender

Although high on today's social agenda it would be quite misleading to imply that sociology had only just discovered time. In fact all the classical theorists wrote about it and so did most major and minor twentieth century thinkers. Marx's theories of commodity exchange and exploitation assume an 'abstract labour time', but he did not problematise the temporal element treated as the basis for conversion and of value. For Weber processes of routinisation and bureaucratisation integral to the transition to modern rational-legal society owed much to abstract chronometric time associated with the Protestant ethic and its institutionalisation. Where Marx stressed commodification, and Weber routinisation, Durkheim emphasised the integrative and social synchronising function of time. For Durkheim and the French school of anthropology with which he was associated time was a collective phenomenon derived from social life, the sum of temporal procedures that interlock to form the cultural rhythm of a particular society (Hassard, 1990).

Time is perhaps more explicitly crucial to Giddens's conceptual framework than to these classical figures. Although the significance and interpretation of temporality have altered as his theory developed, time has been central to Giddens's theories of structuration, as well as to his concepts of sedimentation, routinisation, 'time–space distanciation', recursiveness of knowledge, commodified time and so on. Giddens conceptualises the repetitive aspect of social reproduction as time and 'any patterns of interaction that exist are situated in time; only when examined over time do they form 'patterns' at all'(1979: 202). Thus Giddens sees time as constituted through the replication of social practices, and order and stability as no more timeless than change and revolution.

These different ways of interpreting time very evidently derive from the overall framework of the particular theorist. Indeed the more one reads the more obvious this becomes, so much so that it is quite possible to extrapolate the theory of time that 'goes with' any given theoretical perspective. Thus there are functionalist, symbolic interactionist, phenomenological, social constructionist and numerous other theories of time which stress different dimensions of temporality and differ in ways that may be easily predicted in advance.

A cursory glance at the wide range of theories reveals them as part of an attempt at 'grand theory', a total conceptual framework which the author posits for interpreting 'society as such'. Time appears often simply as an epiphenomenon of the overall framework, included only so as to achieve a truly comprehensive theory. And so, apart from a few notable exceptions, such as Bourdieu's (1963) work on the Kabyle of Algeria, and Zerubavel's (1979, 1981) on hospitals and the calendar, many theories of time are relatively devoid of substantive content, or use historical or empirical material merely as illustrative of a theory formulated in the abstract.

This is a general criticism of approaches where the prime concern is internal coherence of the theoretical construct and where greater zeal is devoted to perfecting this than to developing its analytical ability in making sense of social process. When approaches take 'the high ground', in this manner, then substantive studies of temporality or other social process come to appear trivial by comparison, 'little' empirical case studies of minor significance. They have no place in the debate between grand designs, even if the grand designers pick and choose amongst such examples to back up their argument. However, when viewed from the perspective of the substantive studies, many 'big' theories of time look dangerously near to megalomaniac projects to incorporate everything in one big scheme.

My readings thus certainly confirm the assessment of Barbara Adam (1990, especially Chapter One), that, in spite of the dazzling array of theories of time, the actual nature of time itself has rarely been a central focus for attention. Many new and different ways of thinking about time were stimulated by my reading, but whether they do more than inform my analysis is open to question. As a means of cutting through a lot of confusion about how to approach time, I found instructive the brief comment of Latour that 'it is the sorting that makes the time, not the time that makes the sorting' (1993: 76). Also helpful was the essay by Elias which does attempt to develop a theory of time itself. For Elias time is a symbol which clarifies one sequence of events by reference to another, an implement or tool invented by humans which permits events that cannot be directly compared to be compared indirectly. Because 'positions and sequences which have their places successively in the unending flow of events cannot be juxtaposed' (1992: 10) a second sequence of recurrent patterns is needed to serve as standardised reference points. Time thus refers to the 'relating together of positions or segments within two or more continuously moving series of events' (Elias, 1992: 10).

But Elias cautions against a confusion common in the literature on time, that of mistaking the measuring instrument for what it is measuring. Time, he emphasises, is:

> neither a conceptual 'copy' of a flow existing objectively, nor a category common to all people and existing in advance of all experience.
> (Elias, 1992: 8)

He illustrates the point by using the analogy of a boat, another humanly constructed implement. No more than the boat constitutes or spatialises rivers and seas whilst navigating around them to establish a cartography, do time instruments structure events. No one would postulate that a boat had the same ontological status as a sea or a river; nor would a boat builder be interpreted as following a transcendental concept of a boat. The same should go for time.[1]

Unlike time in general, work-time *has* been a subject for much substantive research, especially by labour and economic historians and sociologists. Many take as their point of departure Thompson's well-known essay charting the transition from task-oriented to clock-oriented work which he postulated as accompanying the establishment of industrial capitalism. Time became an instrument for social control, imposed by employers on their workers as a means of industrial discipline. Following Marx, Weber and others who had highlighted the connection between the extension of the sphere of commodities, the Protestant ethic, and time-thrift, Thompson drew attention to how time came to be used as an instrument of class domination, a means of subordinating and controlling industrial workers. A corollary of the new pre-eminence of clock time, and of consolidation of the separation between home and work, was that the new distinction between work and life also involved a distinction between work-time, now seen as belonging to employers, versus own-time or free-time. As Thompson put it:

> *Those who are employed experience a distinction between their employer's time and their 'own' time. And the employer must use the time of his labour, and see it not wasted: not the task but the value of time when reduced to money is dominant. Time is now currency: it is not passed but spent.*
> (Thompson, 1967: 61)

It will be important for the discussion of women's work/time later in this chapter to remember that the notion of time being 'free' or one's 'own' can have meaning only in opposition to time that is bought and sold, in circumstances where time is commodified. Otherwise there is nothing for time to be 'free from'. It is also worth signalling here the covertly gendered nature of Thompson's and later writers' discussions of work/time: they tend to presume (illegitimately) that the conditions and experience of male industrial workers have also been common to women. However, when certain groupings of women worker are placed at the centre of analysis, the distinction between task and clock oriented work may not appear quite so absolute.

So how does gender fit into these various theories, and what of feminist theories of temporality? As yet (perhaps surprisingly, given the concern of researchers with the 'second shift' and 'dual roles', as with the life-course and the body), this is a relatively undeveloped field. None of the grand theories (unsurprisingly), and few of the historical accounts, attempt a serious consideration of the gendering of temporality. The few feminist studies of women's time draw attention to the embedded character of women's time as opposed to decontextualised abstract time as the medium for exchange value (Adam, 1995: 99; Davies, 1990). The focus shifts to women's capacity to generate and 'give' time as a resource rather than simply spending or using it up, so establishing a new emphasis on women's creation of time for themselves and others through emotion work (Hochschild and Maching, 1990).

Bringing a gender perspective to the analysis of time should not imply that there is a 'female', or a 'male', experience of time common to all women or all men. Yet some feminist critiques of E.P. Thompson and approaches to time (Forman and Sowton, 1989),[2] come dangerously close to essentialism by reworking the modernist dualism of cyclical versus linear time (Kristeva, 1981) as a gendered division. From this perspective women's time is conceptualised as cyclical or following biological rhythms and phases of life while men's is linear and progressive, approximating more closely to industrial time.

In addition to its essentialist leanings, this line of thinking also tends to downplay women's situation as wage workers and the conflicts over control of time in paid employment which have affected them equally as men, even if in specific and gendered ways. Whether they are assembly line workers, whose employers try to squeeze productivity out of every second of the time they are paid for,[3] or, at the opposite end of the spectrum of exchange between time and money, whether they are domestic servants with no formal contract of employment, whose hours of work are open-ended and whose labour employers can demand virtually at any time of day or night,[4] they all have a gendered temporal relation to waged work. If even paid work-time is differently organised, reckoned, experienced and challenged for and by women in different occupations and industries (there is no common relation of women workers to working time) then this is much more the case for the relation of women in general to time as such.

I hope that the discussion of weavers' and casual women workers' relations to temporality will make very clear that differences exist *between* women in the gendered structuring of time. Part of the analysis concerns chronometric or clock time, in which amounts of linear time can be counted and measured, added and substracted. However, since weavers' and casual workers' differing relation to time extended far beyond the clock and daily routine I shall also be looking at other broader differences in temporal modalities.

'Economy of time'

My observations relating to clock time will be concerned with what might usefully be termed an 'economy of time'. Time can be conceptualised, as the foregoing discussion has suggested, as a medium of exchange that is broader or wider than money. Time may be bought and sold as a commodity. It may be a scarce resource, with potential conflicts over its allocation and use. Exchanges of time may be equal or unequal; some people may be in a position to appropriate or exploit other people's time, or use of time, or products of time. Time would constitute an integral dimension of power in relationships where some people possessed more control over it than others or had the ability to determine what was done with it (both their own and that of others). Many exchanges of time do involve money, as in the case of formal paid employment when money is exchanged directly for labour time. Money may also buy time indirectly, as in the purchase of the products of labour. But, whether direct or indirect, money exchanges far from embrace all exchanges of time. Many labour activities involve exchanges of time or particular allocations of time use that have no financial dimension.

Developing a framework for analysing labour along such lines, in contrast to a framework confined solely to monetary exchange, would provide not only a much broader conception but also one that is more appropriate to taking seriously women's labour and gender differences in work. Using time as the basis for an umbrella notion of labour activity provides a means of conceptualising and acknowledging as 'work' domestic labour, voluntary work, as well as the many kinds of caring and other non-waged work, alongside paid employment. Using time as the common standard of measurement has much to recommend it: it enables inputs of labour to be quantified regardless of whether or not they are paid. By the same token it also provides a potentially novel means for calculating appropriations of labour (possibly even 'exploitation'?) that could quantify 'who does what for whom' regardless of differences in work relations or the economic spaces in which they occur.

But caution is necessary since this advantage may also contain its own disadvantage. Quantification could only be achieved by effectively homogenising all labour activities. Time can be operationalised as a yardstick for comparison only if a standardised form of time is abstracted out of the very different temporalities that do in fact characterise activities undertaken within different socio-economic relations. Thus appreciation of differences between kinds of work that was made possible by a time perspective could immediately be lost again in a reductionist attempt to construct a unidimensional model to incorporate all of them. This would undermine precisely what the attention to time set out to achieve, namely recognition of differences between different forms of labour, which must also include their different temporalities.

Time has no neutral or objective existence, and this applies even to working time that is reckoned according to the clock.[5] So, in talking of an 'economy of time', care must be taken to avoid crediting time with any natural or causative properties. Furthermore, once viewed from a perspective broader than that of the exchange of commodities, time cannot really be seen as a homogeneous medium, such as Marx confined himself to in his concept of 'abstract labour time'. Indeed even Marx, within this narrowed focus, considered abstract labour time – broadly equivalent to chronometric time – as established or verified through market exchanges.

It is possible (although by no means inevitable) for time-use studies[6] and time-budgets[7] also to operate with a simplistic notion of measurement in terms of standard units, whereby one hour of assembly line working, for example, is equated with one hour of, say, walking the dog, as if this conversion were unproblematic. But the expenditure of time in different economic spheres or social relationships may well be incommensurable. It is certainly not homogeneous; nor can it be straightforwardly converted or 'clocked' since there is no common external standard for conversion, other than clock time itself. It is one thing to consider chronometric time as a frame within which events occur according to different temporalities, but it would be quite another to treat it as the universal standard for counting, measurement and conversion. Walking the dog and working on an assembly line are activities that involve such different temporalities that to count an hour spent on each does not really tell us very much. Although both activities *can* be measured by linear time they cannot be equated, since no medium exists for equivalence. Attempting to do so risks the problem of Elias' boat and river, that is, of reifying the measuring instrument and thereby confusing it with what it is intended to measure.

This problem of clocking can be further exacerbated when multiple activities are undertaken simultaneously. Take the case of a woman doing the ironing. At the same time she is watching television. A load of washing went into the washing machine about half an hour ago and will soon be ready to be transferred to the dryer. So she is keeping an ear open for the washing machine, and also an eye on the oven where a meal, prepared earlier, is now cooking. And all this is being done not in her own house but in the home of her elderly aunt, and they are chatting together the while. Clearly our friend is undertaking many different activities at the same time, productive and reproductive labour in the case of cooking, washing and ironing. She is also caring; watching television could count as leisure though it might more appropriately be considered as a medium for caring and emotion work. But none of these activities is differentiated from each other in reality. What is most significant about them is temporal integration of the multiplicity of tasks, an issue posing problems which time study budgets are now taking on board.

If no neutral objective external framework exists from which to view time we should be wary of flattening the distinctive temporalities of different kinds of work and thereby obscuring their varied qualities, experience and meaning. It is probably not possible to add up inequalities in exchanges of time that occur in commodity production to those occurring in the household economy since no common or universal market exists by which *equivalences* of labour time could be established for all labour. The attempt to develop an overall system of time-accounting for all the varied forms of work would inevitably reduce all to the single dimension of clock time and so foreclose precisely those advantages offered by a temporal perspective in the first place. If time is quantified along a single dimension just like money, then the value of studying time use is in danger of being negated.[8]

Dimensions of temporality

The central sections of this chapter return to differences between weavers and casual women workers but focusing now on time. I want to show that the two groups vary as regards three dimensions of temporality which will be examined in turn. They differ, first, as regards the temporal structure of their work/time in waged work, in both formal and informal economies, in domestic labour, and leisure. Second, different temporalities of life-course events structured weavers and casual women workers' experience. Lastly, the division between public and private was also distinct for the two groups, temporality constituting a central aspect of this distinction.

It is worth keeping in mind some points from the earlier discussion. We are dealing not only with experiences and understandings but also with different structures of temporality. Although these are ascertained primarily through the experiences of the women, the temporal structure cannot be reduced to, or understood solely in terms of, how it was experienced. Also, there are many different forms of temporality, of which linear chronometric standard time is one. Certainly clock time is pre-eminent in contemporary life; but its dominance is an effect of a particular kind of temporality, rather than a cause of it. Nor does the dominance of clock time wipe out other temporalities and temporal dimensions of social processes and relationships. They are not mutually exclusive. As chronometric time coexists with many other forms of temporality there is no need for an either/or approach to the issue. What is of particular interest is the area of significance of chronometric time, the nature of those temporalities, and the intersection between the different kinds.

Exchanges of time, money, labour

The casual workers, it will be remembered, engaged in a multiplicity of jobs, some of which were part-time. Taken together these amounted in time to at least the equivalent of a full-time job, often considerably in excess of the ten hour day. Their waged work spanned both formal and informal employment relationships: formal when they did night cleaning or working in a pub, informal when they performed services like washing or childcare for other women. They also did all their own domestic labour, with very little assistance from their husbands, and on a highly labour-intensive basis.

A prime example was Mrs Preston whom we have encountered several times already. She worked through the night as a cleaner, cared for her own family of five, and did washing for two other women at the municipal wash-house for pay. In terms of time, it is significant that this service-performing element of her paid work was not separated off from her own domestic labour since she did her own washing in the wash-house at the same time.

The same was true for those who looked after other women's children, or who prepared cooked dinners for others. Such work activities were not distinguished temporally for a casual worker from performing her own domestic labour. Moreover, the absence of any formally set hours marking off domestic labour time from leisure or 'free' time meant that no meaningful distinction could be made between periods of time allocated to paid work, domestic labour and leisure.

This is not to say that the casual workers I interviewed felt no pressure of time. On the contrary, and as Mrs Preston suggests, it was a rush to fit everything in. All gave detailed accounts of their daily and weekly routines for cleaning, cooking, washing and childcare. They emphasised the need for a pre-planned efficient method in order to get everything done in the time available and the necessity of a regular routine and rational ordering of tasks during the day and week.

Rigid gender division also extended to social activities. Many husbands returned home for their meals only to go out again to the pub, once they had eaten, and spend the evening drinking with other men. Women's leisure time was much more restricted than that of their husbands and their activities not so formalised, often being spent at home in the company of other women. Although many regularly went to the cinema they rarely frequented the pub.[9] Thus, in contrast to their wives, male time was strictly divided into work time, as purchased by the wage, versus leisure time, as their *own* time, when they were serviced by women or could go out on the town.

As Mrs Preston had put it:

> The man's place was in the work and the woman's was in the home. It was supposed to be all done by the time he came in from work and all he did was come in, have a wash, sit down and his meal would be put in front of him and that was it, wasn't it?

Her words were echoed by Rose Whitely, whose husband often worked night shifts:

Q: *Did your husband help at all?*

Rose Whitely: *Well no. My husband had the attitude it was all your job. He had nothing to do with that. His job was to bring the wage in and that was him finished.*

Q: *You can't have seen much of each other?*

Rose Whitely: *We didn't, no. It was hello, goodbye. And he worked six nights a week. He used to start work Sunday night to Saturday morning, home Saturday morning and then he'd go for a drink Saturday dinner and he'd be out Saturday night. Ten years I brought the kids up myself.*

Despite her husband doing night work and Mrs Whitely's many jobs, money was short. Forty years on she still remembered exactly how she had to budget for food so as to last the week:

> Rose Whitely: We laugh now and the children laugh when I tell them. I used to buy a joint at weekend, lamb for Sunday and that lamb used to last until about Wednesday or Thursday. Because we had roast on Sunday, and then we would have cold meat on Monday. Tuesday it would be potato hash. Wednesday would be just potatoes but I just used to put more spuds in. And Thursday they would probably just get a crust on it. It had to last because the wages were so low.
>
> Q: What about Friday and Saturday then?
>
> Rose Whitely: Well you got your wages and it would be a chippy thing on a Friday.

Within the household men contributed wages but appropriated their wives' labour and their time, while wives contributed income, labour and time to the household. But casual women workers' time was also appropriated by their employers, and by the other women for whom they performed services in addition to their husbands. The gendered inequalities of their waged work and domestic labour were mutually reinforcing, time being an integral component of the inequalities. Whether given, sold or exchanged, they were on the losing side of any equation. Thus their work/time constituted a distinctive gendered temporality which was experienced as such.

The situation of weavers was quite different. They engaged in full-time 'standard' formalised employment. Many worked continuously over a lifetime, from the time they left school until retirement age, with only short breaks for childbirth. Their wages were sufficient for many to purchase consumer durables and prepared food, and to pay other women for childcare and laundry services. Their families were smaller than those of the casual women and their husbands were more likely to take some responsibility for cooking, cleaning and childcare.

In their accounts of 'work' domestic labour assumed much less significance for weavers than for the casual women workers, and it was often difficult to get them to say anything about it. Lily Hunt (Chapter 3) had summed up her domestic arrangements in a brief matter of fact manner. And Kath Hinton's[10] account is even less expansive:

> Q: And how did you manage with your housework and everything when you were working?
>
> Kath Hinton: Well that was done at night, when the children were in bed.
>
> Q: Did you have a different night for different things?
>
> Kath Hinton: No, there was no set routine, I just did it as I felt like it, but something got done every night.

Kath Hinton was unusual in being so explicit about her lack of routine. Like the casual women, Lily Hunt and all the other weavers interviewed emphasised the necessity of having an organised routine, with time slots specifically ear-marked for the various domestic tasks on an hourly, daily or weekly basis. But, importantly, for many weavers, unlike the casual women, this organisation of domestic labour also included their husbands' time.

However, most weavers clearly thought that such routines were unworthy of detailed description. Given this reticence, it was notable how much more expansive they were about outlining their mothers' routines, a generation earlier, than their own. For example, 'JP', the Bolton weaver born in 1908 had given a detailed day-by-day account (quoted in Chapter 4) of the housework she had to do as a teenager after she came home from paid work in the mill. The timing of tasks and days remained clearly imprinted on her memory at a distance of more than 60 years.

Clearly circumstances had changed by the time 'JP' and the other weavers were grown women with children of their own. Looking after the home had been more arduous for their mothers' generation, and on that account perhaps more memorable also for the daughters than their own domestic labour. With no access to consumer durables (most did not yet exist), nor the ability to buy other women's labour, their mothers had relied on them.

It should now be evident that weavers and casual workers did not share an identical relation to time. They differed with respect to their use of time and their degree of control over time both in relation to their paid employment and to their household responsibilities.

The working day was structured differently for each group with work time, domestic labour time and non-work time being far more distinctly demarcated from each other for the weavers as separate time-periods or blocks of the day, and far less so for casual workers. The weavers conducted all their paid labour in a 'place of work' under contractual conditions of employment and so had a clear temporal (and spatial) cut-off point between what they treated as 'work' and the rest of the day which they were less likely to describe as work. Of course this was partly because they were in a position to buy time with money through purchasing services or consumer durables, and also partly because their use of time did not differ so markedly from that of their husbands. Weavers were thus in a stronger position than casual women workers to convert time and money in either direction: not only could they buy time with money but they could also buy money with time by means of their relatively higher earning capacity in paid employment.

But for the casual women workers different kinds of labour activity were not structurally or temporally differentiated from each other. Paid servicing work and domestic labour might be undertaken simultaneously and not in a formal workplace but rather in the wash-house or in their own home. The activities and relationships of paid work were thus inextricable from other non-work activities and relationships. Their commodified time was embedded in time that was not commodified so that they were in effect constantly negotiating the relationship between these two dimensions of work time, unlike the weavers whose commodified time was distinct from non-commodified time. (I shall return later to this important characteristic of casual women workers' time and its analytical implications since they bring into question the unitary conceptualisation of working time prevalent in texts on modernity and industrialism.) Less formal and less temporally separate hours of work for the casual women made the distinction between time allocated to work/domestic labour/leisure one that held little meaning for them. However, in their case, their husbands' relation to these same activities and time-use was very different from their own. No time was allocated by husbands to domestic labour, and their paid work-time remained absolutely distinct from leisure-time.

Turning now to the question of *control* over time, it might appear, at first glance, that the casual women had an advantage over weavers. Certainly weavers enjoyed greater control over the disposal of household time: they had more call than the casual women on their husbands' time to undertake housework, and they could 'acquire' time by spending money to substitute for their own labour. But weavers' control over time in the domestic sphere was predicated on the very absence of an equivalent ability to control time in their paid employment. While in the weaving sheds or mills weavers were not in a position to determine or organise their own use of time. The payment system, usually piece-rates, put them under extreme pressure to work as fast as possible and gave little opportunity for flexibility over time-use. This is only to state the obvious: weavers worked under classic conditions of wage labour, selling the use of their labour-time and receiving a wage in exchange. There was a pay-off between these two parts of their lives, where extreme pressure on time in one gave the possibility of less pressure in the other.

The casual workers, on the other hand, seemed to enjoy greater control over their paid work, being able to determine when and how they accomplished it. Because they fitted jobs in, 'boxed and coxed', exercised some choice over their hours of formal employment so as to suit themselves, and could undertake the various tasks on different days or at different times of the day with a certain degree of latitude, casual workers appeared to have more control to determine how they organised their working day than weavers. But this would be a superficial interpretation: since it was just as much a necessity for casual workers to sell their time in order to acquire money, their greater flexibility over the disposal of labour time related only to the management of time rather than conferring any real control over its disposal.[11] They enjoyed some flexibility with regard to time management, but it would be quite misleading to conclude from this that they actually controlled the time or 'possessed' it themselves any more than the weavers.[12] They worked also under time-pressure and against the clock, but in a different way.

These variations between the two work situations lend weight to the earlier point about the incommensurability of time-use when labour is undertaken under differing economic relations. Qualitative temporal differences between different kinds of work make it innappropriate to measure or equate or add up or subtract in any quantitative manner time-uses and time-exchanges when they occur across different economic spaces.

In their exchanges of time weavers and casual women workers differed along two dimensions: first, in their paid work with their employers, regardless of whether these involved formal or informal economic relations; and second, in domestic labour with their husbands and with other women. In terms of chronometric or clock time, granted their greater economic vulnerability and poverty, more of the casual women workers' total time was up for exchange.

They hardly had an idea of 'free' time, and if they did, there was not a lot of it. To make ends meet more of their time had to be at the disposal of others. In this sense they were more dominated by an 'economy of time' than the weavers. And even if it did not all add up to a grand total, because their work was performed under a variety of exchange relations, more of the total was absorbed by labour exchanges.

No single causal factor determined these variations in control over the disposability of time between the two occupational groups. It was not down to their employers nor to their husbands. Rather, as argued in Chapter 3, the women's lives were like a jigsaw where the different pieces fitted together and mutually reinforced each other. Control over the disposal of time comprised one element in such a configuration, caused and reinforced by the other elements and in its turn also reproducing and making them viable. The variation in control over disposal of their own time between weavers and casual women workers, although not carved out by them, gave those with more of it greater opportunities and more power to determine the rest of their lives.

Modalities of experience of time and the life course

Analysis of weavers' and casual workers' testimonies suggests that their different relation to temporality was wide-reaching and deep-rooted. Far from being restricted to the daily routines and work already outlined, it extended to the life course and to the very structure of memory.

In discussion weavers placed far less emphasis than casual workers on age or stages of life, and marriage was not presented as their major life-changing event. Life seemed less punctuated and more continuous through time for them since it was not divided up into temporal units defined in terms of marriage and fertility. Neither personal nor world events were remembered as being before or after marriage, or before and after having children. On the contrary, they used historical events independent of their own experience (local, national and international) as an external time grid by which to fix the temporal sequence of events in their own lives. So when recalling the time their mother died, they moved house, changed job, and so on, they positioned these personal events in relation to a historical calendar, as having occurred 'before' or 'after' the war, 'about the time' the National Health Service was established, 'soon after' a particular mill closed down.

By contrast, the memory of casual workers did seem to rely much more heavily on locating events in terms of the temporal sequence of rites of passage. They positioned events in terms of proximity to a timed reference point in their own personal past, and most notably referred to the marriages, births and deaths of their immediate family and close neighbours or friends. The times when they began 'courting' their husbands, their own and others' illnesses, the onset of frailty of parents, were also frequently mentioned. It was as if such life course events formed the basic frame of time reference, or personal calendar, by which they fixed all other events and changes.

To a certain extent this privileging of personal rites of passage did mirror the casual workers' experience of life through time: marriage did represent a watershed for them in a way that it did not for the weavers. Before they married or before they had children, all had worked full-time in standard conditions of paid employment, whereas afterwards they did not. They had also performed domestic labour for their parents, whereas afterwards they did not. The operation of a marriage bar actively excluded many from the job they had done until then. Getting married thus involved a double life transition, both in personal life and in work, the former inevitably bringing about the latter. Rituals and parties marked the work rites of passage, as wedding celebrations did marriage. Many firms adopted the formal custom of giving a bread knife to women they were forcing to leave, in clear symbolic acknowledgement of their new status.

Change in marital status or becoming a mother made much less difference to weavers' 'working' life. Paid employment spanned their whole lives, changing the impact of life course events by providing a continuing and constant backdrop for personal changes and life transitions.

The lives of weavers and casual women workers were thus subject to quite different temporalities, different orderings of events through time. Their 'lifetimes' were blocked differently; within the blocks they experienced distinct temporalities; and transitions between the blocks were registered more or less strongly. For casual women workers the life course was more chopped up into distinct and successive segments, the transitions between them being of such momentous significance that they were marked by rites of passage. In the intergenerational cycle of family life, the transition from being a daughter in the family of origin to being a wife and mother in the new family they formed assumed a significance for casual women workers that it could not hold for weavers. Analysis of the household economy in earlier chapters involved a predominantly cross-sectional perspective, looking at how it 'worked' synchronically, at any given point in time. The patterns were then approached diachronically in the dynamic of the intergenerational cycle of exchanges and obligations, which has its own rhythm and temporality. The 'actor' (sic), however, is unlikely to think of her household economy independently of its placing in time: at any stage in her life she is also always at a particular point in an ongoing intergenerational cycle. Participants are more likely to think in terms of the cycle than of the cross-section, and the temporal structure of their life-course made this much more so for casual women workers than for weavers. Their more sharply demarcated life transitions predisposed them to greater rootedness in an ever ongoing family cycle which linked their mother's generation to their own, and their own to their children's. They located themselves as a daughter, young wife, mother or grandmother in this cycle, as evidenced by the highly personalised and family cycle character of their time grids.

To be fully understood, these variations in lived experience and understanding of temporality between the two groups must be seen as one aspect of a larger set of circumstances which encompassed not only paid work and domestic labour but also their friendship, neighbourhood and community networks to which I now turn.

Temporality of the division between public and private

Although weavers' community and workplace overlapped in so far as co-workers often lived near each other, and neighbours and relatives also worked in mills, friendship and social networks appeared to be rooted more in their situation of working in the same place than in living nearby, while those of casual workers seemed more strongly linked to a community base of women living in close proximity to each other.

The centrality of the neighbourhood to the lives of casual women workers meant that they were more subject than weavers to community norms and rules, including those regulating the timing of domestic tasks. In most local communities there were established norms laying down which day of the week washing, drying and ironing were to be done, which day the steps were to be 'donkeyed' and so on. Monday was customarily allocated for washing. It was acceptable to bake on Sunday but not to wash. In Bolton house-cleaning duties for younger women were to be done on Friday night but in Rochdale on Thursday. Friday and Thursday were known respectively in Bolton and in Rochdale as 'bucket' night and 'hellfire' night, when teenage daughters were expected to stay in and help with housework.[13]

The force of community constraints reinforces the argument that casual women's control over time was more apparent than real given that their latitude in the management of time was subject to external constraints setting down the right order and day to do things on. The weavers, however, appeared not to be constrained by such regulations: there was no regularity about the days they allocated for specific chores. Many did their washing on Sunday.[14] Nor were they concerned about possible criticism from their neighbours, or more general social opprobrium that might be elicited by their irregular domestic routines.

This different type of rootedness in neighbourhood and community throws light also on the different sources and forms of self-esteem available to the two groups. As already discussed, weavers' self-esteem was associated with their role as skilled workers while that of the casual workers was tied up with how well they coped in comparison with others in their community in making ends meet. When presenting success in keeping the family fed and clothed on very meagre resources as their greatest achievement, they deployed these same criteria in judgement of their friends and neighbours.

This discussion of community may be reworked in terms of the division between public and private, a distinction long central in feminist theory, now increasingly addressed also in sociological reappraisals of modernity. Weavers and casual women workers were subject to both private and public regulation of time. But, more profoundly than this, I want to suggest that temporality was constitutive of the private/public split.

For weavers the distinction between home and work on the one hand and private and public on the other overlapped with each other. 'Home' was a private sphere where they undertook domestic labour at times to suit themselves, unlike the public sphere of work dominated by an externally imposed clock time. Home was a zone where they regulated their own time with a latitude not open to them at work. At home they had autonomy over a certain range of activities: what they did and how they did it were down to personal decision, and individualised. They could organise cleaning, clothes washing, childcare, and leisure pursuits without reference to an external public. Public and private were thus distinguished by a different relation to time.

Despite their relative autonomy over the home and domestic matters, weavers, as discussed in the previous section, positioned their 'private' lives and personal events by reference to 'public' historical events. This demonstrates the depth and strength of the temporal split and its inscription in the public/ private distinction. Their accounts operated with two series of sequences, the time ordering of one being used as the basis for sequentialising the other.

No such neat temporal split between spheres existed for the casual women workers. Theirs was a much messier situation where divisions between home and work, private and public, were less distinct. Their waged work spanned the division with more interweaving and a less rigid dichotomy. Although less subject to clock time in their informal work, they were constantly juggling and moving between differing temporal orders. They got the children ready for school, and prepared their husband's meal in line with the clock time regulation of school and timings of male employment.

The centrality of local networks and the local community to their lives made the structure and the boundaries of the division between public and private quite different for them than for the weavers. And temporality was differently constitutive of their structure of public and private. If the public sphere for casual women workers was seen as comprising the local community and other women, rather than formal workplaces and distant world events, then it could be also argued that for them the public was predominant over the private: they were subject to community norms about the right way of doing things; gossip represented a means of social control; respectability was conferred by community consensus. Many activities which weavers considered to be their own private business were undertaken 'in public' by the casual women.[15] For them the realm of the 'private' was relatively undifferentiated or undeveloped.

The difference between the two groups comes across graphically in the language of their testimonies. Describing their domestic labour Lily Hunt, Kath Hinton and all the other weavers always spoke in the first person, saying 'I did this'. If they said 'we did that' they were including their husband. The casual women workers were more likely to stress that 'we did X or Y', or 'it used to be done like X', the implied others being their mother and sister, or their neighbour and friend, that is, a collectivity of other local women.

Part of what binds the community as a community is the imposition of a temporal order: everybody does the same thing on the same day so they share a common daily or weekly cycle. It is through the medium of doing things that the community is constituted and the doing of things includes their temporal regulation. Although the public/private split is easier to conceptualise as spatial I hope to have suggested how it may also be temporal. If we ask the question of over what area or network of social relations a form of temporality can be organised, how extensively it applies, the temporal dimension of the spatial becomes clearer.

What comprised the public sphere thus differed for the two groups of women. For weavers it was formal employment, the wider society of bureaucratic institutions and the state; for casual women workers it was the local community. And the division between private and public also differed: for the weavers it was more distinct, while the two were more interpenetrating for the casual women.

Differences in the structure and experience of temporality may be seen as one aspect of the division between public and private. If there is a strong split between public and private, there may also be a split in the form of temporality. Conversely if there is no such strong split, as was the case for casual women workers, then one form of temporality, neither distinctively public or private, is more likely to permeate every aspect of their lives.

To summarise, weavers and casual women workers differed with respect to these three dimensions of temporality: time regulation of paid work versus unpaid labour, life course structuring of time, and public and private regulation of time. Each dimension has a distinctive temporality, with differing rhythms and orderings of events. In combination the differences deepened and mutually reinforced each other. Under such circumstances it is not surprising that each group constructed the division between home and work differently, according a different importance to each, and placing different emphases on home and work as potential sources of identity. Their different modes of structuring of time were central to the place accorded to the passage of time in constructing their own identities.

Time ending

In this final section I return to more general and conceptual issues.

Although it is true that casual workers were more tied up with 'female' life events and the life course than weavers, the reason for this was the overall social structuring of time, and not because casual workers were somehow 'closer to nature'. There was nothing 'natural' about the circumstances of either group, and it would be quite misleading to view one, by implication, as more 'womanly' and the other as less so.

And, if casual women workers were no more 'womanly' than weavers, neither were they more backward, pre-modern or a leftover from the pre-industrial era. Yet such an interpretation could easily be suggested by the view, common in the sociological literature, that the modern industrial era is characterised by the dominant temporality of the clock, such that work time is commodified time. Following Giddens (1979, 1987: 140–65), Adam (1990: 112–20) implies that an individual's work time is all of one kind, either commodified or not, industrial or not.

Yet casual women workers provide a clear instance of workers who simultaneously engage in both kinds of work: their 'commodified time' (in Adam's and Giddens's terms) could not be distinguished from the non-commodified time within which it was embedded. Yet they could in no way be contrasted with weavers as ancient versus modern, the one a traditional 'leftover' from a pre-industrial epoch, the other archetypical industrial workers. Casual women workers were as much a lynchpin of the local economies of which they were a part as any other worker: their distinctive pattern of involvement with formal and informal employment, waged and unpaid labour, made viable the conditions under which their husbands worked. Many weavers also relied on buying the services of casual women workers in order to engage in their pattern of permanent standard full-time employment. If the various forms of labour activity and modes of engagement depended on each other then it makes little sense to characterise them as typifying different stages of development, either pre-industrial as opposed to industrial, or pre-modern as opposed to modern. That casual workers' commodified time was embedded in non-commodified time signals rather the inadequacy of the conceptual division if the two are deemed as necessarily mutually exclusive.[16]

Casual women were constantly juggling different forms of temporality, including the clock times of others and community driven weekly cycles, and shifting between them, with apparent ease. This might suggest, in contrast to the pre-modern argument, that theirs was, on the contrary, a postmodern existence before its time. The multiple temporalities they were negotiating bear an uncanny resemblance to those marshalled in evidence of 1990s 'new times' and temporalities.

But, rather than either of these possibilities, what the situation of the casual women workers does suggest is that an ungendered conceptualisation of industrial or standard time has dominated the literature. The ten or eight hour working day, five or six day week, with a clear cut-off between work and not work, work-time and 'own' time, may well, until recently, have been standard for the majority of male employees. But women's patterns of working time have always been more diverse than men's and many women workers have engaged in several simultaneously. Domestic service work, homeworking, part-time work, twilight shifts: none of these conform to standard work/time despite their long history and the millions of women affected. To define any of these as 'non-standard' implies a standard based on the male norm.

Realisation that the apparently non-gendered discourse of standard working time is in fact highly gendered could also induce a bit of scepticism about the supposed arrival of postmodern time: only when the prevailing pattern of men's work/time changed, becoming more like that long prevailing for women, did working time became a subject for such concern. I am *not* suggesting that contemporary forms of casualisation and insecurity hark back to the pre-modern era anymore than it could be seriously suggested that casual women workers were pioneers of a postmodern multiple work temporality. To argue any of these positions would involve anachronistic denial of historical change and specificity. The main point is that multiple temporalities have always existed. To recognise their existence only in the current period betrays an ungendered perspective on time and on work.[17]

Introducing temporal analysis adds an important dimension to the 'total social organisation of labour', complementing its earlier presentation as an 'anthropological' view of the totality of labour. Exchanges of labour, complementarities of tasks, reciprocities of obligations are all established in a definite succession, in cycles or various forms of order and sequence. They necessarily constitute and structure their own temporal frameworks. In this sense, it is regularities in successions of exchanges, events, socio-economic relations that order time and produce the specific temporality, rather than the other way round. The form of organisation of labour makes clock time dominant rather than the reverse.

In answer to the questions posed at the outset, exploration of the temporal dimension has provided valuable and distinctive insights. Differences in temporal modalities of life, and in control over the disposal of time, undoubtedly represented an important area of variation between the two groups of women researched. It could, therefore, be fruitful to extend this type of analysis to other groups of women and men. Examination of different dimensions of temporality and the correlative experience of time made possible by a broader conception of work provides a distinctive perspective on difference between women. It also draws attention to specific forms of appropriation and subordination that may not otherwise be revealed. Adopting this wider perspective thus opens up the possibility of analysing inequalities generated by unequal exchanges of time both between genders and within them.

Although this analysis focused especially on work as a particularly salient feature of social temporality, I want to emphasise that labour is not the only organising principle of temporality, and that other facets of social life also have their own temporalities[18] (as was suggested in discussion of the structuring of the life course and of memory, and of the public/private distinction).

The historical specificity of the temporalities analysed here suggests that history is not to be thought of as an envelope of time in which events take place. On the contrary, the ordering of events forms the temporality of history. And, if all temporalities are historically specific, then any a priori conception of temporality is impossible. Temporalities are as they are, as we find and analyse them historically and empirically, rather than instantiations of a transcendental notion. Returning to the earlier comments about the relation between abstract theory and substantive research, it follows that no abstract theorisation of time could anticipate or configure specific historical temporalities and that theorisation of temporality can only be premised on analysis of substantive examples. While it might be possible to assert, a priori, the existence of multiple temporalities, this could not lead on to an understanding of their principles of ordering.

Notes

1   According to Elias time achieves a high level symbolic synthesis 'by means of which positions in the succession of physical natural events, of the social process and of an individual lifespan can be related together' (1992: 16). He provides a fascinating analysis of the development of calendars in these terms, as a grid for synchronising past and present on a world wide scale. I am far less taken with the role of time as a 'civilisatory mechanism' although this way of conceptualising it does provide a means of thinking about symbolisations of time as indicators of the degree of differentiation and individualisation of the society they are found in.

2   Forman seeks an elusive balance that affirms women's biological difference from men but without celebrating women's natural cycle (viz. Holmes, 1994: 6).

3   For assembly line workers conflict over time (centred on intensification, speed-up and Taylorism) was between employers and employees. It would have a gendered dimension if male rate setters or supervisors gained from work intensification for women workers. But this would be a gendered conflict (between different sections of the work force) interlinked with another kind of conflict (between women workers and their employers).

4   It was notable that women assemblers I interviewed (Glucksmann, 1990) who had previously worked as domestic servants stressed the advantages of their new employment in terms of the relative freedom of time they gained.

5   On this point see also Whipp's (1987) criticisms of E.P. Thompson (1967).

6   See Sullivan (1997) for a recent example avoiding this problem.

7   One of the most successful and comprehensive attempts is Gershuny's notion of 'chains of provision' (1988). This provides a model for analysing the interconnection between technical innovation, production in the money economy, informal production and consumption, and historical changes in time use between them.

8   The main point being made here is that temporality has many dimensions and these require different modes of access and methods of analysis. It is not intended as an argument against time-budget studies, or a criticism of their value or use.

9   Davies (1992b) provides a vivid and detailed account of leisure activities of the time and place which highlights their highly gendered character.

10   Also a weaver, Mrs Hinton went on to work in engineering factories assembling computers when the weaving sheds closed down in the 1960s.

11   The situation with regard to household income and finance was similar: managing money did not confer control or ownership over it (see Pahl, 1989).

12   A study of the growth of domestic servants in contemporary Britain comes close to such an interpretation. Imprecise definition of the term leads Gregson and Lowe (1994) to imply that cleaners enjoy more 'control' over their work, notably over the amount of time they work and their organisation of working time, in comparison with nannies who are not only professionally qualified but also command considerably higher rates of pay.

13   Evidence of these weekly routines from my own interviews is corroborated for Rochdale by Abendstern (1986), and for Bolton in the large oral history project, *Growing Up in Bolton* (1981–3).

14   The Mass Observation (1939) investigation into 'motives and methods' of clothes washing in Bolton (see Chapter 2) reveals variability in washing routines amongst weavers, and also between weavers and Bolton women more generally. However, because it treats all women homogeneously as 'housewives', regardless of their paid occupations, these variations are hardly commented on, except in terms of the 'efficiency' or 'intelligence' of particular women. As the report's author deems certain methods and traditions (including the communal rule of Monday as washday) as outdated and 'unintelligent' she would certainly view weavers with their greater flexibility as more 'modern' and 'rational' than those women who remained constrained by prevailing local customs.

15   Again, clothes washing would be a good example. For weavers it was a private matter, an unemotive topic, over which they had made a personal decision. They might use bagwash, a laundrette, their own washing machine, or pay another woman. Their identity was in no way tied to the cleanliness of their washing. But the casual women workers discussed washing at great length. They often did it in company, at the wash-house where everyone could see what everybody else was doing. Clean washing, visible to others, was a source of pride and congratulation. It was easy to understand their resistance to having their own washing machine at home.

16   This is not the only problem with the notion of 'commodified time'. It also presses too many issues together in one concept, and thereby effectively reduces time to one of its aspects. With the development of capitalism it is labour power that is commodified rather than time as such, although this of course has consequences for the organisation of time. (Marx talks not about the commodification of time but rather makes the issue of time and its control and organisation dependent on commodified labour.) The 'regularising' of time is also a response to the consequences of commodification and individuation of labour but it is a process distinct from 'commodification'. It frequently has its origins in the state rather than the market, viz. legislation on hours of work, night shifts, etc. which sometimes seeks to moderate the consequences of commodification of labour. Writings on 'commodified time' often seem to be using this term as a proxy for 'commodified labour'. Thanks to John Holmwood for teasing out these issues.

17   Employers' ability to loosen up and 'flexibilise' time involves for employees not only an extension of commodified labour and hence time, but also enforced adaptation to work/ time regimes where the employment equivalent of 'just in time' replaces the standard working day and overtime, and also exposure to new forms of regulation and surveillance of time. In this way, the multiple temporalities of today represent no less a dominant form of temporality than the single form that supposedly preceded it.

18   The role of religion in establishing the timing and cycle of routines, especially in rural communities, is well known to historians. The leisure media represent an important contemporary organising principle of temporality: as ever wider sections of the population acquired radio and TV in their own homes, whole nations plugged into clock time and GMT, watching the same programmes at the same time.

Chapter 6
So near and yet so far

Explorations in space

'Phoebe Street'

'I was born just over there, about 25 yards from here' was Hilda Walker's answer to the question 'Where do you come from?'. She pointed out of the window to show where she meant. 'This row of houses was Phoebe Street'.

'Here' was a comfortable and well-decorated bungalow in the sheltered accommodation section of a council estate of low-rise houses in the Ordsall part of Salford. But, looking out of the window, interviewee and interviewer 'saw' quite different things. It was clear that Hilda still saw Phoebe Street as it had been when she was young: its back-to-back houses, the narrow road, grocer's shop and the little library. All I could see 'there', across the main road, was a dismal row of boarded-up shops, which looked as if they had been derelict for some time, their broken windows protected by sheets of plywood, the doors and remaining plate glass covered with metal grilles. Behind them, all around, obscuring the horizon, were blocks of high-rise flats. From our ground level position, only the lowest six of the 20 or so storeys of the nearest block were visible, and this was the main view from Hilda's front room.

The image of Hilda pointing out of that window stuck in my mind. It said so much about her attachment to Phoebe Street, literal and emotional. Despite the fact of it having been totally transformed, Hilda could see the area as it had been many years ago, while to me, according to my research diary, 'it looked like wasteland, urban anomie incarnate'.

Hilda was born in 1917. 'So I've not moved much', she said, 'twenty-five yards from where I was born.' She has lived in and around the no-longer existing Phoebe Street all her life, but only since 1970, after slum clearance and rebuilding of the area, in housing with a purpose-built bathroom, inside toilet and running hot water.

Of course, Hilda also saw the place as it is now. So much so, in fact, that she and her friend Agnes Brown insisted I move my car within direct view of the window so that we could keep a constant eye on it. Kids had taken to setting fire to tyres, they told me, and three cars had been burnt out in recent days. They kept breaking off from the interview to check outside, even though it was broad daylight and we were on a main road with buses.

The picture of Hilda looking out of her window is suggestive of two themes to be explored in this chapter. 'Uneven development' in the modernisation of housing might be a short-hand summary of the first, and here the terms 'patchwork' and 'leapfrogging' will be introduced to help refine the analysis of unevenness. The general focus will be on spatial variation in the condition of housing, the provision of domestic infrastructure (gas, electricity, sewage, running hot water), the state of domestic architecture (purpose-built bathrooms, inside toilets and kitchens), and the extent to which women used technological domestic appliances. All these factors are crucial to the performance of domestic labour, their nature and, indeeed, their presence or absence having far-reaching effects for those charged with doing the domestic labour. At a social structural level they also have far-reaching implications for the manner in which the household economy is connected to the formal economy of markets, commodities and wages. The difference in housing conditions between the Greater Manchester area and the South East where I had conducted my previous research was quite dramatic. In the Greater London area the majority of people I interviewed had moved into new suburban housing from the 1930s, whereas many in the North West endured very poor conditions for a further 30 to 40 years. This difference suggests the importance of the spatial dimension to the process of transformation in the relation between household and market economies. In addition to this large regional difference, considerable variation also existed, with respect to all the aspects of the modernisation of housing mentioned above, even within my small sample from Greater Manchester, so indicating a 'patchwork' of local spatial division.

The provision of infrastructural facilities in the home is normally understood to be the precondition for labour-saving domestic appliances. There is not much sense in getting a fridge unless you also have the electricity or gas to run it. In order to fulfil their function hot water taps rely on a source of power. But are the stages of what follows what really so straightforward or unilinear? Does the trajectory of housing – infrastructure – facilities – appliances always follow the same pattern? If, as the evidence of some of the weavers suggests, it is possible to 'leapfrog' a stage or two, or if, as some casual women workers suggested, the same person might be extremely positive about acquiring some new facilities in the home while being equally negative about others, then we might need to think again about the arrival and history of the 'ideal home'. I hope to show, therefore, that bringing a spatial perspective to bear on such questions, may enhance their analysis more generally.

The second theme concerns people's rootedness in and attachments to places and localities, their sense of 'home' and accounts of 'what it's like round like'. Here I shall argue that appreciating the significance of locality and of locally-based discourses is a quite different matter for researcher and researched. For the researcher it involves standing back and placing the actors' discourses within a broader analysis of that particular locality, its specific characteristics, how it came to be formed as it is, whether and how it is to be distinguished from other localities. To do so does not involve counterposing a 'structural' against a 'cultural' approach since people's understandings of locality are integral elements of that locality, and may be actively constitutive of it, especially in memory. But it is nevertheless possible to think about why localism is more salient in some localities than others. Nor does a focus on localities need to imply the 'locality determinism' that was so heavily self-critiqued by geographers in the early 1990s. Suggesting that a local area is distinctive does not mean suggesting that the distinctiveness is endogenously 'caused' by what is local to the area. Very few places, surely, are hermetically sealed, and certainly none contain within themselves their own hermetically sealed explanation. Such an analytical perspective, however, although quite unexceptional theoretically, departs from the implication of much of the testimony I collected, when people's accounts of where they lived seemed very often to suggest that the place contains its own explanation.

Space, place and time

Before embarking on these matters, however, it may be helpful to discuss further the approach to be adopted.

As an academic discipline geography appears to have undergone dramatic change over the last 20 years, its most basic concepts up for questioning. Geopolitical realignments of world power blocs in the 1980s; advances in information and communication technology which permit places all over the world to be instantly in electronic contact with each other; the break-up of the Soviet bloc; the emergence of new 'units of belonging', and their attendant new nationalisms, regionalisms and ethnicities and the wars fought on their behalf, particularly in Europe; the rise of new zones of power, both economic and military, notably in the Far East and Pacific Rim. It is obvious that developments like these would have an enormous impact on spatial relations, reshaping the world in fundamental ways which are only partially captured by the buzz phrases that gained popular usage such as 'globalisation', 'the local and the global', the 'stretching' of time and space. In coming to terms with these changing realities geographers were remarkably open to other disciplines and especially to the new ways of thinking emerging in philosophy and cultural studies.[1] The ideas of such diverse thinkers as Raymond Williams, Clifford Geertz, Pierre Bourdieu, Michel Foucault and Stuart Hall cropped up regularly in the texts I consulted for this chapter, and geographers seemed as (or more?) concerned with discussing 'metaphors of travel and home' and contributing to debates about embodiment and landscape, or the heritage industry and 'invented tradition', as with their more mainstream subject matter like patterns of international capital, spatial divisions in economic restructuring, the city and urban environment, or the journey to work.

Not only did geography open up and out in the most fruitful and stimulating ways, but its new perspectives were also been taken up by emergent fields of study in the realignment of social science disciplines in the 1990s. Perhaps it became easier for others to acknowledge the significance of the spatial once disciplinary barriers were lowered and geography liberated from its traditional concerns.[2] Certainly sociology adopted spatial concepts – superceding those of biology or linguistics on which it had relied in earlier times to describe social relations and process. The ubiquitous 'mapping' springs immediately to mind, but so too do terms such as 'locating', 'inscription', 'zones', 'sedimentation', 'boundaries', and more.

But is there also a downside to the profound self-scrutiny to which geography subjected itself? Eagerness to deconstruct basic concepts and avoid using terms which were previously undertheorised could well involve a tendency to throw out the baby with the bath water, to deny that there is anything distinctive about spatial relations, or even that place could be a legitimate subject for study.

Feminist geographers have long been at the forefront of critique, from the early publications of the 'Women and Geography Group' to the more recent work of Doreen Massey, Linda McDowell and Gillian Rose. All have demonstrated the thoroughly gendered nature of geography's frameworks and substantive concerns, and attempted to reformulate the agenda.[3] Gillian Rose, for example, draws attention to masculinist thinking underpinning the two quite distinct approaches of time geography and human geography. The former is criticised for 'social scientific masculinism', its belief in the transparency, and infinite knowability of space, and its unproblematised and naturalistic search for totality and perfect representation. These characteristics of time geography, Rose argues, effectively deny the domestic and private, and exclude consideration of possibilities that may be opaque, unamenable to measurement, Other, and women (Rose, 1993: 38–40). Humanistic geography, on the other hand, suffers from what she terms 'aesthetic masculinity', a different kind of masculinist thinking which does acknowledge the feminine, but only as undifferentiated 'Woman' rather than as women. Its humanistic concern is with places, conceived as laden with meaning and significance which call for reflexive interpretation. This approach, Rose suggests, 'feminizes its notion of place' (1993: 45) with claims 'that home is the exemplar of place' (1993: 53). The home/place of humanistic geography is an essentialist, conflict-free, nurturing idealisation that few women would recognise. The conflation of Woman and place denies both difference between women and the multiplicity of possible relationships of actual women with home and place, thus effectively erasing women:

> Place becomes the feminized Other in the discourse of humanistic geography, idealized as 'Woman', spoken of in terms of the (lost) mother. (Rose, 1993: 60)

Rose's unmasking of the hidden conceptual underpinning of 'place' should act as a deterrent against any innocent use of the term. Even more damning were the plethora of arguments marshalled against the notion of 'locality'. 'Locality' was rejected as a flawed concept, by writers representing a variety of different political and philosophical positions, on account of its connotations, variously, of essentialism, nostalgia, romanticism, timelessness, Being (as opposed to Becoming), and localism (as opposed to global factors) as well as for its implication that places exist as bounded, internally coherent and internally explicable entities.[4]

But out of such critiques emerged new and more positive ways of conceptualising space and place, more adequately theorised and capable of addressing new realities without the old problems. It is this new reconstructed geography, premissed unequivocally on the salience of the spatial dimension,[5] that I have found the most helpful for approaching the questions of spatial organisation arising in my research on Lancashire, and especially the work of Doreen Massey. Massey insists on the centrality of both gender and time to thinking in spatial terms, and her starting point (following Henri Lefebvre) is that spatial organisation makes a difference to how society works and how it changes. The spatial form of the social has 'causal effecticity' (Massey, 1994: 255). Thus, rather than being negatively defined in terms of lack, absence or stasis, space is to be conceived as 'a moment in the intersection of configured social relations' (Massey, 1994: 265), constructed out of the complex interlocking of networks of relations across all scales from the most global to the most local. Viewed thus, space could not be conceived as static, any more than time can be conceived as spaceless.

At a more concrete level, this way of thinking about space suggests a relational conception of 'place' as a differentially-located node in a network of relations, unbounded and unstable, as:

> ... particular moments in ... intersecting social relations, nets of which have over time been constructed, laid down, interacted with one another, decayed and renewed. Some of these relations will be ... contained within the place; others will stretch beyond it, tying any particular locality into wider relations and processes in which other places are implicated too.
> (Massey, 1994. 120)

No internal causality here. This is an anti-essentialist conception which acknowledges places, but as open and porous networks, whose understanding must draw on links beyond their boundaries. To recognise the place-based character of social relations does not entail seeing them as place-bound (Massey 1995: 184). The local cannot be explained solely in terms of the local. And, as for the 'identities' of local areas, these are constructed precisely through their interaction with other places rather than by counterposition to them. Such identities may be dominant, they may be multiple, they may be contested, and they change. That the 'character of an area' is not the product of an internalised history, however, does not rule it out as a legitimate subject for investigation.

I have summarised at some length the spatial framework proposed by Massey since it points such a refreshing way forward that is especially pertinent to thinking about Bolton and Salford as localities and to coming to terms with the local identification of many people who lived there. This sort of approach was already implicit in the way issues of place have been treated in earlier chapters. However, it may be worth drawing out more explicitly some of my key 'points of perspective' since they inform the analysis to be developed in this chapter.

First, the central concern when discussing local labour markets and cultures in Chapter 3 was to focus on what it is that goes into the making of a particular locality, to analyse what distinguishes one from another, and what specifically it is about a locality that might make it localistic. Rather than starting at the other end of the chain, and assuming that a locality produces its own locality, this focus requires an explanatory framework sensitive to the mutual interaction of 'inside on outside' and 'outside on inside', which might affect the very boundary between inside and outside.

Second, as with temporality, we are dealing not only with experiences of place, and identities built on that experience, but also with a structure of spatial relations. That structure cannot be reduced to, or understood solely in terms of, how it was experienced, even if the experience is an integral element of the structure.

Third, there is no envelope, or pre-given context, of space into which people and things are fitted. Rather it is the arrangement of things in space, their spatial linkage, that constitutes place. In this connection, Latour's comment on time (Chapter 5) might usefully be paraphrased to suggest that 'it is the arrangement that makes the place, not the place that makes the arrangement.'

Finally, it is evident already that place involves time. Hilda Walker's sense of Phoebe Street was about both past and present. It would be impossible to think about the distinctiveness of localities or the significance of localisms outside of their historical time. Or again, the regional variation in social housing conditions between North West and South East was simultaneously a temporal division, one region experiencing generalised improvement long before the other. Uneven development was thus both spatial and historical. And, a third example, spatial difference in the linkages between infrastructure and appliances, and between household and formal economies, is inseparable from a difference in temporal sequence. Everything substantive, then, that has been said about place so far in this chapter, also involves time, and necessarily so since these two co-ordinates always frame social relations together.

Much that was said in the chapter on time, then, was also, often explicitly, about place. The discussion of the different temporalities of weavers from casual women workers, for example, could also be written in terms of place. It has been difficult, generally, to decide what to discuss where, whether under the heading of temporality or spatiality, since often both are at issue. As with all problems about how to 'slice the cake', there is no ideal solution, and the two chapters are best read in conjunction.

Place matters

Place has already had to be central to the analysis of women's working lives. To gather all spatial analysis together in one chapter, and exclude it from all others, is, interestingly, an unachievable and nonsensical project, for even the compartmentally minded. Thus, comparison of the local employment structures of Salford and Bolton provided a spatial slant on the difference between weavers and casual women workers, without which it would be impossible to understand their respective configurations of home and work. Similarly, the debate about commercialised leisure before the war, and whether or not it formed an important element of Lancashire youth culture, was settled only by focusing on differences between towns. Analysis of juvenile employment statistics revealed, not unexpectedly, that in towns on which social historians based a claim of little change in youth culture since the late nineteenth century, rates of youth unemployment were high. Conversely, they were low in Manchester where cinemas, dance halls and other commercialised leisure activities were most strongly in evidence. The structuring of age could thus be seen to have a spatial dimension and also to have a further spatial effect, adolescence being more strongly demarcated as a separate stage of the life course in some towns, while in others the division between youth and adult was less marked, and generations were defined more on the basis of marital status.

But spatiality is crucial in a more fundamental, and also a more obvious, way. Physical structures and people are linked in space as well as in time and are connected to each other in particular ways which combine to characterise a particular place and to differentiate it from others. A single industry mill town will differ from one where there are both coal mines and weaving sheds. As we have seen, a labour market structured by the proximity of mine and mill has effects for the gender relations of both paid employment and domestic labour, that are absent when weaving is the main occupation for men and women alike.

The decision to site an enormous industrial complex in what became Trafford Park was not just chance. Consideration must have been given to the spatial advantage of the site. Access to Salford docks and to the port of Liverpool via the Manchester–Liverpool canal would be important both for bringing in raw materials and for transporting finished products to their markets. The availability of a suitable labour supply, located conveniently for access to the site, was also important. In the early decades of the twentieth century, the eventual complex of factories and purpose-built avenues of housing in straight lines, brought together tens of thousands of workers and their families within an area of a few square miles. Ford, Kellogg and other American firms produced the most modern of products, including the Model T car and cornflakes, using the most technologically advanced methods of production (Stevens, 1947; Trafford Library Service, 1982; McIntosh, 1991). The workforce was predominantly male and included many migrants, lured by the promise of work from areas of underemployment elsewhere in the country, and notably from Ireland. Primary schools, pubs and churches were also built on the site, and hawkers sold fish, meat and groceries. People who lived there conjured up for oral historians the image of a place that was almost self-contained.

Here was a locality whose character was clearly shaped by its spatial features, local, national and international. Its connection to Detroit, Michigan and other North American industrial centres was crucial to its being. So were the Irish Catholic origins of some of its inhabitants, and the resulting, sometimes uneasy, cohabitation of English and Irish, and Protestant and Catholic (Fielding, 1992). The physical proximity of work to home meant that many men would know each other both as workmates and as neighbours. The absence of work opportunities for married women on the site was also a feature of the place. Wives, unlike their husbands, would either have to travel to work, or to find some informal employment locally. So the women of Trafford Park would be more likely to relate to each other as neighbours. All these spatial characteristics played a part in making Trafford Park the distinctive place it was, and in shaping the diverse experiences of the people who worked and lived there.

Contrast this with nearby Salford. Proximity to the docks was more crucial here than in Trafford Park since it provided one of the main occupations for men, but in casualised conditions like most of the other jobs. Global and local factors intertwined as men who lived within walking distance of their work unloaded imports from all over the world, from the Spanish orange boxes Agnes Brown remembered to heavy engineering equipment from the USA. But, unlike the Trafford Park men who also lived close to where they worked, the Salford homes were back-to-back rows of terraced housing lacking the basic facilities that were built into the new Trafford Park houses.

The irregularity of male income in Salford put pressure on wives to bring in an income, but this was an area where little regular industrial employment was available for married women. Hence the long hours of work, the multiple sequences of jobs, the informal and casual work of married women. The linking in one place of casual work for both men and for women, and the homogeneity of circumstances shared by many, is partly what constitutes the specificity of the locality. Spatial connection produced particular effects which to some extent were accidental. Casual work for men and for women are not inherently complementary but when brought together they produce a particular configuration which combines with other aspects of their social existence (the poor domestic facilities and the municipal wash-house) to structure people's experience and understanding of the place in a distinctive manner.

In each case then (and I have deliberately chosen two places that on the face of it were not so different from each other) the local specificity was shaped by the conjunction of particular sets of spatial relations. If Trafford Park and Salford were distinct localities where similar ways of working and living were common to large sections of inhabitants, then these are what constitute local cultures and local communities. Place does matter, the particular form of spatial connections being both constitutive of and constituted by social relations. Connectivity in space does produce effects, even if that connectivity is itself only a point of space/time intersection.

From her window, Hilda Walker saw both time and place. But her view was also gendered. It was of the street and the houses, of 'home' as the domestic location where she and her family lived, the place where she played as a child, where she came home from school to, where her grandmother and mother went shopping, and where she still lived. It is not simply that such living space was the domain of women but rather that what was remembered as 'home' was rooted in the domestic situation of the house and street she lived in, not Salford docks nor the town centre, nor Trafford Park where she had spent many years as a clerical worker at Metrovicks. It was thus a gendered remembering now of a past that was also gendered. This street, where she came from and where she felt she belonged, was central to Hilda's identity. For her friend, Agnes Brown, the bus conductress, however, the 'private' domestic living aspect of life remembered was not nearly so salient. In telling her life story the relation between past and present seemed much more fractured. Although she was also a lifelong Salfordian, with vivid memories of childhood living conditions, there was no focal point of reference like Hilda's Phoebe Street. Agnes talked far more about Salford in general, the docks, the hospital, the state of sanitation, but usually in relation to the changing circumstances of her own growing up and subsequent working life. Listening to her, the place in the past was long gone. It could not be recaptured by looking out of any window, but nor would Agnes seek to recapture it.

The next two sections look at some of the varied interconnectivities of people and place, exploring and bringing together different dimensions both of locality and localism, the forms of attachment and identifiction with place. The intention is not to define what Salford or Bolton, or anywhere else, were like; rather, it is to see how certain dimensions of localities and localism hang together, for instance how the defiant pride of some Salfordians is part of – not just a discourse about – the locality, and just as situated in place and time.

Spatial divisions of domestic living

Communities of women

Although most pronounced in Salford, all the women interviewed detailed customs local to their area. This contrasted markedly with my earlier research on women's assembly line work in the new mechanised industries of south-east England where there had been no such reference to local customs. None of the women I interviewed in the Greater London area had ever spoken of 'what its like round here' or of community-based traditions. When talking of their childhoods or their mothers' domestic routines, they were more likely to elaborate a notion of family culture, referring to what had happened in their own particular family ('Mum expected the girls to ...'); or they spoke in terms of 'the' past, contrasting this with the present ('in those days we used to ...'), but this was a past that was not rooted, in their description at least, in a particular place. The portrayal of domestic routines by women in Salford, Oldham, Rochdale or Bolton was quite different. Here depictions of 'bucket night', of washing methods and standards, of donkeying the steps, or of the acceptable limits on husbands' drinking or gambling all suggested local customs carrying the force of a rigidified social rule, or at least strong informal pressure.

However, it is important to appreciate that the operation of such norms depends on certain circumstances, and that these will not affect equally everyone living in the same area. A similar point was made in Chapter 5 in relation to the temporality of the public/private division when I suggested that casual women workers were more rooted than weavers in community and neighbourhood networks. Home and work, and public and private, intersected differently for the two groups and this affected the significance of their immediate locality for each. For casual women workers there was considerable overlap of family, home, neighbourhood, work and community, while for weavers these were more differentiated. For weavers, washing was just washing, a practical household matter. Unlike the casual women workers, they did not consider the whiteness of their linen either as source of self-esteem or any business of their neighbours.

The phrase 'communities of women' enjoyed wide currency during the first decade of feminist history when attention to the private and domestic lives, especially of working class women, 'uncovered' networks of support in which women living in conditions of urban poverty, male supremacy or other shared straightened circumstances helped each other out on a regular basis with mutual aid of all kinds, practical, financial and emotional. Within a perspective which saw women and men as inhabiting the 'separate spheres' of private and public, exploration of informal but collective forms of organisation of women drew attention to a place where women did wield some power and possess some authority. This redressed an earlier somewhat 'victim'-oriented focus on women's exclusion from formal and public arenas for the exercise of power and decision making. Powerful matriarchs (Chinn, 1988) were seen as counterweights to male domination, and the role of gossip was highlighted as a means of enforcing local norms and as sanction against those who did not conform. Later work along these lines (e.g. Ross, 1989; Tebbutt, 1992) largely avoids the earlier romanticism by situating reciprocal networks in the context of the specific circumstances which engender and perpetuate them.

However, to interpret local networks as 'communities of women' still risks essentialising place. More precisely, in terms of the present discussion, it risks essentialising locality as female. It also implies that communities of women were homogeneous, comprised of women who were all in the same boat, confronting similar sets of problems in similar conditions. But this was certainly not the case for the buyers and sellers of domestic goods and services outlined in Chapter 3. I argued there that domestic service type relations between women living in the same neighbourhood should not be viewed in terms of simple reciprocity or redistribution between equals. Rather, a hierarchy of inequalities existed between working class women in the same locality. This did not mean there was no network. On the contrary, those who bought childcare or washing services relied on the sellers of such services in order to engage in their own employment, just as much as the sellers relied on the buyers for their owns means of livelihood. A network based on women in dissimilar economic circumstances, which ties them together in a particular, but unequal way, is just as much a network as any other. But whether or not such a community-based network could be called a 'community of women' (with its connotations of equality) is less certain.

'Uneven development'

'Uneven development' between regions[6] shaped not only industries and job opportunities, and the formal indicators of economic expansion or decline. Housing and the basic conditions of domestic living were also affected. Thus, economic development in the areas where new industries were located also brought with it the construction of new housing and the beginnings of mass consumption of domestic consumer products. The processes were interconnected. They complemented each other, as integrated features of the new 'total social organisation of labour' which emerged with the consolidation of mass production and consumption. When analysing the spiral of interconnections between women's role in both production and consumption of new domestic products (Glucksmann, 1990: 226–8), the regional dimension was perhaps insufficiently highlighted. Concentrating on the 'upward' spiral, I did not follow through the implications for housing and domestic standards in areas where the spiral was downward. In fact these reached deep into the fabric of people's homes, their domestic power supply, their water system, and their toilets. It took the research in Lancashire to reach a fuller appreciation of the connections.

Several allusions have been made to the very poor living conditions experienced by many interviewees. Perhaps the most extreme example was Ernie, born in 1899, who started working in a mill at the age of 12 and remained employed in mill work as a ring spinner, then overlooker, for the next 63 years. He and his wife enjoyed few mod cons at home. Their first access to an inside toilet and bath came only when they moved into sheltered accommodation in Oldham in 1981, when Ernie was already 81 years old.

It was not quite so bad for most of the people I interviewed, but a very high proportion of those, particularly, but not only, in Salford, lived in run-down privately rented accommodation into the late 1960s. Landlords made few improvements to the houses, and if residents wanted gas appliances, fireplaces rather than ranges, a bath or modernised kitchen they had to organise and pay for it themselves. Amy Fowler heated water in a copper and used a tin bath until 1966. Her husband Harry lived in the same two-up two-down house from birth in 1923 until he was rehoused in a slum clearance programme in 1968. Only then did Harry have proper heating, a bathroom and toilet. His parents had brought up seven children in the house, and his mother took in washing to make ends meet, using a boiler to heat water and hanging linen and clothes to dry in the kitchen. Electricity was installed just before the war, but only for lighting. When his mother was ailing Harry used the light socket for an electric fire to warm her bedroom. Mary Gouden, the senior secretary at Metrovicks, bought two gas rings during the war for her mother to cook on and later had a gas geyser installed. The landlord would put a gas fire only in the front room. The first two of Vera Rogers' five children were born into a house with no hot water or bath and only gas lighting. She had to heat water on a stove and paid for the installation of a modern fireplace. Agnes Brown's husband put in a gas boiler to replace the old brick one and she paid for electricity to be laid on, but had to wait until after the War. But she had no bath or toilet until she was eventually rehoused. By the early 1970s most had been rehoused in high-rise council blocks. Several went straight into sheltered accommodation as they were already pensioners.

The list could go on, but let it finish with an example I was particularly struck by, Flo Nuttall's 'best birthday present' when she turned 40. She described the cold and dark outside toilet where:

> we used to take candles in and have lighted paper. They had a window with a little ledge and you stick your candle there, and there was all candle grease running down ... And you didn't have toilet paper, you tore newspaper up with a string. You never had toilet paper did you?

But:

> For my fortieth birthday I'd been working and I came in. I had a small boy that next door used to look after while I was out, and I thought 'he's lit a fire in the the toilet'. I could see a red light coming from underneath it. And I went and opened the door, and inside there was a big piece of cardboard 'Happy Birthday'. Me brother had been and put a light in. It was the best birthday present I had ...

The year was 1956!

These instances provide ample evidence of the housing side of spatial inequality and 'uneven development'. The conditions which persisted on a quite extensive scale until well into the 1960s in parts of the North West were to be found only in smaller pockets in more prosperous areas of the country. Of course they did exist elsewhere but usually as the exception rather than the rule. In both research projects I had asked retired women workers when the main changes had occurred in their lives. Virtually all those in the Greater London area highlighted the War, and drew a clear distinction between before and after the War. Their conditions of living improved dramatically between the late 1930s and early 1950s. For the majority in Lancashire, however, the

War held no such significance. They drew the line between old and new much later, in the 1960s or 1970s, or whenever it was they acquired modernised homes.

The 'patchwork' of Greater Manchester

It would be as wrong to generalise about housing conditions across Greater Manchester in the 1930s as about the incidence of unemployment. The time-scale of rounds of restructuring differed between places that were quite close to each other. Early in the twentieth century, the back-to-back houses in Ancoats, in city centre Manchester, which Engels had described as new replacements for the unhygienic hovels of the industrial revolution were already becoming slums, due for replacing again.[7] No doubt the Salford houses which survived until the 1960s had been built much later than those in Ancoats. Thus, while poor housing was commonplace in Salford in the middle decades of the twentieth century, the conurbation as a whole resembled a 'patchwork', conditions varying quite considerably from one part to another, depending partly on their particular histories and their position in a cycle of expansion and decline.

Variation in the time-scale of rounds of economic restructuring was probably the most important factor underlying the patchwork of housing quality. In Manchester a diversified set of new industries, including many in the retail and service sectors, had been established from the early years of the twentieth century as the cotton textile industry declined (Clay and Brady, 1929; Daniels and Jewkes, 1932; Pullen and Williams, 1962; Smith, 1969). The earliest and largest industrial estate in the world, Trafford Park, was at the forefront of economic development, attracting inward investment from across the UK and the USA (McIntosh, 1991). And so it was only to be expected that in parts of Manchester there would also be a renewal of housing in the inter-war years, involving extensive slum clearance and the building of municipal housing estates in the suburbs. The experience of central Manchester with respect to these connected developments was arguably more similar to that of London than to the towns surrounding Manchester where dependence on cotton was not relieved by equivalent economic restructuring.

By no means all the 35,000 people who worked at Trafford Park in 1935 lived in the 'village' on the estate.[8] A vast network of trams, trains and buses serviced the site, and many came by bicycle. Given the size of capital investment and the large numbers of workers and residents who spent their waking lives in Trafford Park, a correlative investment in shops and canteens might have been expected. But in this respect there was a disjunction between the development for production of goods and for the daily reproduction of workers and residents. Although very modern in one way, it was quite old fashioned in another. True, Trafford Park estate houses were purpose-built and contained all the latest basic facilities of their time, which were so attractive to would-be tenants. Churches, schools, doctors' surgeries and other communal services also came, contributing to the self-contained 'village' atmosphere described earlier in this chapter. But first-hand accounts of residents collected by the Manchester Studies Group shortly before demolition of the houses in the early 1980s are surprising for their portrayal of a street life which seems strangely at odds with living adjacent to one of the most advanced industrial sites. Outdoor games, local football teams, allotments, a thriving pawn shop, the wash-house, mutual support between women, the barrel-organ woman, the lamp-lighter and the knocker-up who knocked on the window for five pence a week: these are reminiscent of an epoch prior to the modern technology on which Trafford Park's reputation was based. While Model Ts were rolling off the production lines, the wives of Ford's employees were buying goods not from shops but from hawkers with ponies and carts:

> Everything came down the back-entries, everything: coal, fish, butcher, greengroceries, they all came down with their carts, some with the little pony, some with the hand-carts, and brought the stuff round. You bought nearly all your eatable stuff ... at the back entry, it was there. They'd just come round shouting out, yes, 'Fish', yes ... On a Saturday night another fella came down with a cart with a chimney on it and you'd buy a bag of peas for a penny, mushy peas; that did well ... Oh aye, there was a lot of things come round ... the wives used to go out and pick the pieces of meat and vegetables, oh yes, they were there ...
> (quoted in Russell and Walker, 1979: 33)

In the absence of canteens some women turned their front parlours into cafés and sold hot meals to workers at lunch time:

> they used to set them out in their front rooms and proper like tables, white cloths and things, and they used to come from the works. My sister was one, she used to go and have her dinner in a private house ... very reasonably priced ... all nicely served. It was just a little way of making money ...
> (Russell and Walker, 1979, Manchester Studies, Lily Brophy Tape, 755)

This sounds similar to the sort of service sold by casual women workers. Later on, though, by the outbreak of war, many firms did open their own canteens and selling dinners dried up as a source of income. The same woman continues:

> When Auntie Lil first opened up there were no canteens, everybody flocked there – as many as it would hold but when the works got their own canteen that's when business fell off you see.
> (Russell and Walker, 1979, Manchester Studies, Lily Brophy Tape, 755)

The uneven development between consumption and production on the Trafford Park estate adds a further complication to the spatial patchwork of older and newer across the conurbation. And it was, evidently, a highly gendered dimension of unevenness, affecting paid employment and domestic labour differentially, and also men and women, since primarily male labour was engaged to operate the advanced technology while women undertook the servicing and domestic labour.

Across the city, on the new Wythenshawe housing estate, more deliberate attempts were being made to reshape domestic life, and with it marital and gender relations. Manchester's municipal authorities undertook a vast rebuilding programme in the 1930s to alleviate the problems of old and overcrowded housing (Hughes and Hunt, 1992). By 1939, 30,000 homes had been built, many in the style of cottages on suburban estates. Wythenshawe, where building commenced in 1930, was the largest of these: it contained a third of all council homes in Manchester built during the decade and by 1939 was home to 35,000. These houses dated from a later period than those of Trafford Park, and their design was influenced by a more explicit ethos of social engineering. Rents were high and the unemployed were barred from tenancy. Thus, most tenants of the new housing were families with a skilled male worker in regular employment rather than families from the cleared slums of inner-city areas. Many of the latter could not afford the rents and moved close to their previous dwelling (Hughes and Hunt, 1992: 79).

Not only were Wythenshawe's homes to be 'fit for heroes', but the tenants were also to be worthy of their new well-appointed dwellings. Integral to the ethos of respectability demanded of tenants was what became widely known in feminist history in the 1970s as an 'ideology of domesticity' (e.g. Hall, 1977). This promoted a division between husband and wife as earner and housewife respectively, a privatised nuclear unit living in a house whose cleanliness and comfort both strived for and took pride in. With the enhanced status of the housewife, the physical layout and equipment of houses assumed a new importance: they had to be modern, efficient and hygienic, facilitating the wife's duties as scientific household manager. Wythenshawe's designer insisted, on the grounds of the health of women and children, that all sculleries should face south, whether this was at the back or the front because 'the housewife spends nine hours in the scullery for one she spends in the living room' (Barry Parker, quoted in Hughes and Hunt, 1992: 83) and they would thus have the greatest exposure to sunshine.

Most of Wythenshawe's residents in the early years were, not surprisingly given the circumstances, families with small children and a non-earning wife. There were few employment opportunities for married women in the vicinity in any case, and most husbands had a much longer journey to work. Although women tenants were full of praise for the design and facilities inside the house, they were critical of the estate's drawbacks: increased expense, a total absence of communal and recreational facilities, and no shops nearby. They felt cut off. The priority given to the provision of private rather than communal public facilities in the eventual design of the estate had been the result of political decision and it was not gained without a struggle. Feminist Labour Councillor Hannah Mitchell's pressure for the public wash-houses to be built in every district led some scurrilous critics to suggest that:

> *Mrs Mitchell would go as far as to omit washboilers and ovens too –*
> *from all future corporation estates, so that communal arrangements for*
> *cooking as well as for washing may become a matter of course.*
> (*The Woman Citizen*, January 1930, quoted in Hughes and Hunt, 1992: 95)

On another new housing estate at Belle Vue, Gorton, which, unlike Wythenshawe, did count a majority of former residents from slum clearance schemes among its tenants, similar criticisms were made. Rents were higher for 93 per cent of tenants, as were fares, and half had further to travel to work (Manchester University Settlement, 1944: 10). On the other hand, the wartime survey appears to underestimate women's enthusiasm for running hot water: the finding that 99.5 per cent of respondents 'liked the method of water heating' is reported as 'general approval for the hot water supply' (Manchester University Settlement, 1944: 12)!

The primacy of private over communal facilities in Wythenshawe, and the disjunction between production and consumption in Trafford Park were imbalances of different kinds, adding to the complexity of the patchwork of 'uneven development' of Manchester. In each case the imbalance had consequences for the relation between home and work for residents, the gendering of those consequences profoundly affected by the spatial characteristics of the respective estates.

'Leapfrogging'

I want to look now at the evidence of domestic modernisation from a different angle, and discuss what was earlier termed 'leapfrogging'. If 'patchwork' is a term designed to indicate the close spatial juxtaposition of 'ancient' and 'modern', 'leapfrogging' is designed to suggest their temporal juxtapositon within the course of people's lives. It is already apparent from the patchy and uneven nature of housing conditions and infrastructural provision that there was no one single preordained route to modernisation and no unilinear sequence of development of housing, followed by infrastructure, followed by facilities and finally appliances. Considerable variation was evident even amongst the people I interviewed. So far in this chapter I have drawn primarily on the experience of people who endured very poor housing conditions until relatively late. The majority had themselves installed facilities so as to modernise power and water systems, buying cookers to replace open ranges, or new style fireplaces, laying on electricity, and acquiring geysers and baths. Modern equipment such as this must have stood in some contrast to the ancient fabric of the housing stock which contained it.

It would be misleading to suggest that all had to contend with poor housing. There was a systematic difference in this respect between casual women workers and weavers, and connected with this, between those living in Salford and those living elsewhere. Many of the weavers had not only bought their own houses, or moved into new housing in the 1930s, but they had also acquired domestic appliances around the same time and almost as soon as these came on the market. Quite a number had washing machines before the war and vacuum cleaners and fridges soon after, long before the people I had researched in the South East. Edith Ashworth was probably the most 'advanced' in this respect: she had bath, fridge and washing machine by 1938. But others were not that far behind, acquiring one or two major domestic appliances in the 1950s. Marjorie Fisher, Alice Foster and Nellie Lynch, all weavers like Edith Ashworth, fell into this grouping, as did Vera Rogers who was not. When looking earlier at this phenomenon my focus was on different modes of domestic labour undertaken by women working full-time. Edith Ashworth and company provided evidence of a pattern of commoditised domestic labour where tasks were achieved on the basis of purchasing either services or, in this case, domestic appliances. Doing their own washing at home with the aid of an electric machine was unusual for the time. In the South East women workers had often used commercial laundries in the 1930s, followed by laundrettes in the 1950s and 1960s, and only later did they emulate Edith Ashworth. Many of the Salford women were notable for their enthusiasm for the municipal wash-house. They did not not want to give it up until forced to by its closure. Indeed, the same Flo Nuttal who was so delighted with the electric light in the outside toilet was vehemently opposed to having a washing machine in her own kitchen, to the extent of giving away the one her son bought her.

The point now to be drawn from these examples is a different one from the ability or otherwise of women to undertake domestic labour on the basis of purchased commodities. It relates rather to the trajectory of domestic modernisation, and to possible misreading of the history of the 'ideal home'. Having a washing machine in a house with an outside toilet would be a clear instance of 'leapfrogging', when one facility precedes another one which would normally be expected to come first. Although this particular example was not very common (only one case), the variety of mismatching heating, washing, and sanitary facilities that women had in their kitchens and bathrooms provided compelling evidence of such 'leapfrogging'. Older and newer pieces of equipment seemed to co-exist in the same house to a surprising extent, and to follow each other in an unexpected order. Present day social historians who look back at the process of domestic modernisation, now long completed, have the benefit of several decades of hindsight and this might encourage a more unilinear account of 'what followed what', or 'what went with what' than is warranted. After all, looking back from the end-point of a finished process, and determining how it was achieved, involves a different set of questions than looking forward from the beginning or intermediate phases when the outcome was uncertain, and other directions could have been taken than those that were eventually. The evidence from Lancashire certainly suggests not only 'leapfrogging' but also a multiplicity of routes rather than a simple, single, neat and tidy sequence of modernising one aspect after another. There was no simple or gradual replacement of old houses and old facilities by the 'ideal home' but rather a renewal that was more jerky and messy, more hiccups than smooth transitions.

Towards what 'ideal home'?

Nor was everybody drawn towards the same goal of an 'ideal home'. Neither Mrs Ashworth and those women who bought washing machines very early, nor Annie Preston, Agnes Brown and the others who were so attached to the wash-house, talked about their houses or household equipment in terms that could suggest pride in the home itself. 'Practically needed it' was Mrs Ashworth's reason for getting her washine machine. Her matter-of-fact tone suggests that for her the machine served only the purpose for which it was technically designed, easing the burden of the weekly wash. It was not part of a project of creating the 'ideal home' nor evidence of a new form of domesticity. Nor was it something to show off to her neighbours, since she saw her washing as none of their business. Similarly, when Agnes Brown or Vera Rogers had their kitchens renewed or Ivy Turner and Mary Gouden installed modern fireplaces, they gave the impression of doing so purely for reasons of convenience and ease. In both cases the notion of the 'ideal home' as an objective to strive for seems inappropriate. It was of little appeal to the better off weavers whose identity was tied more closely to their working lives than to their domestic situation, and unrealistic for the women whose poor quality housing placed limits on improvement.

This should not be surprising in so far as promotion of 'ideal homes' (by construction companies, firms manufacturing domestic equipment, and women's magazines) formed part of an ideological package[9] which also included a 'non-working' 'housewife', and a particular form of privatised domesticity, which were characteristic of neither group of women. The weavers were in a financial position to buy consumer durables: being employed was both a condition of their purchasing power and also the reason why they 'needed' the labour-saving equipment. In no sense did they go out to work *in order to* buy modern appliances. Nor was there any hint from the poorer women that they would have desired all the modern accoutrements of the home even if they could have afforded them. Indeed, Flo Nuttall's attitude to the washing machine suggests the contrary, as did her and others' fulsome eulogies of the municipal wash-house. These women enjoyed the sociability and did not want to do the washing in their own kitchens when they could get it washed, dried and ironed in one sitting in the wash-house in company and have a bath at the same time. Thus they discriminated between the different equipment facilitating household tasks: although certain aspects of modernisation and particular appliances were warmly welcomed there was no blanket desire to have them all, and certainly not inside the home.

The same was true also of the Belle Vue residents: despite being so positive about running hot water, their appraisal of inside toilets, for example, was far more equivocal

> There is general dissatisfaction with the position of the w.c. 33.3% of the tenants would rather have it upstairs than down, and 41.6% would like it to be outside the house altogether ... Many do not like it to be near the kitchen or the living room because of the noise of the flushing cistern. A few dislike the publicity of a lavatory near the front door.
> (Manchester University Settlement, 1944: 11)

If Hannah Mitchell had had her way perhaps the history of the modernisation of domestic labour might have taken a different course, with more public facilities, and contemporary equivalents of the washhouse. Certainly it would have been easier to separate out the benefits and drawbacks of the equipment from the division of labour between husband and wife, and social separation of private from public that linked 'ideal housewife' with 'ideal home'.

'Uneven development' involved far more than the division between South East and North West. It was complicated by the existence of many kinds of interconnectivities and by the complex patchwork of variations, the very concept itself being rendered problematic by the multiplicity of routes to and forms of 'modernisation'. Changes in consumption and the acquisition of domestic appliances appeared to be less dependent on housing improvement in the North West than the South East. At one level, the transition of the relation between market and household economy, and, at another, between married women's paid employment and the purchase of labour-saving consumer durables, had different trajectories in the two regions, and even within different parts of the same region, especially in the North West. The different elements had different time-scales and meshed together in different temporal sequences. Here again we come across the impossibility of abstracting spatial variation out of time and differences of temporality from space and place.

Localism

'What it's like round here.'

I was immediately struck when listening to people's testimonies at how frequently they referred to 'what it's like round here'. All the people I interviewed explained their situation in such terms whether in Oldham, Little Hulton, Salford, Bolton or anywhere else. Localism seemed central to every dimension of their existence and also to structure their understanding of life. They gave highly articulate accounts of local culture and tradition, often prefacing what they had to say about women's methods of washing household linen, the leisure activities pursued by young people, whether husbands gave housekeeping allowances or 'tipped up', whether or not married women worked, by 'well, you see, round here we ...'. And in their accounts it seemed as though Bolton just was 'like this' and Salford just 'like that', Salford especially acquiring mythic status in the representation of its inhabitants. Local traditions were elevated almost to explanatory principles, and presented as if *sui generis* and in no need of further explanation.

People seemed not to have been familiar with the very different, but apparently equally immutable, local customs or with the different job opportunities in towns less than 15 miles away. Some of the women interviewed in Oldham, who had been unemployed as cotton workers during the depression of the 1930s, described having 'walked their feet off', or said they had worn out numerous pairs of shoes looking for work in the local mills. But their search was limited to places with which they were already familiar. They did not consider travelling the 20 minutes to look for work in Manchester where unemployment was comparatively low and a variety of jobs were available for young women. Their horizons were restricted to a radius of a few miles only. They may well have had good reasons for not looking further afield, such as the cost of transport, or as skilled workers they may naturally have been reluctant to look for employment of a lower level. But what was significant was that no reasons were offered, as if explanation was unnecessary. They did not mention alternative possibilities, implying either that they had been unaware of them, or had discounted them because they were not in Oldham.

Beliefs about local tradition also included the diverse and divergent notions of femininity and masculinity that I described in relation to weavers and casual workers. In Salford the widely acknowledged expectation was for the man to think and act as 'boss' of the house; paid work was integral to Bolton women's self-identity in a way that it was not in Salford. In Salford a sharp distinction was drawn between married and unmarried women, but not in Bolton where marriage appeared not to have the same significance as the rite of passage to a different kind of life.

The depth of belief about local identity, and the strength of localism, tell us much about the significance of place in the various towns, and about the specificity of that significance. Here I discuss some of the problems involved in confronting, and suggest ways of interpreting and assessing, the varying importance of 'localisms' (in the plural), especially for women, bearing in mind that varieties of localism exist both within and between places.

Although Hilda Walker and Agnes Brown were both from Salford I have suggested that the meaning of the locality was different for each of them, Hilda being attached to the Salford streets of her childhood, while Agnes viewed Salford as the town, its landmarks and institutions. These are minor differences, yet indicative of the differing intersection of home/work/community in the life experience of the two women. Very many of the Salfordians I interviewed referred to actual buildings, streets, pubs and factories in their descriptions of life in the past. In Bolton and Oldham, by contrast, the 'what it's like round here' seemed to relate to people and what did they there (couples went to the pub together on a Saturday, weavers farmed out their children during the week), to customary practices (which night was bucket night), so that the locality was defined not so much by its physical structure but rather by what people did there, common activities and ways of doing things.

Would it be an exaggeration to interpret these as different kinds of localism? Certainly an argument could be made in favour of such a variation between Salford and Bolton. A single industry was much more dominant in Bolton than in Salford, employing a significant proportion of the population, and notably married women as well as men. So 'what its like round here' for Bolton women might mean 'what we cotton workers do', suggesting local traditions that were shaped partly by the working experience common to many residents. Although in their working lives Salfordians were dispersed across a broader range of industries, their living conditions were fairly homogeneous. Women, as we have seen, often saw themselves as wives and mothers first and foremost, irrespective of their waged work, and they were more rooted in their home than their work life. Localism, in such circumstances, may well be a localism of neighbourhood culture, the traditions understood as belonging to a few streets, or a ward, or the whole of Salford, while the Bolton traditions were formed also by association with its working culture. This impression of contrasting localisms, based primarily on oral testimony, was reinforced by an admittedly highly selective reading of autobiographies. Alice Foley's (Foley, 1973) account of childhood in Bolton, for example, contrasts markedly from Elsie Oman's (Oman, n.d.) of her early days in Salford. Foley's description of daily family life is permeated by their worlds of work and the effects of this on the household and its members. She outlines in some detail her own experience of shop and mill work. Employment comes over as an integral element of the conditions of living. But in Oman's memoirs waged work, even her own, seems merely incidental. Her account centres on life in the street, and on the relationships between people living there, the front steps, the pawn shop, the man with the barrel organ.

Whether or not the distinction is as clear cut as I have delineated or even valid at all, it does seem important to be sensitive to variations in the content of localism, in what 'the local' is thought to consist of, and to be aware of connections between the kind of localism and the local conditions in which it is found. If this is far-fetched, then more far-fetched, by a long way, was J.B. Priestley's throwaway explanation for the Lancashire popular culture (presented as if were was identical throughout the county), encountered during his 'English Journey' in 1934

> *Between Manchester and Bolton the ugliness is so complete that it is almost exhilarating. It challenges you to live there. That is probably the secret of Lancashire working folk: they have accepted the challenge; they are on active service, and so, like the front-line troops, they make a lot of little jokes and sing comic songs.*
> (Priestley, 1934: 248)

'Salfordian and proud of it'

If their fiercely expressed loyalty to the city is to be taken at face value, Salfordians would probably have felt particularly insulted by such blanket condemnation. Many of the people I interviewed introduced themselves as 'Salfordian born and bred', 'Salfordian and proud of it', or distinguished themselves by 'No, I'm not Mancunian, but a true Salfordian'. Amy Fowler, and her husband Bill spoke in such terms, as did also Annie Preston, Flo Nuttall, Agnes Brown and Hilda Walker. In some cases their parents had migrated to Salford from Ireland, Sheffield, Derbyshire; others' grandfathers had settled in the area after coming to work on the construction of the ship canal. Their civic pride in and identification with a locality, thus, was not based on a family association dating back for hundreds of years. An identity as Salfordian came over equally strongly from first, second or third generation immigrants, if such terminology is appropriate. It seemed to have less to do with their own backgrounds and more to do with Salford, and what was distinctive about the city and its history. Salford was, and is, a city in its own right, as against a suburb or quarter of Manchester, even if separated only by the width of a river. People in Bolton and Oldham also revealed a strong sense of their town, and of their own identification with it. But it was particularly pronounced in Salford and the following discussion takes the most extreme example as its point of departure.

Why should people express such loyalty to a place? What is the researcher to make of it, and how seriously should it be taken? I suspect that attentiveness by social scientists to local identification is much greater now than a decade or two ago. I found myself interpreting what I heard as a form of local 'chauvinism', as a 'marker of difference' or of 'inclusion/exclusion' from those living in other towns nearby, even seeing parallels between local identification and ethnic identification. It would be too extreme to think of a Salfordian (or Boltonian, or Mancunian) *ethnicity*, but the meaning and the effect of a highly localistic identity may partially overlap with ethnic identity. The focus on identity, and on different forms of identity, which has been so central to contemporary social science, raises questions that may also be asked of localism, and indeed suggests a line of thinking in relation to local identity. What is the specific gravity of localism as a form of identity? This seems the most fundamental question to ask in this connection, and it might best be approached by contrasting local identity with other forms of place and people identification. To assist in weighing the specific gravity of localism I shall draw in discussions of ethnicity and place, of 'whiteness' and 'home' that have been developed across a range of disciplines since these may help put into perspective what is distinctive about localism as a form of identity.

The experience of the former Yugoslavia lies behind one strand in the thinking underlying any suggestion of a parallel between local and ethnic identity, especially the division of Bosnia and Croatia into smaller and smaller units where nearby towns claim their own distinctiveness as conferring the right to self-government. The complex intertwining of ethnicity and locality, on the surface unproblematic in Yugoslavia for many years, was prised apart by the process of 'ethnic cleansing' in altered political conditions of renewed nationalism. The reshaping of areas claiming sovereignty and the shifting significance of differing units of territory (continents and regions as opposed to nation states) over recent decades stimulated much thinking and writing about nations, national identity and 'imagined communities'. The issue of whether other units of 'belonging' than the nation state are becoming more significant, and of how ethnicity connects with a territorial base are high on this agenda, and addressed by political theorists (e.g. Gellner, 1983; Hobsbawm, 1990; Anderson, 1991; Smith, 1991; Ignatieff, 1994) and new-style geographers alike.

Via a different route, from the study of 'race' and ethnicity, came the long overdue recognition (e.g. Roediger, 1991; Hall, 1992, 1993; Frankenberg, 1993) that majority groups and 'host' populations, have an ethnicity too. It is not just immigrants and their descendants, and minority groups, who should be thought of in this way, but also the colonisers and natives of the metropolis. British colonials, after all, gained much of their own self-confidence and sense of superiority in their own whiteness and Britishness by contrasting themselves with the Irish, Africans and Indians. The history of British colonialism is imbued with its whiteness, and for the most part, its Englishness. A shift of perspective thus opens up dominant national groupings, and white English, including white English working class women, to being considered in terms of their ethnicity in a way they have not been before (Hall et al., 1999, Chapter 4).

A further area of investigation that has recently exercised cultural theorists and geographers (Cohen, 1993; Sarup, 1994; and ongoing joint research by Back, Cohen and Räthzel), concerns the meaning of 'home'. Linked in a fairly obvious way to the other developments, this focuses on the many and different ways in which 'home' may be deployed as a marker of identity, both literal and metaphorical, and on national, local, ethnic and gender variations in its usage.

It is a long way from the assertion of 'Salfordian, and proud of it' to questions of national belonging and ethnic identity. However, there are connections helpful to assessing localism, even if they exist only in the mind of a researcher familiar with strands of thinking from other directions. That they came from Salford was clearly of importance to many of my interviewees, but how important, and whether it was of any consequence or affected their behaviour is not so clear. Their attachment could not be dismissed simply as nostalgia; local identity did seem to function as a marker by which people could distinguish themselves as a group from others. Salfordians (unlike the rather less generous British generally) did seem to admit first generation migrants to the identity. But it is difficult to imagine 'coming from Salford' or 'coming from Lancashire' ever acquiring the social or political significance of being Bosnian, Serb, Catalan or Basque. To be Salfordian was not an essentialised or exclusive identity, and was compatible with being from Lancashire and England. Salfordians, moreover, had many other, unspoken, identities than their place identity. People would (hopefully) not kill or die for Salford. A Salford identity thus had definite limits. Since people express pride in a place from within, and since that pride is not normally tested, it is difficult to know exactly where those limits to pride lie. To an outsider, Salfordian identity did not appear hostile; it seemed rather to consolidate a sense of difference and to highlight allegiance to Salford as opposed to Manchester, thus expressing a form of non-conflictual adjacency to other localities. Though strongly expressed, the markers of local difference in Greater Manchester were relatively benign, their importance largely restricted to those who identified with them, and having little broader significance or impact for the wider world. Clearly, what is done with markers is not determined by the markers themselves. Paradoxically, the strong Salfordian identity expressed (also by those passing through for a generation or two) may have been born out of adversity, connected closely with the conditions of casualism and insecurity that affected so many of its citizens, and distinguishing Salford from its more illustrious, prosperous and larger neighbour. In that sense, it may be a compensatory identity, associated with the circumstances, but it would be the worst kind of romanticism to see Salfordian identity as defending insecurity and casualism.

Perhaps I am mistaken in making so much of Salfordian identity. After all, the people I interviewed were elderly and they were also those who had stayed while many others had left the area, not only in the depression of the 1930s but also more recently. The 1930s emigrants would obviously not have been available for interviewing, and included in the later leavers were many sons and daughters of the people who did talk to me. In other words, though typical of the women I wanted to meet, my sample was highly selective, biased towards those who had lived in Salford all their lives and from whom a strong attachment was only to be expected.

Living with representation

But a further consideration is involved in interpreting the importance of Salford to its inhabitants, namely the representation and self-representation which Salford has enjoyed for over a century and a half, and this complicates matters. Engels' study *The Condition of the Working Class in England* contains detailed description of Salford in the early 1840s as an 'unwholesome, dirty and ruinous locality' (Engels, 1892: 95) and of housing standards as bad as any he encountered in the Manchester area where people lived in conditions of filth, excrement, heaps of debris, and putrid water. Roberts' accounts (1971, 1976) of life in Salford in the first quarter of the twentieth century depict in some detail the stratification of working class life, and codes of respectability. Equally influential in establishing Salford's emblematic standing as an archetypical northern working class town are the writings of Walter Greenwood, his autobiography and, especially, his novel *Love on the Dole*. First published in 1933, it evokes the desperation of unemployment, and the social and personal desolation it caused Greenwood's characters both directly and indirectly. Although the novel brought Salford to national public prominence, many Salfordians remain equivocal even today about the exposure, feeling that he brought shame on Hanky Park by focusing only on the negative, and bitter that he became rich and famous on the backs of other people's misery. Community myths, critical of Greenwood's personal life and authorship of the book, that have been handed down over the years since the 1930s, are still used to question the validity of his work (Davies, 1991).

A generation later, Shelagh Delaney's play *A Taste of Honey* dealt with contemporary postwar themes (single parenthood, teenage sexuality, homosexuality) against the backdrop of Salford. The black and white film made on location by Tony Richardson in 1962, starred Rita Tushingham as the pregnant girl and Dora Bryan as her brassy and irresponsible Mum. It gives an atmospheric feel of run-down industrial and urban decay with little for young people to look forward to, but where remnants of an older and now outdated culture nevertheless survive.

Salford has figured in other media too. Now collected together in their own special museum in Salford, L.S. Lowry's paintings of 'matchstick people' in industrial landscapes and local street scenes were familiar to the people I interviewed, as was Alan Price's popular song of the same title.

Coronation Street is perhaps the best known representation of life in Salford, as well as being Britain's longest running and most successful soap opera. 'Weatherfield' is a caricature of 'northern working class life' with its self-contained and cosy community revolving around the street, its pub, shop, garage and factory. Most of the characters appear to live out their lives within the highly restricted social and economic space of a few streets. Many are depicted as self-employed and working locally in occupations (hairdresser, betting shop, school teacher, paper shop, café) where they service other locals. In recent years a few black faces have appeared (and usually disappeared quite soon), and attempts have been made to suggest that a world exists beyond Weatherfield. But despite the city centre pub, shopping trips and the prison, the 'outside' remains hazy and insignificant to the characters, who disappear into it as if into a black hole. They only seem real when they are in Weatherfield. As is general in soaps, the women of *Coronation Street* continue to play their allotted role at the centre of the community, keeping it together (Dyer *et al.*, 1981; Geraghty, 1991) and transmitting the culture and informal rules which bind it from one generation to the next. The soap operates through stereotype. Seen in the context of the localistic sentiments I encountered in Salford, the localism which is so fundamental to *Coronation Street* is intriguing. All the people I interviewed would have been familiar with the series and its (unrealistic) representation of how people in Salford interact and make a living. I hope it is evident that the localism they expressed was of a different kind than that portrayed in *Coronation Street*, centred on a civic loyalty and sense of shared history and culture, but lacking the premiss on which the series is based that all of people's economic and social aspirations or needs could or should be fulfilled by what goes on in the space of a few streets. Neither form of localism seems to touch the other. But neither should they be expected to since realistic portrayal is not the aim of a soap.

I mentioned early in Chapter 2 my unease with the impression that Annie Preston and her friends were conscious bearers of the history of Salford, concerned to uphold its reputation with details from their own experience which confirmed its characterisation as the 'classic slum'. The stories they told could not be interpreted at face value as being only their own personal accounts, since they were well aware of the role of reminiscence and oral history in keeping a place alive. That group of three women were the most active local historians I came across, but they were by no means an exception. Many others were also members of local history groups. The 'snowball' method of making contacts seemed here to involve being propelled into a network of amateur local historians. The majority of people interviewed were familiar with the various depictions of Salford. Several recommended books I should read, exhibitions or collections of photos to be seen, or local libraries where useful records could be found. Indeed local history figures prominently in the local public libraries as well as in the more specialist Working Class Movement Library.

Clearly more is involved in Salford people talking about Salford than just telling their own story. Layers upon layers of past and present representations of various kinds, reputations, public histories and collective memories lie behind their own telling of life in Salford. And, by implication, more must also be involved in interpreting what they said. It would be impossible to abstract out their own personal accounts from the context of narrative ambience in which they also were located. Many of the quite personal accounts of family life did not sound like spontaneous answers to a question they had never really focused on before (not that even the most naïve oral historian would be expecting direct access to someone's memories). But if the impression was correct that private stories had been chewed over, told many times before, and were consciously connected in the minds of the tellers to the public histories and representations which formed Salford's collective memory, then this should be taken into account in any interpretation. If personal and public accounts co-mingled, as they appeared to, ought the arguments I have developed about Salford localism be revised, or toned down? I think not, because the coincidence of local pride on the one hand and the extent of public representation and self-representation of the town on the other is no accident. People identified with the place very actively, but in so doing they were also contributing to the maintenance of its identity. Expressions of local attachment were not mere reflections of an independently existing public image.

Locality and localisms

Finally I return to the contrast between the North West and South East which was greater than those within the North West. Clearly there was a connection between, on the one hand, the very different geographical structure of London and its labour markets and the Lancashire towns and their labour markets, and, on the other hand, the different experiences of life and locality, and discourses of localism. It is beyond my scope to do more than suggest some factors that would be relevant to an analysis. Slum clearance, new housing estates, and the establishment of trading estates and factories on greenfield sites in the London suburbs had resulted in considerable geographical dislocation and mobility, and in a custom of searching for work, and establishing social networks, over a wide spatial area. Moreover, a significant proportion of the population of London was migrant, having moved within the last generation from Scotland, Wales and other distressed areas in the search for work. Women as well as men travelled long distances to work, sometimes right across London. The structure of labour markets in the conurbation was complex, heterogeneous and multi-layered. All this was far removed from the relative homogeneity, dominance by a few industries, and discrete and restricted labour markets that were distinctive features of the Lancashire towns.[10] Although in decline by the 1930s, the Lancashire textile industry was long established: things were 'like that' partly because they had endured over a long time span.

A crucial effect of this difference was to make locality and localism a far more salient feature of social and economic life in Lancashire, encouraging the predisposition to accept local traditions without questioning their particularity and to place greater emphasis on 'what its like round here'. The experience of Londoners being less localised and homogeneous (aside from important exceptions like the docks and the East End), they were also much less likely to think in terms of 'what its like round here'. Thus, although place was just as structured and as significant in London as in Lancashire, it was differently structured and differently significant.

Life was more localistic in Lancashire than in London, people being locked into the particular and limited patterns of living that existed there. For women in Salford especially, there were not many different possible ways of being a casual worker, but rather one dominant mode. Similarly, those who lived in one-trade towns were less likely than Londoners to bump up against the many different patterns linking gender divisions of household and paid employment, a larger proportion living within a smaller number of dominant patterns. That people universalised the particularity of their own situation indicates their inescapability from an enduring way of life that they, and often their parents before them, had grown up with, and which they knew as 'what it's like round here'.

But contrasting Lancashire with London is hardly appropriate since it involves comparing unlike with unlike. The spatial difference was also a difference of time in terms of change and development, and because of this a focus on place makes sense only in its historical context. During the inter-war years London and the South East were centres for the establishment of new industries, where new kinds of economic organisation were developed and new occupations emerged, accompanied by new forms of housing, transport and consumption. Patterns of working and living that appeared here in the 1930s prefigured what was to become more widespread nationally after the Second World War, though not for many decades, if ever, in the North West. But Lancashire, its traditional textile industries well into decline by the 1930s and not replaced by any new industry, experienced none of this transformation. Patterns of working and living endured. The difference of place between London and Lancashire in the 1930s was entwined with the historical developments that also separated them.

The view from her window would probably not have held such great significance for Hilda Walker if the run-down industries of the area had been replaced by a viable alternative. Absence of renewal undoubtedly contributed to the strong sense of the past of places expressed by so many.

Exploring even a few aspects of spatial relations has demonstrated that 'place matters'. The spatial dimension was most obviously implicated in the formation of localities and forms of localism. But spatial variation was integral also to uneven development, both within and between regions, and between the modernisation of factories and houses, and production and consumption. More than that, though: if place matters, so too does a spatial framework of analysis. This was the precondition for comprehending issues involved in locality and localism and trajectories of domestic modernisation alike.

Notes

1   Soja (1989) and Harvey (1989) are amongst the most influential rethinkers of geography. See Robertson et al. (1994) for an example of cultural travel geography.

2   The collection edited by Gregory and Urry (1985) provides a good flavour of work at the boundary between sociology and geography.

3   Useful overviews of the progress and preoccupations of feminist geography are to be found in Rose (1993), McDowell (1993), Women and Geography Group (1984), Massey and Allen (1984), Massey (1995), Bondi (1990), Bowlby et al. (1989). Gender, Place and Culture, a journal of feminist geography, appeared from 1994.

4   There are many definitions of locality and as many critiques and debates. See, for example, Massey (1994, especially Chapter 5, The political place of locality studies), Cooke (1989), Warde (1989), Urry (1987), Duncan (1989) and Sayer (1991). For debates about locality, and its explanatory role, see Duncan and Savage (1989, 1991). On household arrangements and locality studies, see Morris (1991), and on gender and locality, Bowlby (1986).

5   Clear and interesting parallels in the mode of debate may be discerned here between geography and sociology. While in sociology, as outlined in Chapter 1, one side of a dualism tended to dominate before giving way to the other, geographers reacted against a political economy approach which was criticised for reading off empirical events from the 'laws' of capitalism. The see-saw then swung the other way in the 'locality studies' (many were ESRC funded) in which local determination or influence was emphasised. Doreen Massey's position clearly represents more of a balance between these two extremes which related to a specific period in the intellectual history of geography when writers had caricatured each other's positions. I should like to thank Diane Perrons for clarifying this context.

6   Viz. Massey's (1984) concept of a 'spatial division of labour' referring to the form of uneven development which results from the combining of a range of concurrent spatial structures.

7   Engels' survey includes a lengthy account (1892: 86–92) of housing conditions in Manchester which he evidently found shocking. He attributed the poor quality largely to building contractors' use of shoddy materials and corner-cutting methods which saved money but ensured that dwellings quickly became run down and had a short life span.

8   The following discussion of Trafford Park draws on a variety of sources, including the oral histories collected by Russell and Walker (1979), testimony in the Bridging the Years project, my own interview with Connie Mitchell, and Fielding (1992, 1993).

9   On the emergence and effects of the 'ideal home' ideology see Cowan (1989) especially, and Wajcman (1991). Useful histories of domestic appliances and architecture can be found in Hardyment (1988), Forty (1986, particularly Chapter 9), Davidson (1982) and Roberts (1991).

10   This is by comparison with London, and not to deny the important variations between
       the Lancashire towns. Some were more self-contained and discrete than others, as
       discussed above, all having different economic histories, industrial structures and labour
       markets. Their individual political and civic histories had also been important in shaping
       the character of each town, its self-representation and the type and depth of meaning it
       held for its inhabitants.

Chapter 7
Fitting endings

The aim of this final chapter is to draw together and make more explicit both the frameworks and the mode of analysis so as to suggest their wider relevance. Although they have been developed here in relation to specific subject matter – women workers in Lancashire, UK during the second third of the twentieth century – the approach could just as well have been elaborated in relation to other substantive material. The value of a relational analysis, which helps to elucidate the configurations and patterning of social relations and to throw light on the interlocking or intersectionality connecting together different social processes, is not restricted to the use to which it has been put here. Rather, it has much to offer any analysis of social life, whether contemporary or historical, local, national or global, a single case or comparative study. Moreover, the mode and method of approaching subject matter suggests a view on the construction of theory and knowledge and a route towards explanatory analysis that might revitalise a sociology still somewhat limping after the critiques of postmodernism and post-structuralism. The problems that these brought so sharply into focus – unreflective grand narratives, uni-causal and universalistic explanations, the nature of 'reality' of subject matter – are real issues for all the social sciences and humanities, sociology and feminism included. But, rather than burying our heads in the sand or abandoning the quest for systematic analysis and explanation, we need to take on the issues, come to terms with them and move forward.

How to 'slice the cake' is as much of a problem at this juncture as earlier, but it arises now because so many of the arguments to be drawn out are interconnected: the overall framework of the 'total social organisation of labour' implies a conception of interlocking relations, institutions, or structures, and so also encourages a relational focus and a relational type of explanation in terms of intersecting social divisions. Similarly, the particular interplay between concepts, theory and substantive material suggested as productive of knowledge embodies a view on the relation of concrete to abstract, individual to social, micro to macro. An alternative to dualistic thinking which views binaries as mutually and inextricably interdependent, rather than as dichotomous or self-standing, is also involved in the approach adopted towards the construction of theory.

Revisiting the 'total social organisation of labour'

The TSOL, used throughout this study as the unifying analytical framework, has been further developed through responding to the challenge of new material. It had to be extended so that it could take into account extra dimensions implicated in the organisation of labour of weavers and casual women workers: informal economic activity and exchange, inter-generational and intra-generational change, temporality and spatiality. These were incorporated into the framework, refining it and strengthening its analytical capacity. This section will now draw out some general conclusions arising from this development of the concept of TSOL.

So what is 'work'?

Informal economic activity emerged as an integral feature of the lives of both weavers and casual women workers, in addition to their paid employment and unpaid labour. Weavers tended to be the purchasers of goods and services supplied by other women in their neighbourhoods, including their own sisters or mothers. Casual women workers, on the other hand, were the main suppliers of services such as childcare, laundry, prepared meals. For both groups the connection between their household economy and the market was mediated by informal work and informal economic exchange. Indeed, for many weavers it was precisely such activity that sustained their ability to undertake full-time continuous employment *and* have responsibility for home and children. Performing such services represented one of the multiple sources of paid employment for casual women workers, and the remuneration an important component of their overall earnings. For both groups of women, then, the articulation of domestic labour with paid employment, which was the original starting point for the research, involved more than just these two forms of work. The connection between domestic and formal economy could not be understood without widening the frame of analysis so as to include informal economic activity. It was this that linked the two groups of women to each other as well as underpinning the connection, for each group, between the work they undertook at home and for pay. In addition to the goods and services they sold for money, casual women workers also exchanged services with each other, one woman looking after her neighbour's or sister's children while the other did her washing at the municipal wash-house at the same time as doing her own. A further point to note in this connection is that the identical task or 'work' activity was undertaken within quite different socio-economic relations, only some of which involved money. But, whether paid, reciprocated or given, all could be placed squarely under a heading of 'informal economic activity'.

Until very recently such activity, in industrial societies at least, has not been recognised as 'economic' and rarely appeared in official statistics relating to the labour force or production. Market relations and exchanges alone were acknowledged as economic, social scientists actively colluding in the extremely restricted constructions of 'work', 'labour' and 'economy' in common usage. Although the term 'informal economic activity' is far too general to capture the enormous variability and heterogeneity of actual 'informal' socio-economic relations, the attention that this 'sector' is now beginning to receive represents a very significant and welcome shift of perspective, not least to feminists, since so much of women's work has been of a non-market variety.

International drugs trafficking, unregulated financial exchanges over the Internet, cash in hand or 'off the books' work, and the so-called 'black economy' in general, local exchange trading schemes (LETS), the expansion of DIY (do it yourself) and self-provisioning, the rebirth of private domestic service – if all these are recognised as forms of economic activity, then existing definitions of 'work' and 'the economy' will eventually be forced to change. 'Satellite' accounting for developing economies is becoming a standard means for the United Nations and other organisations of estimating the contribution to production of labour undertaken outside of the core 'market' sector (United Nations, 1995; Goldschmidt-Clermont and Paganossin-Aligasakis, 1995). A European Commission report in 1998 claimed that the 'black economy' accounted for between 7 and 19 per cent of gross domestic product overall in the European Community, representing between 10 and 28 million jobs. This prompted the policy question of whether in the future member states' financial contributions to the EU should reflect their total GDP, including the 'black economy', rather than the GDP calculated for the regulated standard economy as hitherto (*Financial Times*, 8 April 1998).

Hopefully such developments, in addition to transforming the way work and labouring activity are conceptualised, will also encourage far more extensive and serious attention to women's 'casual' work, bringing it out of obscurity and highlighting its past and continuing economic contribution and social significance.

The TSOL represents one amongst these new and more inclusive ways of thinking the 'economic'. Although the foregoing discussion, drawing on the analysis of gendered economies of home and work, centred on the connections between unpaid domestic labour, paid employment and 'casual' labour that might be paid or unpaid, the more general point that I hope to have demonstrated is that the analytical approach is one that may be applied to numerous other, completely different situations. Unlimited by any notion of 'work' as an activity which takes place only in certain institutions or organisations, or occurs only within certain social relationships, the TSOL can be used to look at any kind of work, and to explore the connections between different kinds of work undertaken under different socio-economic relations within the same society. For example, 'voluntary work' has remained significant in many western industrial societies throughout the postwar period of the liberal democratic welfare state (and indeed has proliferated in many countries into a multiplicity of differing forms). But it has played a greater role in some countries than others, more perhaps in the UK and Netherlands and less in the Nordic countries. Much 'social work', including major areas of ancillary health care and care of the elderly and children, that is done as paid employment in the latter is achieved on a voluntary basis in the former. The TSOL would permit not only both to be seen as work, but provides a means of analysing the linkage between this kind of work (paid or voluntary) and other 'sectors' of work and social organisations of labour in the particular society (market, domestic, communal and so on).

In addition, the TSOL provides the potential of a perspective where work and especially employment may be viewed against the broader institutional and societal context of which they form a part. Employment, unemployment, youth employment and the gendered pattern of participation in employment all interconnect with and are regulated by public policies, labour market institutions, social welfare and taxation systems. All of these vary between countries and over time, resulting in differing configurations connecting employment with public and social policy. There are strong parallels between this 'institutional totality' dimension of the TSOL approach and recent work in the field of social policy, especially analyses (e.g. Orloff, 1993; Levitas, 1998) of changes in the connections between state, welfare state, and economic policy regimes that are being forged or loosened in the post-welfare state era.

It is clear that this framework could also be developed further in relation to other areas of major, yet largely unacknowledged, transformations of the nature of work, for example, retail and the retailing sector and its growth, diversification and gendering over the twentieth century. Goods are sold as well as being produced and consumed. Yet the work that occurs during this integral phase in the circuit of production and consumption (not to mention its gigantic expansion and transformation in recent decades) has been seriously under-recognised both by a political economy focus on production and labour process and by a cultural studies focus on shopping and shoppers. Many of the goods and services that are sold by a predominantly female labour force in a proliferating range of retail 'outlets' are not only made by women, and bought by women, but may also substitute goods that used to be produced in the home and which therefore were never 'distributed'. As well as acknowledging selling as work, the TSOL framework would facilitate analysis of the shifting boundaries of work, and of the changing nature of the overall circuit of production–distribution–consumption implied by these historical developments.

Temporality and time

As well as the strengthened substantive focus on informal economic activity, the TSOL has also been conceptually extended by the addition of a temporal dimension. Temporality enters the TSOL in a number of ways. First, time offers a powerful means of comparing different forms of labour undertaken within a variety of socio-economic relations where none or only some involve financial transactions, since it can be used as a standard measure of equivalence. Adopting this approach revealed how weavers and casual women workers differed in their exchanges of time for labour both in their paid work with their employers and in domestic labour with their husbands, and also in their exchanges with each other. Comparing the two groups made clear that a higher proportion of casual women workers' total available time was absorbed by (frequently unequal) exchanges of labour, and that, unlike the weavers, they hardly had an idea of 'free' time.

Looking at time helped also to illuminate gendered generational differences in relation to work. As young adults the women I interviewed invariably had to undertake domestic chores at home after a full day in the factory or weaving shed. Expectations of their brothers were much lower on this score, but a 'double shift' was normal for girls. Their dual contribution to the household economy of time and wages was crucial to many working-class families' ability to maintain a basic standard of living. But household economies, like people, pass through a life cycle. Viewed longitudinally, as opposed to frozen at one point in time, the time versus wage inputs of household members can be seen to vary, differing before and after children are born, during the stage when working children are still living at home, and again in old age when unmarried daughters often became a source of financial support for a parent who 'in turn' performed unpaid domestic labour. Moreover, the household life-cycle also changes historically. What was normal for the casual women workers and weavers in their families of origin during the 1920s and 1930s was no longer so by the 1950s. Unlike their mothers they did not expect their own children to devote much time to household labour; nor did they expect to receive an unopened wage packet from a working child still living at home.

Introducing an 'economy of time' into the TSOL framework thus provides a much broader conception of labour and one that is more appropriate to theorising gender differences in work. Time, as a common standard for quantifying inputs of labour regardless of whether or not they are paid, represents a powerful means for calculating 'who does what for whom'.

Attempting such quantification, however, has definite limits and becomes highly problematic when work relations are embedded in disparate other social relationships or processes, as they so often are, or occur in different and incomparable economic 'spaces'. Comparing how long tasks take to complete can tell us only that – when other aspects of their temporal organisation may be far more significant than the number of minutes or hours spent on them.

Clock or chronometric time, thus provides only one view of temporality. Even in the case of weavers and casual women workers there were many other differences of temporality between them than chronometric time. Their experience of time differed. Their daily lives and their life courses were 'blocked' differently, and their memories of the past were structured by different kinds of 'calendar'. The differing division between public and private between the two groups also included a strong temporal dimension, the casual women workers being subject to 'public' neighbourhood norms which determined *when* they should do domestic tasks that were treated as 'private' and personal matters by the weavers. More than the weavers the casual women workers also juggled different forms of temporality and time expended in commodified and non-commodified labour, shifting between the clock times of their husbands (meal on the table at 5 pm sharp) and children's school hours, their own temporally indistinguishable paid servicing work and unpaid domestic labour, as well as the weekly community driven cycles.

With the introduction of the temporal dimension into the TSOL perspective, exchanges of labour, complementarities of tasks and reciprocities of obligations can be seen as established in a definite succession, in cycles or various forms of order and sequence. A more general lesson emerges from accepting that 'it is the sorting that makes the time' rather than the reverse. Treating temporality as an integral component of social process, rather than as an external envelope within which social relations occurs, may provide new insights and a distinctive analytical slant on difference, that is not restricted to the specific instances examined here.

Spatiality and place

Similar remarks apply also to spatiality. Since the organisation of labour embodies a definite spatial dimension the introduction of a spatial perspective cannot but enhance the analytical capacities of the TSOL framework. Space, like time, should not be conceived as a context external to social process, but rather as an integral component of it. Social relations and social processes are active constituents in the construction of place, to be seen as productive of spatiality rather than as occurring within a spatial envelope that does not need to be brought into the understanding of what happens 'inside' it.

Introducing a spatial dimension demonstrably aided understanding of the diversity of circumstances encountered in inter-war Lancashire. For example, configurations connecting gendered divisions of home and work held together over a limited spatial range. Casual employment for men and women are not inherently complementary, but when brought together, as in Salford, they produced a particular configuration which structured people's experience of and attitude towards the place in a distinctive manner, resulting in the fiercely held Salfordian identity. In Bolton, women's employment was far more highly concentrated in a single industry, cotton manufacture, where work was both higher skilled and paid than in Salford. Employment opportunities for Bolton men were not only more heterogeneous in range and skill level than for Salford men but also included some occupations and workplaces that were relatively unsegregated by gender.[1] A grasp of the specific features of these spatial co-variations between men and women in the two towns throws considerable light on the otherwise puzzling distinctive discourses of locality and links between domestic sharing and gendering of occupations.

Although adjacent to Salford, life for those who worked and lived on the Trafford Park industrial estate differed in significant ways, the local specificity of each being shaped by the conjunction of particular sets of spatially organised relations. One of these related to housing quality, Trafford Park residents enjoying newly built houses in the 1930s complete with mod cons while many Salfordians had to wait until the 1970s for bathrooms, inside toilets and running hot water. Unevenness such as this turned out to be characteristic of Greater Manchester as a whole. Clashing juxtapositions of development and decline provide a further dimension to spatiality, adding depth to local specificity. Not only housing stock and amenities, but also industrial decline and growth, rates of unemployment, and employment opportunities for married women varied markedly between places that were very close to each other, resulting in a 'patchwork' of uneven development. Even the structuring of age had a spatial dimension, adolescence being more strongly demarcated as a separate stage of the life course in some towns, while in others the division between youth and adult was less marked, and generations were defined more on the basis of marital status.

That people were unaware of the particularity of their own circumstances, and of the different experience of those living only a few miles away, revealed just how insulated and discrete local labour markets and local cultures could be, even though the work connected residents directly with a global colonial economy, as when assembling Model T cars at Ford, weaving cotton from Egypt destined for export to India, or unloading fruit from the tropics. Reinforced by discourses of 'what it's like round here', localities were portrayed by their inhabitants almost as self-producing, as if their features were generated from within and did not require explanation.

During the second third of the twentieth century uneven development between regions was a far greater public worry than the patchwork within the

North West. Concern focused on the growth of new industries and expansion of jobs in the South East, which stood in such sharp contrast to the industrial decline and high rates of unemployment of the North West. But regional disparity extended further than this, to conditions of living not so frequently commented on at the time, such as the fabric of housing and the infrastructure of power, water and sanitation. The absence of laid-on gas and electricity in Lancashire, at a time when they were already a normal feature of domestic architecture in the South East, had an enormous impact on home life, prolonging for decades the demand for arduous labour-intensive domestic labour, and reducing the scope for consumption of domestic consumer goods and appliances. In this way 'uneven development' between South East and North West was complicated by many kinds of interconnectivities and complex patchworks of variations. Introducing a spatial perspective into the TSOL framework enabled the analysis to grasp the various connectivities in the spatial networks they inhabited and constructed.

Comparing South East with North West brings home again the intertwining of spatial and temporal and the impossibility of thinking about spatial variation outside of a historical context. Thus the spatial difference between Lancashire and London in the 1930s was entwined with the historical developments that also separated them. However, when thinking in terms of space and time it is important not to conceive of spatial difference and change occurring in linear temporality and of regional developments in production and consumption following identical trajectories. There was no single unilinear route which some places just travelled along later than others. Rather there was a multiplicity of routes to, and forms of, 'modernisation'. Changes in consumption and the acquisition of domestic appliances appeared to be less dependent on housing improvement in the North West than the South East. Both the transition of the relation between married women's paid employment and the purchase of labour-saving consumer durables, and, more generally, that between market and household economy, had different trajectories in the two regions, and even within different parts of the same region, as we saw for the North West. The different elements had different time scales and meshed together in a different temporal sequences.[2] This is just one instance, that could be endlessly replicated for quite other situations, places and times, of how impossible it is to abstract spatial variation out of time and differences of temporality from those of space and place. Temporality and spatiality have to be 'thought' in conjunction with each other in the broadening out of the conceptual frame of the TSOL.

Summary

The intention of this section has been to draw out the analytical power of the conception of a 'total social organisation of labour'. As an umbrella framework it can be used at any level of generality, micro, meso or macro, to explore the organisation of labour within a single household or workplace, or within a particular area, town, region or country, at any historical conjuncture, and to compare and differentiate between differing organisations of labour across and between each level, geographically, synchronically and diachronically. Even when focusing on a single household, the TSOL looks at it exhaustively, that is, in terms of its total interconnectedness, rather than suggesting that the household is itself a totality.

The conception of labour is inclusive: the work may take any form, occur in any institution, be undertaken within a wide variety of socio-economic relations, be more or less strictly demarcated from other activities, and more or less differentiated from or embedded within other non-work social relations and processes. The purpose of the approach is precisely to investigate the linkages existing between different kinds of work that are connected to each other, and the nature of the overall configuration constituted by their combination.

Relational analysis: intersectionality and configurations

Intersecting divisions of labour of husbands and wives, mothers and daughters, cottons and casuals; *connections* between local employment structures and local cultures; *networks* of linkage between production and consumption, or between paid employment and domestic labour; *configurations* of home and work for different individuals and occupational groupings; *patterns* that change over the life course – these have been the main focus of research.

Relationality and intersectionality have been the central analytical frames used in this study for focusing on inter-relationships and intersecting processes and divisions. The approach attempts to reveal how different sets of social relations, socio-economic processes and social divisions 'fit' together, investigating their component processes, the connections that constitute them and give them their specificity, and the manner and circumstances of their conjoining. A procedure like this, which analytically unjoints and then rejoints sets of relations and processes that are interlocked or intersect with each other, offers an important mode of explanation, one that is further strengthened when coupled with a historical exploration of the various component strands and parts that combine to make up a particular configuration.

Within a relational perspective the intersecting of different kinds of social division is of particular significance. In recent years sociologists have increasingly recognised the extent to which social divisions overlay and criss-cross each other, reinforcing or cross cutting each other in such a way that explanation in terms of a single self-standing social division can no longer be considered sufficient. For instance, class relations in western industrial societies have to be conceptualised as also gendered and ethnicised. Or, it may no longer be helpful to conceive of gender, class or ethnicity as 'pure' processes having an effectivity that is unaffected by each other and their interconnection. Investigating intersectionality is thus of special interest for an analytical approach that privileges relationality. Divisions are generated by relations between people rather than by distinctive traits or properties of people. Relationality is a way of looking behind 'constituted groups' and attempts to avoid any taxonomic or categorising approach to social divisions.

The 'fit' between the component parts of a configuration, it must be stressed, could well be contradictory, involving conflict or uneven processes. For example, the divisions of domestic labour and of paid employment for casual women workers and their husbands in Salford involved considerable tension, kept at bay only by the wives' adoption of strategies to avoid the outbreak of open marital warfare. The coincidence of the latest technology and most modern production methods in the Trafford Park industrial estate with a simultaneous absence of shops or facilities for consumption that might have 'matched' those of production, provides an example of imbalance or unevenness. Thinking in terms of linkages, therefore, should *not* be taken to imply a vision of functional unities or tension-free webs of connection devoid of internal contradiction or conflict.

A further point relates to which actual intersecting divisions are under consideration. The interlocking social relations that were examined here could not be universalised. Although relevant in this study they would not necessarily apply anywhere else, and certainly not everywhere else. Which particular relations and divisions are the most relevant to investigate will depend directly on the subject matter. For cotton and casual workers the key relationships to go under the microscope were gender, occupation, place and time, formal market economy, household economy and informal exchange. The resulting analysis demonstrated how, in particular places and at particular times, different kinds of division of labour intersected in particular ways for particular individuals, occupational groups, and genders. In another study, perhaps sexuality or religion might be the key parameters, or ethnicity/race and age, or class, rather than gender, occupation and so on. And the actual manner of interrelating and intersecting is also an open question, to be determined for each case and the specific circumstances under scrutiny.

Individualising the social and the non-particularistic particular

Other theoretical implications flow from the relational approach, of broader relevance to social analysis. For instance, focusing on an individual person or studying the particular may contribute to the general understanding of social dynamics and power relations. If the particular is conceived as a distillation of interacting forces and reactions to these, or a nodal point of multiple intersecting socio-economic processes, then investigating the particular reveals insights of far wider significance than the individual case. Thinking about Hilda Walker pointing out of her window to the now non-existent street where she was born led to suggestions about configurations of gender, place and memory that extended far beyond Mrs Walker herself. The importance of the temporal dimension to social analysis was demonstrated by comparing weavers' and casual women workers' experiences of temporality. Studying the particular, in other words, need not result in particularistic understanding.

Preferring complementarity

Throughout this study an attempt has been made to think in ways that are complementary and both/and rather than binary and either/or. Bringing two sides of a supposed dualism into play can reveal just how interdependent they might be and consequently how much more elucidating it is to consider them as complementary rather than as mutually exclusive frames of interpretation. The teenage years of Marjorie Fisher and Edith Ashworth provide a good example with respect to the binary of 'materiality versus meaning'. Both women had worked extremely hard. During the depression, when their fathers and brothers were unemployed, they became the main source of financial support for their families despite being only in their mid-teens. However, the way Mrs Ashworth and Mrs Fisher experienced similar material circumstances was quite distinct. Youth employment held an entirely different meaning for each woman, and their discourse about it differed accordingly. For Mrs Ashworth it was 'exploitation'; she was resentful, feeling she had been 'used' while still too young to appreciate what was happening to her. She remained bitter throughout her life towards her mother who had 'taken every advantage she could'. By contrast, Mrs Fisher, who actually was the sole financial support of her family in the early 1930s, had only positive memories about her experience. She went out of her way to praise her father and explain why he should have been driven to drink.

A narrowly materialist interpretation of the two women, focusing on their 'objective' similarities, might draw general conclusions about youth exploitation and the appropriation of labour, time and money. The alternative interpretive frame, according primacy to the meaning attached by actors to their circumstances, might not recognise any similarity at all between the two women, and consider it illegitimate for the researcher to accord to the women's experiences a meaning or significance at odds with their own. Positing these alternative interpretations as mutually exclusive is to set up a false dualism since it is clear that each captures something but is also missing out on something. These were similar material circumstances differently experienced, and it is entirely unproblematic to accept them as such, acknowledging both aspects as parts of a picture which can incorporate both meaning and materiality, or words and things.

In order to explain *why* the women should have accorded such different meanings to their situations would of course involve recourse to additional factors, and notably the quality of their particular family relationships. But attending to this explanation would not undo the material similarity. Similarly, attempting to explain the role of juvenile labour in the inter-war years, also by recourse to other factors, would not conflict with accepting the women's own memories and interpretations.

Detailed examination of particular individuals was central to my overall analysis, the circumstances and views of Mrs X or Mrs Y being important for what they tell about the dynamics of social and economic processes in certain places. Conversely, an understanding of institutions and structures throws light on why Mrs X and Mrs Y say what they say, live as they do, and their subjective understanding of that experience. The casual women workers' identity as mothers and wives was an example of why not to take everything at face value: placed in the context of the generally low social esteem accorded to the kind of work they did, this way of defining themselves made complete sense. Methodologically, making sense of this had called both for close attention to individual transcripts as well as attempting to 'place' it by reference to other sorts of evidence which could help explain the particularity of their situation.

Counterposing the cultural to the social or to structure was a dominating theme of much 1990s social and feminist theory. For research on work and employment this often had the unfortunate effect of erecting an opposition between a focus on work cultures on the one hand and a focus on structures of work on the other. Yet, cultures of work may be closely associated with other, non-cultural, dimensions of the conditions in which they are found. As we saw in Salford and Bolton distinct traditions, customs and expectations closely linked with the particular characteristics of the local employment structure (especially its degree of homogeneity or heterogeneity) and the nature of the jobs available (and their degree of gender segregation). Wives' expectations of married life and the 'proper' role of husbands in Salford 'made better sense' in the context of a relatively insulated employment structure where a large proportion of both men and women worked in insecure, unskilled, manual, low paid, casual work highly segregated on the basis of gender.

Thus, cultural and economic processes were viewed as interrelated dimensions of the object of study, analysis of the economic being better informed by an understanding of its cultural facets and vice versa. 'Local culture' could not be seen as self-standing, suspended in mid-air. Understanding its specificity necessitated reference to the wider relational web of processes, institutions and relationships within which it was operative.

Simply stated, it is the connectivity between two sides of a supposed dualism, rather than their internal dynamics considered separately, that is crucial to an understanding of what goes on within each.

Diversity and inequality

Diversity and difference have been at the heart of feminist concern, both theoretically and politically, since the black critique of white feminism. Attention to difference within gender, and between women, represents a necessary complement to, but does not displace, concern with difference between genders. Appreciation of the multiplicity of femininities and feminine identities (that is, of difference *within* genders) has been a great stimulus to the construction of theories which can take account of the variable significance of gender, the different kinds and strengths of gender division, and its different modes of intersection with other social divisions, both in discourse and in social process. Initial studies concentrated on the differing experience of slavery, imperialism, and racism for women of different nations, ethnicities, classes and colours in the colonising and colonised world (so redressing the white 'first world' bias of 1970s feminism). Now writings on the gendering of whiteness, the ethnicity of gender and divisions between white women (Hall, 1992; Ware, 1992; Frankenberg, 1993) (this study of white working class women all living in the same small area being just one) have joined the burgeoning literature on gender and post/coloniality, attesting to the ability of feminist analysis to rebuild itself on a less ethnocentric base and its continuing vibrancy.

Questions about inequalities and how to conceptualise them follow swiftly on from a focus on difference, diversity and division between women. Casual women workers and weavers, I suggested, were not in an equal economic relation to each other, even though each depended on the other and many talked in terms of 'she helped me and I helped her'. Weavers had more economic power than the casual women workers whose services or products they bought. They had more choice, could buy commodities, and so did not rely on having to employ casual women workers. The casual women workers, however, had to sell their services in order to survive.

To view this kind of inequality as 'class' or as 'class' within 'class', would be to overstate it, probably raising more definitional problems than it solves. It is not clear that anyone was appropriating anything from anyone else or that any surplus was involved. But although an informal exchange of money for labour is not the same as that between wage labour and capital, it is still an employment relation. The existence of unequal economic transactions even amongst the same gender in the same broad category of 'manual working class' is evidence of a particular form of intersection of class and gender relations. It could make sense to analyse this in class terms but only if class is conceived as a relation of exchange (Glucksmann, 1990: 18–20, 261–2, 279–80), the specific nature of which will vary according to the case in question, rather than as a location or position on an already predetermined grid or map.

The picture becomes far more complicated if we widen the view so as to include, in addition to the unequal exchange relation between them, all the other exchanges in which the two groupings of women were also involved with husbands and with more formal employers, and all the inequalities implied in them. If we then recognise that some exchanges were of money and some of time it becomes more complex still. The problem arises of how, or whether, to connect all these different kinds of inequality. Some may be incommensurable as I argued in relation to time. It may not add anything, or make much sense, or be possible, to squeeze into a unitary scale of measurement differing forms of inequality even when all may be at play at the same time. However, inability to add up different kinds of inequality should not imply giving up on the attempt to understand their interconnection. It just means further developing the analytical framework of intersectionality, and going beyond earlier notions of 'class as a context for gender' etc. (Anthias and Yuval-Davis, 1992) or 'matrices of domination' (Collins, 1990).

Differences and diversities of different kinds, multiple forms of divisions intersecting in different ways, disparate experiences for proximous people. Despite all the complexity and variability, diversity and uniqueness are as amenable of explanation as anything else. Indeed, a central argument throughout this study has been the *systematic character* of the differences between weavers and casual women, the different *patternings* and *combinations* of features, the *structure of connections* between different dimensions, and the possibility of producing an explanation of them.

Acknowledgement of multiplicity, difference, particularity or fragmentation should not entail the end of systematic analysis. Maybe the old explanatory frames (certainly all those traditional binaries) were not up to the job. But the choice is not between now discredited modes of explanation and nothing. On the contrary, the construction of new, more adequate frameworks is called for, capable of dealing with the complexities, of analysing diversity and fragmentation. These may not look like what was on offer in the past, but instead they may provide, in place of 'grand narratives' or monocausal determinisms, the means to conceptualise interconnections and entanglements of a broad plurality of factors, and also to conceptualise the history and formation of the interconnections and entanglements, that have gone into making whatever is the object of investigation.

Developing theory through substantive analysis

Last but not least, the concept of relationality applies reflexively to the knowledge process behind the production of this book which has involved the intersection of an 'intellectual trajectory' with certain historical and sociological material. The general argument for developing theory on the basis of substantive material has been a constant theme, providing the motivating force for this work. So, for example, the theoretical concept of a 'social inscription of temporality' was both made sharper and given a higher level of generality through confronting empirical data than might have been gained by further abstract refinement of theoretical constructs of time. Similar remarks apply to uneven development and divisions of labour. Producing an interpretation of substantive material for which none yet exists calls for theoretical labour as, if not more, difficult than any 'purely theoretical' work, and it can equally result in new ideas. It means confronting non-theorised, even recalcitrant, material and cannot be achieved simply by extrapolating from existing theories or criticising one approach in terms of another. Taking on this challenge engenders a respect for the empirical that appears to be absent from many self-defined theoretical works of sociology.

In contrast to a view of refining theory that relies on procedures which apply theory 'to' empirical data, use empirical material to 'prove' a theory, or in some other way counterpose concepts, theory and substantive data, the perspective I prefer sees theoretical development as occurring in relation to the production of new empirical material through inventive methodologies which are capable of providing shocks to one's own best loved or well worn ideas. Theories are constructed and refined in a dynamic interplay which connects concept and data, abstract and concrete in a complex and repeated interactive traffic loop. A broad conceptual schema forms the basic framework for the analysis of substantive data and in so doing for the development of theory and the refinement of the schema. The 'total social organisation of labour' is an example of just such a construct: a conceptual framework used, in this case, for analysing the divisions of labour affecting textile and casual women workers but which was itself changed and refined as a consequence of the analysis. Although based on a TSOL conceptual schema the analyses did not 'illustrate' or 'prove' it since the TSOL has no abstract existence in itself outside of the analyses of particular substantive material.

Linkages and conceptual frames are an emergent characteristic of ongoing knowledge interactions, and so they can be expanded, deepened, extended as different empirical challenges are faced, by looking at areas such as retail, informal or voluntary work. The concepts themselves are relational, processual, and their worth derives from what they articulate.

Notes

1 The co-variation of employment for men and women which resulted in similarity within couples (both husband and wife in casual work or both in more secure and better paid work) resonates with late 1990s concern about polarisation between couples whose employment or unemployment circumstances rendered them either 'time rich and money poor' or 'money rich and time poor'.

2 This calls for a genealogical approach to the analysis of historical change, which looks backwards from a configuration or constellation of features in order to trace the histories of the different elements and how they combined together.

Appendix

The most important sources for the research comprised:

1. Local projects, labour and oral history groups and libraries. These included: Salford and Ordsall local history libraries and groups; 'Growing up in Bolton 1900–1940', an oral history project of 300 hours of tape collected 1981–83, mostly transcribed and held by Bolton Libraries Archives and Local Studies Services; 'Bridging the Years' oral history project in Ordsall docks; Manchester Women's History Group; Manchester Studies project on Trafford Park; Documentary Photography Archive; the Manchester Jewish Museum; Salford Working Class Movement Library.

2. Other types of material and contacts were gleaned through the following organisations and agencies: Manchester Employment Research Group; General, Municipal and Boilermakers Trades Union branches; Workers Education Association in Manchester and Bolton; local newspapers; Age Concern; Citizens Advice Bureaux. Most interviewees came through these contacts.

3. Contemporary surveys provided another kind of data source, for example: J.L. Harley's 1937 M.Ed dissertation on leisure activities of Manchester school leavers; A. Fielder's 1932 Diploma in Social Studies thesis on adolescents and the cinema; research by the Manchester Settlement on Ancoats prior to slum clearance of this part of central Manchester which included useful household budgets; Mass Observation surveys, books, and photographs of Worktown (Bolton).

4. Recent unpublished PhD theses were also useful, including: David Fowler (Manchester, 1988) on young wage earners in inter-war Manchester; Andrew Davies (Cambridge, 1989) on leisure, gender and poverty in inter-war Salford; Michele Abendstern (Essex, 1986) on gender and leisure in inter-war Rochdale; Ian McIntosh (Manchester, 1991) on Trafford Park.

5. The interviews: 28 separate interviews of approximately two hours each were conducted with 25 women and three men. Some were conducted in groups or pairs, including one mother and daughter pair. Thirteen were done in Salford (contacted mainly through local history projects), eight in Bolton (contacted through the GMB, and WEA and personal contact), five in Oldham, and two in Timperley, with women who had previously lived in Rochdale and Trafford Park.

   In addition two group interviews/discussions were held in Oldham and Bolton, of six and eight people respectively, in sheltered accommodation and at a pensioners' club.

Bibliography

Abendstern, M. (1986) 'Expression and Control. A Study of Working-Class Leisure and Gender 1918–1939: A Case Study of Rochdale using Oral History Methods', Unpublished PhD Thesis, University of Essex

Abrams, M. (1961) *Teenage Consumer Spending in 1959*, London: Press Exchange

Adam, B. (1990) *Time and Social Theory*, Cambridge: Polity Press

Adam, B. (1995) *Timewatch. The Social Analysis of Time*, Cambridge: Polity Press

Alexander, S. (1994) *Becoming a Woman*, London: Virago Press

Anderson, B. (1991) *Imagined Communities*, London: Verso

Anderson, M. (1971) *Family Structure in Nineteenth Century Lancashire*, Cambridge: Cambridge University Press

Anderson, M. (1984) 'The social position of spinsters in mid-Victorian Britain', *Journal of Family History*, Vol. 9, Winter, pp. 377–93

Anthias, F. and Yuval-Davis, N. (1983) 'Contextualising feminism: gender, ethnic and class divisions', *Feminist Review,* Vol. 15, pp. 62–75

Anthias, F. and Yuval-Davis, N. (1992) *Racialised Boundaries*, London: Routledge

Barrett, M. (1987) 'The concept of difference', *Feminist Review*, Vol. 26, pp. 29–41

Barrett, M. (1992) 'Words and things: materialism and method in contemporary feminist analysis' in M. Barrett and A. Phillips (eds) *Destabilising Theory*, Cambridge: Polity Press

Beauchamp, J. (1937) *Women Who Work*, London: Lawrence and Wishart

Benjamin, D. and Kochin, L. (1979) 'What went right with juvenile unemployment policy between the wars: a comment', *Economic History Review*, 2nd series, Vol. 32, No. 4, pp. 523–8

Bondi, E. (1990) 'Progress in geography and gender: feminism and difference', *Progress in Human Geography*, Vol. 14, pp. 438–51

Bourdieu, P. (1963) 'Time perspectives of the Kabyle' *Mediterranean Countryman*, Vol. 6, pp. 55–72; reprinted in J. Hassard (ed.) (1990) *The Sociology of Time*, London: Macmillan

Bowlby, S., Foord J. and McDowell, L. (1986) 'The place of gender in locality studies', *Area*, Vol. 18, pp. 327–31

Bowlby, S. *et al.* (1989) 'The geography of gender', in R. Peet and N. Thrift (eds) *New Models in Geography*, Volume 2, London: Unwin Hyman, pp. 157–75

Bradley, H. (1996) *Fractured Identities*, Cambridge: Polity Press

Brah, A. (1996) *Cartographies of Diaspora*, London: Routledge

Branson, N. and Heinemann, M. (1973) *Britain in the 1930s*, London: Panther

Bridging the Years (1989) Oral History Project in Trafford Park; (1990–) Newsletters, Salford Quays Heritage Centre

Brockway, F. (1932) *Hungry England*, London: Victor Gollancz

Bruley, S. (1993) 'Gender, class and party: the Communist party and the crisis in the cotton industry in England between the two world wars', *Women's History Review*, Vol 2, No. 1

Buxton, N.K. and Aldcroft, D. H. (eds) (1979) *British Industry Between the Wars. Instability and Industrial Development 1919–39*, London: Scolar Press

Calder, A. and Sheridan, D. (eds) (1984) *Speak for Yourself: a Mass-Observation Anthology, 1937–49*, London: Jonathan Cape

Caradog Jones, D. (ed.) (1934) *The Social Survey of Merseyside*, 3 volumes, Liverpool: University Press of Liverpool

Census of Population (1931), General Report; General Tables; Industry Tables; Occupation Tables, London: HMSO

Census of Population (1951), General Report, London: HMSO

Chandler, A. (1980) 'The growth of the transnational industrial firm in the US and the UK: a comparative analysis', *Economic History Review*, 2nd series, XXXIII 3, pp. 396–410

Chinn, C. (1988) *They Worked all their Lives. Women of the Urban Poor in England*, Manchester: Manchester University Press

Clay, H. and Brady, K. (1929) *Manchester at Work*, Manchester: Sherratt and Hughes

Cohen, P. (1993) *Home Rules: Some Reflections on Racism and Nationalism in Everyday Life*, University of East London: The New Ethnicities Unit

Cole, G.D.H. and Cole, M. (1937) *The Condition of Britain*, London: Gollancz

Collins, P.H. (1990) *Black Feminist Thought*, London: Unwin Hyman

Cooke, P. (1989) *Localities*, London: Unwin Hyman

Cowan, R.S. (1989) *More Work for Mother*, London: Free Association Books

Crompton, R. (1997) *Women and Work in Modern Britain*, Oxford: Oxford University Press

Daniels, G.W. and Jewkes, J. (1932) *An Industrial Survey of the Lancashire Area*, London: HMSO

Davidoff L., Doolittle M., Fink J. and Holden K. (1999) *The Family Story: Blood, Contract and Intimacy 1830–1960*, London: Addison, Wesley and Longman

Davidson, C. (1982) *A Woman's Work is Never Done*, London: Chatto and Windus

Davies, A. (1991) 'From "Love on the dole" to "The classic slum": Representations of Salford', Unpublished paper delivered to Manchester–Liverpool Economic History Conference, May

Davies, A. (1992a) *Leisure, Gender and Poverty: Working-class Culture in Salford and Manchester, 1900–1939*, Buckingham: Open University Press

Davies, A. (1992b) 'Leisure in the classic slum 1900–39', in A. Davies and S. Fielding (eds) *Workers' Worlds. Cultures and Communities in Manchester and Salford, 1880–1939*, Manchester: Manchester University Press

Davies, A. and Fielding S. (eds) (1992) *Workers' Worlds. Cultures and Communities in Manchester and Salford, 1880–1939*, Manchester: Manchester University Press

Davies, K. (1990) *Women and Time. The Weaving of the Strands of Everyday Life*, Aldershot: Avebury

Delaney, S. (1958) *A Taste of Honey* (play)

Delphy, C. and Leonard, D. (1992) *Familiar Exploitation*, Cambridge: Polity Press

Demos Quarterly (1995) *The Time Squeeze*, Issue 5

Desrosières, A. (1991) 'How to make things which hold together: social science, statistics and the state', in P. Wagner, B. Wittrock and R. Whitley (eds) *Discourses on Society: Volume XV*, Dordrecht: Kluwer Academic Publishers

Desrosières, A. (1993) *La Politique des Grand Nombres: Histoire de la Raison Statistique*, Paris: La Découverte

Desrosières, A. (1994) 'Official statistics and business: history, classifications, uses', in L. Bud-Frierman (ed.) *Information Acumen: the Understanding and Use of Knowledge in Modern Business*, London: Routledge

Duncan, S. (1989) 'What is locality?' in R. Peet and N. Thrift (eds) *New Models in Geography*, Volume 2, London: Unwin Hyman, pp. 221–52

Duncan, S. and Savage, M. (1989) 'Space, scale and locality', *Antipode*, Vol. 21, No. 3, pp. 179–206

Duncan, S. and Savage, M. (1991) 'New perspectives on the locality debate', *Environment and Planning A*, Vol. 23, pp. 155–64

Duquenin, A. (1984) 'Who doesn't marry and why?', *Oral History*, Vol. 12, No. 1, pp. 40–7

Dyer, R. *et al.* (eds) (1981) *Coronation Street*, London: British Film Institute

Elias, N. (1992) *Time: An Essay*, transl. E. Jephcott, Oxford: Blackwell

Engels, F. (1892) *The Condition of the Working Class in England*, 1969 edn, London: Panther Books

Fielder, A. (1932) 'Adolescents and the Cinema: Report of an Enquiry', unpublished Diploma in Social Studies, University of Manchester

Fielding, S. (1992) 'A separate culture? Irish Catholics in working class Manchester and Salford, c. 1890–1939', in A. Davies and S. Fielding (eds) *Workers' Worlds, Cultures and Communities in Manchester and Salford 1880–1939*, Manchester: Manchester University Press

Fielding, S. (1993) *Class and Ethnicity. Irish Catholics in England, 1880–1939*, Buckingham: Open University Press

Finch, J. (1989) *Family Obligations and Social Change*, Cambridge: Polity Press

Finch, J. and Groves, D. (eds) (1983) *A Labour of Love: Women, Work and Caring*, London: Routledge and Kegan Paul

Finch, J. and Summerfield, P. (1991) 'Social reconstruction and the emergence of companionate marriage', in D. Clark (ed.) *Marriage, Domestic Life and Social Change*, London: Routledge

Foley, A. (1973) *A Bolton Childhood*, Bolton: Workers' Educational Association

Ford, P. (1934) *Work and Wealth in a Modern Port*, London: Allen and Unwin

Forman, F.J. and Sowton, C. (eds) (1989) *Taking our Time: Feminist Perspectives on Temporality*, Oxford: Pergamon

Forty, A. (1986) *Objects of Desire. Design and Society since 1750*, London: Thames and Hudson

Fowler, D. (1988) 'The Life Style of the Young Wage-earner in Inter-war Manchester', Unpublished PhD Thesis, University of Manchester

Fowler, D. (1992) 'Teenage consumers? Young wage-earners and leisure in Manchester, 1919–39', in A. Davies and S. Fielding (eds) *Workers' Worlds, Cultures and Communities in Manchester and Salford, 1880–1939*, Manchester: Manchester University Press

Frankenberg, R. (1993) *White Women, Race Matters: the Social Construction of Whiteness*, London: Routledge

Frow E. and Frow R. (1970) *The Half-Time System in Education*, Manchester: E.J. Morten

Gales, K. and Marks, P. (1974) 'Twentieth century trends in the work of women in England and Wales', *Journal of the Royal Statistical Society*, Vol. 137, Part 1, pp. 60–74

Garside, W.R. (1977) 'Juvenile unemployment and public policy between the wars', *Economic History Review*, 2nd series, Vol. 30, No. 2, pp. 322–39

Garside, W.R. (1979) 'Juvenile unemployment between the wars: a rejoinder', *Economic History Review*, 2nd series, Vol. 32, No. 4, pp. 529–32

Gellner, E. (1983) *Nations and Nationalism*, Oxford: Blackwell

Geraghty, C. (1991) *Women and Soap Opera: a Study of Prime Time Soaps*, Cambridge: Polity Press

Gershuny, J. (1988) 'Time, technology and the informal economy', in R. Pahl (ed.) *On Work*, Oxford: Blackwell

Gershuny J. *et al.* (1986) 'Preliminary analysis of the 1983/4 ESRC time budget data', *Quarterly Journal of Social Affairs*, Vol. 2, pp. 13–39

Giddens, A. (1979) *Central Problems in Social Theory. Action, Structure and Contradiction in Social Analysis*, London: Macmillan

Giddens, A. (1987) 'Time and social organisation', in *Social Theory and Modern Sociology*, Cambridge: Polity Press, pp. 140–65

Gittins, D. (1982) *Fair Sex: Family Size and Structure 1900–1939*, London: Hutchinson

Gittins, D. (1993) *The Family in Question. Changing Households and Familiar Ideologies*, 2nd edn, London: Macmillan

Glucksmann, M. (1990) *Women Assemble: Women Workers and the 'New Industries' in Inter-war Britain*, London: Routledge

Glucksmann, M. (1994) 'The work of knowledge and the knowledge of women's work', in J. Purvis and M. Maynard (eds) *Researching Women's Lives from a Feminist Perspective*, Brighton: Falmer Press, pp. 149–65

Glucksmann, M. (1995) 'Why "work"? Gender and the "total social organisation of labour"', *Gender, Work and Organisation*, Vol. 2, No. 2, pp. 63–75

Glucksmann, M. (1998) 'Organisation sociale totale du travail: une nouvelle approche pour une analyse sexuée du travail', *Les Cahiers du Mage* (Marché du Travail et Genre), CNRS, Paris, 3-4/97, pp. 159–70

Goldschmidt-Clermont, L. and Paganossin-Aligasakis (1995) *Measures of Unrecorded Economic Activities in Fourteen Countries*, New York: United Nations Development Programme working paper

Gollan, J. (1937) *Youth in British Industry*, London: Victor Gollancz/Lawrence and Wishart

Graham, H. (1983) 'Caring: a labour of love', in J. Finch and D. Groves (eds) *A Labour of Love: Women, Work and Caring*, London: Routledge and Kegan Paul

Granovetter, M. (1985) 'Economic action and social structure: the problem of embeddedness', *American Journal of Sociology*, Vol. 91, No. 3, pp. 481–510

Greenwood, N. (n.d.) *How the Other Man Lives*, London: Labour Book Service

Greenwood, W. (1933) *Love on the Dole*, 1969 edn, Harmondsworth: Penguin

Gregory, D. and Urry, J. (eds) (1985) *Social Relations and Spatial Structures*, London: Macmillan

Gregson, N. and Lowe, M. (1994) *Servicing the Middle Classes: Class, Gender and Waged Domestic Labour in Contemporary Britain*, London: Routledge

Growing Up in Bolton (1981–83) Bolton Libraries Archives and Local Studies Services

Hakim, C. (1979) *Occupational Segregation by Sex*, Research Paper No. 9, Department of Employment, London: HMSO

Hakim, C. (1980) 'Census reports as documentary evidence: the Census commentaries 1801–1951', *Sociological Review*, Vol. 28, No. 3, pp. 551–80

Hall, C. (1977) 'Married women at home in Birmingham in the 1920s and 1930s', *Oral History*, Vol. 5, No. 2, pp. 62–83

Hall, C. (1992) 'Missionary stories: gender and ethnicity in England in the 1830s and 1840s', in *White, Male and Middle Class*, Cambridge: Polity Press

Hall, C. (1993) ' "From Greenland's icy mountains ... to Afric's golden sands": ethnicity, race and nation in mid-nineteenth century England', *Gender and History*, Vol. 5, No. 2, pp. 212–30

Hall, C., McClelland, K. and Rendell, J. (1999) *Defining the Victorian Nation: Class, Race and Gender and the Reform Act of 1867*, Cambridge: Cambridge University Press

Hardyment, C. (1988) *From Mangle to Microwave. The Mechanisation of Household Work*, Cambridge: Polity Press

Harley, J.L. (1937) 'Report of an enquiry into the occupations, further education and leisure interests of a number of girl wage earners from elementary and central schools in the Manchester district, with special reference to the influence of school training on their use of leisure', unpublished M.Ed thesis, University of Manchester

Harvey, D. (1989) *The Condition of Postmodernity*, Oxford: Blackwell

Harvey, M. (1999a) 'How the object of knowledge constrains knowledge of the object. An epistemological analysis of a social research investigation', *Cambridge Journal of Economics*, Vol. 23, No. 4, pp. 485–501

Harvey, M. (1999b) 'Economies of time: a framework for analysing the restructuring of employment relations' in A. Felstead and N. Jewson (eds) *Global Trends in Flexible Labour*, London: Macmillan

Hassard, J. (ed.) (1990) *The Sociology of Time*, London: Macmillan

Hewitt, P. (1993) *About Time. The Revolution in Work and Family Life*, London: IPPR/Rivers Oram Press

Higgs, E. (1986) *Domestic Servants and Households in Rochdale, 1851–1871*, New York: Garland

Higgs, E. (1987) 'Women, occupations and work in the nineteenth century censuses', *History Workshop Journal*, Vol. 23, Spring, pp. 59–80

Higgs, E. (1991) 'Disease, febrile poisons, and statistics: the census as a medical survey, 1841–1911', *Social History of Medicine*, Vol. 4, No. 3, pp. 465–78

Hobsbawm, E. (1990) *Nations and Nationalism since 1870*, Cambridge: Cambridge University Press

Hochschild, A.R. and Maching, A. (1990) *The Second Shift: Working Parents and the Revolution at Home*, London: Piartkus

Holden, K. (1996) 'The Shadow of Marriage: Single Women in England, 1919–1939', Unpublished PhD Thesis, University of Essex

Holmes, K. (1994) 'Making time: representations of temporality in Australian women's diaries of the 1920s and 1930s', *Australian Historical Studies*, Vol. 26, No. 102, April, pp. 1–18

Holmwood, J. (1994) 'Postmodernity, citizenship and inequality', in R. Blackburn (ed.) *Social Inequality in a Changing World*, Papers presented to Cambridge Social Stratification Seminar, pp. 7–27

Home Office (1930) *A Study of the Factors which have Operated in the Past and those which are Operating Now to Determine the Distribution of Women in Industry*, Cmd. 3508, PP 1929, London: HMSO

Hufton, O. (1984) 'Women without men: widows and spinsters in Britain and France in the eighteenth century', *Journal of Family History*, Vol. 9, Winter, pp. 355–76

Hughes, A. and Hunt, K. (1992) 'A culture transformed? Women's lives in Wythenshawe in the 1930s', in A. Davies and S. Fielding (eds) *Workers' Worlds. Cultures and Communities in Manchester and Salford, 1880–1939*, Manchester: Manchester University Press

Hutt, A. (1933) *The Condition of the Working Class in Britain*, London: Martin Lawrence

Ignatieff, M. (1994) *Blood and Belonging*, London: Vintage

James, H.E. and Moore, F.T. (1940) 'Adolescent leisure in a working class district', *Occupational Psychology*, Vol. XIV, No. 3, July

Jeffreys, S. (1985) *The Spinster and her Enemies: Feminism and Sexuality, 1880–1930*, London: Pandora Press

Jennings, H. (1934) *Brynmawr: a Study of a Distressed Area*, London: Allenson

Jephcott, P. (1942) *Girls Growing Up*, London: Faber and Faber

Jewkes, J. and Gray, E.M. (1935) *Wages and Labour in the Lancashire Cotton Spinning Industry*, Manchester: Manchester University Press

Jewkes, J. and Jewkes, S. (1938) *The Juvenile Labour Market*, London: Victor Gollancz

Jewkes, J. and Winterbottom, A. (1933a) *Juvenile Unemployment*, London: Allen and Unwin

Jewkes, J. and Winterbottom, A. (1933b) *An Industrial Survey of Cumberland and Furness*, Manchester: Manchester University Press

Kiernan, K. and Wicks, M. (1991) *Family Change and Future Policy*, York: JRMT

Kristeva, J. (1981) 'Women's time', *Signs*, Vol. 7, No. 1, pp. 16–35

Latour, B. (1993) *We Have Never Been Modern*, Translated by Catherine Porter, Hemel Hempstead: Harvester Wheatsheaf

Levitas, R. (1998) *The Inclusive Society? Social Exclusion and New Labour*, London: Macmillan

Lewis, G. (1996) ' "Black women's experience" and social work', *Feminist Review*, Vol. 53, pp. 24–56

Lewis, J. (1984) *Women in England 1870–1950*, Brighton: Wheatsheaf

Lewis, J. (1992) *Women in Britain since 1945*, Oxford: Blackwell

Lewis, J. and Meredith, B. (1988) *Daughters Who Care*, London: Routledge

Liddington, J. (1984) *The Life and Times of a Respectable Rebel: Selina Cooper (1864–1946)*, London: Virago

Liddington, J. and Norris, J. (1978) *One Hand Tied Behind Us. The Rise of the Women's Suffrage Movement*, London: Virago

McDowell, L. (1993) 'Space, place and gender relations. Part 1: Feminist empiricism and the geography of social relations. Part 2: Identity, difference, feminist geometries and geographies', *Progress in Human Geography*, Vol. 17, No. 2, pp. 157–79 and Vol. 17, No. 3, pp. 305–18

M'Gonigle, G.C. and Kirby, J. (1936) *Poverty and Public Health*. London: Gollancz

McIntosh, I. (1991) 'Ford at Trafford Park', Unpublished PhD Thesis, University of Manchester

MacKenzie, D. (1981) *Statistics in Britain, 1865–1930*, Edinburgh: Edinburgh University Press

Madge, C. and Harrisson, T. (eds) (1938) *First Year's Work 1937–38 by Mass-Observation*, London: Lindsay Drummond

Madge, C. and Harrisson, T. (1939) *Britain by Mass-Observation*, Harmondsworth: Penguin

Manchester University Settlement (1944) *A Survey of Housing and Amenities on Belle Vue, Gorton, New Housing Estate, 1942–1943*

Manchester University Settlement (1945) *Ancoats: a Study of a Clearance Area*

Mark-Lawson, J., Savage, M. and Warde, A. (1985) 'Gender and local politics: struggles over welfare policies 1918–39', in L. Murgatroyd *et al.* (eds) *Localities, Class and Gender*, London: Pion

Marquand, H. (1932) *Industrial Survey of South Wales*, London: HMSO

Marshall, B. (1994) *Engendering Modernity*, Cambridge: Polity Press

Mass Observation (1939) *Clothes-Washing Report: 'Motives and Methods'*, London: Victor Gollancz

Mass Observation (1943) *The Pub and the People. A Worktown Study*, London: Victor Gollancz

Massey, D. (1984) *Spatial Divisions of Labour: Social Structures and the Geography of Production*, London: Macmillan

Massey, D. (1994) *Space, Place and Gender*, Oxford: Blackwell

Massey, D. (1995) 'Places and their pasts', *History Workshop Journal*, Vol. 39, pp. 182–92

Massey, D. and Allen, J. (eds) (1984) *Geography Matters!*, Cambridge: Cambridge University Press

Maynard, M. (1994) ' "Race", gender and the concept of difference in feminist thought', in H. Afshar and M. Maynard (eds) *The Dynamics of 'Race' and Gender*, London: Taylor and Francis

Meara, G. (1936) *Juvenile Unemployment in South Wales*, Cardiff: University of Wales Press

Mess, H.A. (1928) *Industrial Tyneside*, London: Ernest Benn Ltd

Metropolitan Borough of Trafford (1981) *Short History of Trafford Park*

Middleton, T. (1931) 'An Enquiry into the Use of Leisure amongst the Working Classes of Liverpool', unpublished MA thesis, University of Liverpool

Ministry of Labour (1934) *Report on Juvenile Unemployment for the Year 1934*, London: Ministry of Labour

Mohanty, C. (1991) 'Under western eyes: feminist scholarship and colonial discourses', in C. Mohanty, A. Russo and L. Torres (eds.) *Third World Women and the Politics of Feminism*, Bloomington: Indiana University Press

Morgan, A. (1939) *The Needs of Youth: A Report Made to King George's Jubilee Trust Fund*, London: Oxford University Press

Morris, L. (1990) *The Workings of the Household*, Cambridge: Polity Press

Morris, L.D. (1991) 'Locality studies and the household', *Environment and Planning A*, Vol. 23, pp. 165–77

Mowat, C. (1955) *Britain Between the Wars*, 1984 edn, London: Methuen

Murgatroyd *et al.*/Lancaster Regionalism Group (1985) *Localities, Class and Gender*, London: Pion

Nissell, M. (1980) 'Women in government statistics: basic concepts and assumptions', SSRC/EOC *Seminar on Women in Government Statistics*, London: Policy Studies Institute

Oman, E. (n.d.) *Salford Stepping Stones*, Swinton: Neil Richardson

Oram, A. (1985) '"Embittered, sexless, or homosexual" attacks on spinster teachers, 1918–1939', in Lesbian History Group (eds) *Not a Passing Phase: Recovering Lesbians in History, 1840–1985*, London: Women's Press

Orloff, A. (1993) 'Gender and the social rights of citizenship: the comparative analysis of gender relations and welfare states', *American Sociological Review*, Vol. 58, No. 3, pp. 303–28

Orr, J.B. (1936) *Food Health and Income. Report on a Survey of Adequacy of Diet in Relation to Income*. London: Macmillan

Orwell, G. (1937) *The Road to Wigan Pier*, London: Gollancz

Osborne, P. (1995) *The Politics of Time*, London: Verso

Pagnamenta, P. and Overy, R. (1984) *All Our Working Lives*, London: BBC

Pahl, J. (1989) *Money and Marriage*, London: Macmillan

Pahl, R.E. (1984) *Divisions of Labour*, London: Routledge

Peet, R. and Thrift, N. (eds) *New Models in Geography*, Volume 2, London: Unwin Hyman

Phoenix, A. (1998) 'Dealing with difference: the recursive and the new', *Ethnic and Racial Studies*, Vol. 21, No. 5, pp. 859–80

Pilgrim Trust (1938) *Men Without Work*, Cambridge: Cambridge University Press

Polanyi, K., Arensberg, C. and Pearson, H. (eds) (1955) *Trade and Market in the Early Empires: Economies in History and Theory*, New York: The Free Press

Pollard, S. (1983) *The Development of the British Economy*, 3rd edn, London: Edward Arnold

Power, J. (1980) 'Aspects of Working Class Leisure during the Depression Years: Bolton in the 1930s', MA Dissertation, University of Warwick

Priestley, J.B. (1934) *English Journey*, 1977 edn, Harmondsworth: Penguin

Pringle, R. (1989) *Secretaries Talk: Sexuality, Power and Work*, London: Verso

Pullen, M.J. and Williams, B.R. (1962) 'The structure of industry in Lancashire', in *British Association: Manchester and its Region*, Manchester: Manchester University Press

Reay, D. (1996) 'Insider perspectives or stealing the words out of women's mouths', *Feminist Review*, Vol. 53, pp. 57–73

Rees, G. and Rees, T. (1982) 'Juvenile unemployment and the state between the wars', in T. Rees and P. Atkinson (eds) *Youth Unemployment and State Intervention*, London: Routledge and Kegan Paul

Rice, M.S. (1931) *Working Class Wives*, 1981 edn, London: Virago Press

Richardson, H.W. (1967) *Economic Recovery in Britain 1932–9*, London: Weidenfeld and Nicholson

Roberts, E. (1984) *A Woman's Place. An Oral History of Working Class Women 1890–1940*, Oxford: Blackwell

Roberts, E. (1995a) *Women and Families. An Oral History, 1940–1970*, Oxford: Blackwell

Roberts, E. (1995b) *Women's Work, 1840–1940*, Cambridge: Cambridge University Press

Roberts, M. (1991) *Living in a Man-Made World: Gender Assumptions in Modern Housing Design*. London: Routledge

Roberts, R. (1971) *The Classic Slum*, 1987 edn, Harmondsworth: Penguin

Roberts, R. (1976) *A Ragged Schooling*, Manchester: Manchester University Press

Robertson, G. *et al.* (1994) *Travellers Tales: Narratives of Home and Displacement*, London: Routledge

Roediger, D. (1991) *The Wages of Whiteness: Race and the Making of the American Working Class*, London: Verso

Rose, G. (1993) *Feminism and Geography. The Limits of Geographical Knowledge.* Cambridge: Polity Press

Ross, E. (1989) '"Fierce questions and taunts". Married life in working-class London, 1870–1914', in D. Feldman and G. Stedman Jones (eds) *Metropolis London. Histories and Representation since 1800*, London: Routledge

Rowntree, B.S. (1941) *Poverty and Progress. A Second Social Survey of York*, London: Longman

Russell, D. and Walker, G. (1979) *Trafford Park 1896–1939*, Manchester Polytechnic: Manchester Studies

Samuel, R. (1986) 'The cult of planning', *New Socialist*, January, pp. 25–9

Samuel, R. and Thompson, P. (eds) (1990) *The Myths We Live By*, London: Routledge

Sarup, M. (1994) 'Home and identity' in G. Robertson *et al. Travellers Tales: Narratives of Home and Displacement*, London: Routledge

Saul, S.B. (1960) 'The American impact on British industry, 1895–1914' *Business History*, Vol. III, No. 1, pp. 19–38

Savage, M. (1985) 'Capitalist and patriarchal relations at work: Preston cotton weaving 1890–1940', in L.Murgatroyd *et al.* (eds) *Localities, Class and Gender*, London: Pion

Savage, M. (1988) 'Women and work in the Lancashire cotton industry, 1890–1939', in J.A. Jowitt and A.J. McIvor (eds) *Employers and Labour in the English Textile Industries*, London: Routledge

Sayer, A. (1991) 'Beyond the locality debate: deconstructing geography's dualisms', *Environment and Planning A*, Vol. 23, pp. 283–308

Scott, J.W. (1988) *Gender and the Politics of History*, New York: Columbia University Press

Sharpe, P. (1991) 'Literally spinsters: a new interpretation of local economy and demography in Colyton in the 17th and 18th centuries', *Economic History Review*, Vol. 44, No. 1, pp. 46–65

Smith, A.D. (1991) *National Identity*, Harmondsworth: Penguin

Smith, D. (1977) 'Interview with Humphrey Spender', *Worktown*, Falmer: University of Sussex

Smith, D.M. (1969) *Industrial Britain. The North West*, Newton Abbott: David and Charles

Smith, Sir H. Llewelyn (1930–35) *The New Survey of London Life and Labour*, 9 Volumes, London: King & Son

Social Politics, International Studies in Gender, State and Society (1994–) Oxford: Oxford University Press

Soja, E. (1989) *Postmodern Geographies: The Reassertion of Space in Critical Social Theory*, London: Verso

Spender, H. (1977) *Worktown. Photographs of Bolton and Blackpool taken for Mass Observation 1937/8*, Falmer: Gardner Centre Gallery, University of Sussex

Stanley, L. (ed.) (1990) *Feminist Praxis. Research, Theory and Epistemology in Feminist Sociology*, London: Routledge

Stevens, T.H.G. (1947) *Some Notes on the Development of Trafford Park 1897–1947*, Trafford Park Estates Co. Ltd

Sullivan, O. (1997) 'Time waits for no (wo)man: an investigation of the gendered experience of domestic time', *Sociology*, Vol. 31, pp. 221–39

Szreter, S. (1984) 'The genesis of the Registrar General's social classification of occupations', *British Journal of Sociology*, Vol. XXXV, No. 4, pp. 529–46

Szreter, S. (1991) 'The General Register Office and the Public Health Movement in Britain, 1837–1914', *Social History of Medicine*, Vol. 4, No. 3, pp. 435–63

Tebbutt, M. (1992) 'Women's talk? Gossip and "women's worlds" in working-class communities, 1880–1939' in A. Davies and S. Fielding (eds) *Workers' Worlds. Cultures and Communities in Manchester and Salford, 1880–1939*, Manchester: Manchester University Press

Thompson, D. (1975) 'Courtship and marriage in Preston between the wars', *Oral History*, Vol. 3, No. 2

Thompson, E.P. (1967) 'Time, work-discipline and industrial capitalism,' *Past and Present*, Vol. 38, pp. 56–97. Reprinted in Flinn, M.W. and Smout, T.C. (1974) *Essays in Social History*, London: Clarendon Press, pp. 39–77

Thompson, F. (1937) 'A Study of the Development of Facilities for Recreation and Leisure Occupation on New Housing Estates, with Special Reference to Manchester', unpublished Diploma in Social Studies, University of Manchester

Thompson, P. (1978) *The Voice of the Past*, 3rd edn. Oxford: Oxford University Press 2000

Tonkin, E. (1992) *Narrating Our Pasts: the Social Construction of Oral History*, Cambridge: Cambridge University Press

Tout, H. (1938) *The Standard of Living in Bristol*, Bristol: Arrowsmith

Trafford Library Service (1982) *Trafford Park – its Growth as an Industrial Estate*

United Nations (1995) *The World's Women 1995: Trends and Statistics*, Social Statistics and Indicators series K, 12

Urry, J. (1987) 'Society, space and locality', *Environment and Planning D*, Vol. 5, pp. 435–44

Vicinus, M. (1985) *Independent Women: Work and Community for Single Women, 1850–1920*, London: Virago

Wajcman, J. (1991) *Feminism Confronts Technology*, Cambridge: Polity Press

Walby, S. (1992) 'Post-post-modernism? Theorizing social complexity' in M. Barrett and A. Phillips (eds) *Destabilizing Theory. Contemporary Feminist Debates*, Cambridge: Polity Press

Walby, S. and Bagguley, P. (1989) 'Gender restructuring: five labour markets compared', *Environment and Planning D: Society and Space*, Vol. 7, pp. 277–92

Warde, A. (1989) 'Recipes for a pudding: a comment on locality' *Antipode*, Vol. 21, No. 3, pp. 274–81

Ware, V. (1992) *Beyond the Pale. White Women, Racism and History*, London: Verso

Whipp, R. (1987) '"A time to every purpose": an essay on time and work', in P. Joyce (ed.) *The Historical Meanings of Work*, Cambridge: Cambridge University Press

Wolff, J. (1995) *Resident Alien. Feminist Cultural Criticism*, Cambridge: Polity Press

Women and Geography Group (1984) *Geography and Gender*, London: Hutchinson

Worktown (1977) *Photographs of Bolton and Blackpool taken for Mass Observation 1937/8*, Falmer: Gardner Centre Gallery, University of Sussex

Yeandle, S. (1984) *Working Women's Lives*, London: Tavistock

Zerubavel, E. (1979) *Patterns in Hospital Life*, Chicago: Chicago University Press

Zerubavel, E. (1981) *Hidden Rhythms. Schedules and Calendars in Social Life*, Chicago: Chicago University Press

Index